Unlearning
PROTESTANTISM

D0557264

Unlearning
PROTESTANTISM

Sustaining
Christian Community
in an Unstable Age

GERALD W. SCHLABACH

BrazosPress
a division of Baker Publishing Group
Grand Rapids, Michigan

© 2010 by Gerald W. Schlabach

Published by Brazos Press
a division of Baker Publishing Group
P.O. Box 6287, Grand Rapids, MI 49516-6287
www.brazospress.com

Printed in the United States of America

All rights reserved. No part of this publication may be reproduced, stored in a retrieval system, or transmitted in any form or by any means—for example, electronic, photocopy, recording— without the prior written permission of the publisher. The only exception is brief quotations in printed reviews.

Library of Congress Cataloging-in-Publication Data
Schlabach, Gerald.
    Unlearning Protestantism : sustaining Christian community in an unstable age /
Gerald W. Schlabach.
        p.   cm.
    Includes bibliographical references (p.   ) and index.
    ISBN 978-1-58743-111-1 (pbk.)
    1. Church controversies. 2. Continuity of the church. 3. Catholic Church—Discipline.
4. Church controversies—Mennonites. I. Title.
    BV652.9.S278 2010
    262.001′1—dc22   2009040098

Unless otherwise indicated, Scripture quotations are from the New Revised Standard Version of the Bible, copyright © 1989, by the Division of Christian Education of the National Council of the Churches of Christ in the United States of America. Used by permission. All rights reserved.

Scripture quotations labeled KJV are from the King James Version of the Bible.

10   11   12   13   14   15   16   7   6   5   4   3   2   1

In keeping with biblical principles of creation stewardship, Baker Publishing Group advocates the responsible use of our natural resources. As a member of the Green Press Initiative, our company uses recycled paper when possible. The text paper of this book is comprised of 30% post-consumer waste.

green
press
INITIATIVE

Dedicated with deep and abiding gratitude
to three from whom I have learned stability,
even amid pilgrim change:

Ivan Kauffman,
partner on the bridge

Stanley Hauerwas,
loyal beyond bluster

Joetta Handrich Schlabach,
wise, pastoral, love of my life

CONCORDIA UNIVERSITY LIBRARY
PORTLAND, OR 97211

Contents

Introduction

THIS BOOK IS not about encouraging people to abandon Protestant churches. It is not a pamphlet to persuade Protestants to become Roman Catholic. Rather, it is about virtues that all Christian communities need to sustain their communal lives, whatever their ecclesial location.

To be sure, I am a Mennonite who has entered into full communion with the Catholic Church. Having sketched out the outline of this book many years before my confirmation as a Roman Catholic at Pentecost 2004, I initially assumed I would have to abandon the project. I feared that it would simply be too difficult to persuade readers that my covert aim would be something other than convincing Protestants to become Catholics. One quick-and-dirty way to describe the project, after all, had always been that the book would be about "what Protestants can learn from Catholics about sustaining Christian community." Sometimes I added, "by hanging in there with each other and the church itself, even when they disagree."[1] Carrying lessons from a Catholic direction to Protestants would hardly seem triumphalistic as long as I myself was "hanging in there" with the church community that had formed me. But now?

Protestant friends and colleagues convinced me to write the book anyway. And I would like to think that the way I have become Catholic without burning my bridges to the Mennonite community has demonstrated a way of "hanging in there" with stability and fidelity. That is for my friends and colleagues to judge, however, and I can hardly prevent the reader from joining them in making a judgment. As I reconsidered this project, what mattered was that Protestant friends and colleagues were disappointed at the prospect that I might abandon it. They wanted the book anyway.

Perhaps their openness owes to the ways that times have changed and Christians are learning from one another in new ways; recognizing both the possibilities and the dilemmas of our new "ecumenical age" will be the first task of this book (chap. 1). The taproot of the entire book is that for many years Roman Catholics have helped me, in moments of frustration, above all to remain Mennonite. Some were peers and professors I had come to know, from the barrios of Nicaragua in the mid-1980s to the seminar rooms at the University of Notre Dame in the early 1990s. Others were figures such as those whose stories I tell in chapter 5, "loyal dissenters" from Yves Congar to Joan Chittister. What inspired me in their witness were a doggedness, a long view, and a loyalty to their church that recast questions of conscience and tradition, of prophetic critique and the role of institutions, in subtle yet significant ways.

As I continued to explore the Catholic tradition, my deepest intuition was that I could neither become a Catholic nor remain a Mennonite without finding or helping to build a bridge between the traditions. This seemed possible because I was increasingly working in the company of Christian leaders and theologians who are so ecumenical that they rarely even bother to label themselves as such. I refer especially to the loose affiliation of Christian leaders who bear some affinity to the Methodist theologian Stanley Hauerwas, whose heroes range from the Mennonite John Howard Yoder to the Protestant Karl Barth to Catholic Pope John Paul II. But even beyond that circle, these days most scholars I know simply take for granted that they must know, and may cite unapologetically, the influential thinkers and schools of thought beyond the tradition with which they identify.

If the question is sustaining Christian community, however, it cannot be simply an intellectual question. And so the first formal way by which I bridged the Mennonite tradition that had formed me and the Catholic tradition that I had begun to appropriate was to become a Benedictine oblate in 1997. Benedictine oblates are not monks, yet they join with a particular Benedictine monastery in serving God and neighbor according to the Rule of St. Benedict, insofar as their nonmonastic state in life permits. I tell some of my story of becoming an oblate in chapter 3.

Other Mennonites I knew were finding both historical links and contemporary connections with Catholicism, however, while Catholics I knew were attracted to the Mennonite witness of service and peace. In 1999, twenty-five of us came together to tell our stories, explore what was happening among us, and ask how we might steward our network. We called our meeting a "bridging retreat," and when we organized to follow up and extend our circle a few years later, we called ourselves Bridgefolk: "a movement of sacramentally minded Mennonites and peace-minded Roman Catholics who come together to celebrate each other's traditions, explore each other's practices, and honor each other's contribution to the mission of Christ's Church."[2] As cofounder and longtime director of Bridgefolk, I am keenly aware that there is no single good way to inhabit a bridge between our traditions. Although a handful of Bridgefolk participants have "crossed the bridge" (as we say in preference to the term "converted") yet found the pastoral and community support to continue affiliating in some way with the church that first formed them, this is hardly the norm. Far more often and with the blessing of Bridgefolk leaders, participants have used our "bridge" to practice an "exchange of gifts" and return to their home churches enriched.

Why I finally did become Roman Catholic would require a memoir to explore, for I have never been able to cite a single reason that would make for a succinct answer. Seeking as a faithful Protestant to live out of and into a biblical worldview, I found myself returning repeatedly to God's covenant-keeping faithfulness even when God's people have gone astray; the biblical history of God's own faithfulness taught me a growing generosity toward Christians whose positions I might once have denounced in the name of prophetic faithfulness. Meanwhile, a long-standing appreciation for the drama of the liturgy slowly grew into a taste (and feel and smell and ear and eye) for sacramentality, which I now recognize as the best way to embrace a robust theology of grace with a full-bodied ethic of community life in the world, centered in God's own nonviolent generosity on the cross and in the Eucharist. Seeking as a faithful Mennonite to

11

witness to this nonviolent love of God—extending even to enemies and reconciling what has been broken by sin—I became convicted that our witness falls short if it becomes the basis for self-definition over against other Christians. Thus we cannot pray "Forgive us our sins as we forgive those who sin against us" if we do not live out this peacemaking vocation vis-à-vis the historic church that many who remain Protestant nonetheless recognize as somehow their "mother church." Behind much of this, I am sure, has been the epoch-making Second Vatican Council. Living out my Christian faith as a young adult in the 1970s and 1980s, I realized that Vatican II had defined my horizons in whichever direction I looked, whether in my early hopes for churchwide neo-Pentecostal renewal, or in my encounter with Catholic social teaching in Latin America, or in the search I found myself sharing with others for what the council called "a completely fresh appraisal of war" and Christian peacemaking in the modern world, or in the vision that the council presented of a truly multicultural and global church.[3]

In a way, I became a Roman Catholic simply because I now could. In other words, I became convinced that the day is dawning in which it is becoming as possible to be a Mennonite Catholic as it is to be a Franciscan or a Benedictine or a Salesian Catholic—identities that map participation in overlapping communities but are *so* unremarkable that no one bothers to use hybrid or hyphenated terms! Yet I have also walked closely with others who cannot in good conscience become Catholic, at least until they see the promise of Vatican II consolidated further, or have their own ministries and community charisms more fully affirmed by the Roman Church. First among these has been my beloved wife, Joetta, who was discerning a call to pastoral ministry even as I was testing a tug toward Catholicism. I know the issues and struggles of such Christians far too well to callously make easy recommendations. So, for example, I do not and cannot ask my Mennonite brothers and sisters to rejoin Catholic communion quickly or en masse. Mennonite peacebuilders around the world know that their task is long and arduous; after all, peace-making differs from war-making precisely in its refusal of quick or simplistic solutions. What I do ask my Mennonite brothers and sisters is this: please recognize that for some of us to explore how it is becoming possible to be Mennonites in full communion with the

Catholic Church is itself a living out of our faith. And meanwhile, if Protestants from still other traditions can use this template to explore fresh new paths of their own toward Christian unity, all the better.

Still and all, as I launch a book on the practice of stability, the virtue of fidelity, and the challenge of sustaining Christian community, I must admit that to "walk the talk" and live out the charge to "hang in there" with my sisters and brothers has sometimes seemed to present me with a catch-22. Would stability require me to remain at all costs with the church that formed me? Or would stability argue for rejoining the church from which my formative church once departed? This puzzle is no doubt why I have come to take comfort in—and begin chapter 1 by reflecting on—Jesus' parable of the shrewd manager who finesses his final week of bookkeeping in a way that raises eyebrows yet draws grudging respect from the boss who is laying him off. Jesus actually praises the shrewd manager for his enigmatic faithfulness. Some puzzles and some sets of trends or circumstance, it seems, have no solution except transcendence. We must use the realities available to us, in other words, to transcend those very realities. Thus if we have inherited a fractured church in which there is no good canonically recognized way to be both Mennonite and Catholic (or Lutheran and Catholic, or Lutheran and Mennonite, I suppose), then we may have to use the fragments available to us to rise above our long-standing impasses more by changing than by resolving the question.[4]

If I inevitably attend somewhat more to what Protestants could learn from Catholics, in the first instance that is simply because such a trajectory has been part of my own learning curve. But I hope more is going on here than that. What I really hope is to change the question from *Who's right?* or *To which church should I belong?* or even *Couldn't we just get along if we stopped quibbling over doctrine?* to something else. Don't get me wrong. I believe there is such a thing as objective truth, and that through human discourse, discovery, *and* humility we can apprehend it. I believe that, historically, the Catholic Church has been very right about certain things, Mennonites have been very right about others, and Martin Luther did us all a service by staking his life on the doctrine of justification by faith. So identity and doctrine do matter; some convictions are right, and others are misleading or outright wrong. But how we work at our differences matters too. The point is not that a pragmatic turn away from ultimate truth-claims or metaphysics and toward process will help us "move on," but that as Gandhi reminded us, the tree is already present in the seed. We must ever endeavor to discern the truth more clearly, but we cannot expect to do so except through truthful means. One—no doubt not the only one, but a crucial one—of those means is the nonviolent and respectful vulnerability that commits to maintaining relationships with one another despite sometimes quite serious disagreements. By shifting the question to *What virtues or qualities does any Christian community need in order to sustain its life together?* I do not intend to leave behind other doctrinal or ethical questions we desperately need to discern together. But I do have a hunch that we will cast new light on fundamental presuppositions if we attend far more carefully to what it means to discern *together*.

Let me state the matter another way by turning from what this book is *not*, to what it *is*. If a book titled *Unlearning Protestantism* is not about becoming Roman Catholic, then what is it?

For Protestants, this book offers a way to address a recurring dilemma of Protestant church life: what may well have been virtues in the early years of the Protestant Reformation have now become vices that corrode community life. The courage that allowed a Martin Luther to stand on conscience has become, in our individualistic age, an all-too-cheap excuse to avoid the hard work of living together in community. Thus I argue that Protestants would do well to relearn certain virtues that all Christian communities need to sustain their communal lives. As Robin Lovin once remarked concerning Reinhold Niebuhr's "Christian Realism," some lessons can be learned too well.[5] This book, then, is about unlearning lessons that might well have been valid at another time. It argues that many Protestant Christians (and some Protestantized Roman Catholic Christians) need to unlearn these Protestant vices. Yet it proceeds not by pamphleteering but by trying to make sense of the less-than-articulate yearning for some new kind of catholicity that Christians of multiple denominations are demonstrating amid a whole series of otherwise puzzling alliances and crossovers. On the way to this goal, chapter 1 begins by explaining how the Protestant Principle has become the Protestant Dilemma, and chapter 2 uses one particular church tradition as a case study for exploring the challenge of sustaining

14

Christian community in the modern era. This dilemma and these challenges suggest why Protestants might want to learn something from Roman Catholics about practices of stability.

For Catholics, this book may simultaneously do a service by naming what they often take for granted. Even as I have said in shorthand that this book is about what Protestants can learn from Roman Catholics, I have faced a major complication: Roman Catholics are not always adept at naming their own strengths, even to themselves. To indicate why Protestants should take note, and to anticipate my argument, here is a quick case in point: when members of the Roman Catholic hierarchy complain about the dissenters in their church, they fail to recognize how good they have it. Through years of straddling the Protestant/Catholic divide, I have observed a subtle quality of the Roman Catholic community—and a corresponding character trait or virtue among individual Catholics—that Protestantism tends to corrode but that Protestants need too in order to sustain Christian community. It is a quality that keeps Roman Catholics together even amid bitter disputes, precisely where Protestants have the ready option of leaving, joining another denomination, or even starting a new one. It is that quality of dogged persistence that I have already mentioned but endeavor to articulate in various ways in chapters 3 through 5.

My working names for this quality are *stability* and *fidelity* in ordinary circumstances and *loyal dissent* in trying ones. In deference to my fellow Christian ethicists, by the way, I distinguish between "stability" and "fidelity" in subtle but important ways. Thus the reader may notice that I speak of *practices* of stability but the *virtue* of fidelity. As ethicists understand the workings of virtue, practices lead to habits that inculcate virtues. Thus practices are to virtue as weight lifting is to muscle strength.

Meanwhile, however, the term "loyal dissent" has other problems, I admit. Perhaps that is why I have needed various angles and multiple chapters not only to name but also to locate it. Many Protestants tend to confuse loyalty with authoritarianism, after all, while many Catholics tend to confuse dissent with disloyalty itself, or even rebellion. To avoid misunderstanding from either direction, I proceed by exploring one formative subtradition within Roman Catholicism that has a track record of stability with flexibility and obedience without

15

authoritarianism (chap. 3). From there I proceed to demonstrate the role that practices of stability have played at a much wider global level as the Catholic Church sought change with continuity at Vatican II (chap. 4), and I name the debt that Catholics owe to loyal dissenters who have contributed to their tradition (chap. 5).

For all Christians, I hope that, in some modest yet significant way, this book promotes conditions for the possibility of greater church unity. In my ecumenical work I have often cited parallel statements by then-Cardinal Joseph Ratzinger, now Pope Benedict XVI, and Cardinal Walter Kasper, head of the Pontifical Council for Promoting Christian Unity. Both have insisted that the proper goal of ecumenical dialogue is not that long-separated Christians move closer to one another but rather that together we grow closer to Christ:

> CARDINAL RATZINGER: History shows us that a superficial unity which jumps the gun without inward preparation through actual living could only prove harmful. Greater unity is really to be found in the fact that . . . separated communities are passionately seeking the truth together with the firm intention of imposing nothing which does not come from the Lord on the other party, and of losing nothing entrusted to us by him. In this way our lives advance toward each other because they are directed towards Christ.
>
> CARDINAL KASPER: The ecumenical aim is therefore not a simple return of the others into the fold of the Catholic Church, nor the conversion of individuals to the Catholic Church (even if this must obviously be mutually acknowledged when it is based on reasons of conscience). In the ecumenical movement the question is the conversion of all to Jesus Christ. As we move nearer to Jesus Christ, in him we move nearer to one another.[6]

The practices of stability that I chart in this book are part of that "inward preparation through actual living" that we need for a Christian unity that is deep and true rather than superficial and harmful. Zealous Catholics may be disappointed that a book titled *Unlearning Protestantism* does not try to argue Protestants into the Catholic fold. They would do well to stop and consider what little good a surge of "converts" would do if they have not already been learning the virtue of fidelity to one another amid the messiness of communal life through time, which is arguably the genius of Catholic tradition. Likewise, firm Protestants may be anxious that even this much talk of tradition and fidelity to one another puts fidelity to Christ himself at risk. They likewise should pause to consider the clarity by which these eminent Catholic prelates agree: the first priority of all must be conversion into Jesus Christ. All I can add—though I take many pages to explain—is that Jesus' own faithfulness to his bumbling, erring disciples is part of what we must also grow into in order to move nearer to him.

And for the world? I will address this question directly in the final chapter. Because of the role that Protestantism has arguably played in creating the modern world, what I call the Protestant Dilemma is in many ways the dilemma of modernity as well. The promise of freedom from the constraints of tradition that Protestantism has spread, together with the Enlightenment, has inspired untold movements for social justice and human rights. Yet those movements have also drawn on the practices, disciplines, and cohesion of communal traditions in ways that the language of rights and freedom rarely accounts for well and thus tends to undermine. For the assertion of rights and the throwing off of shackles to result in civil society rather than raw and cynical struggles for power, therefore, society also needs practices of stability and citizens to have patience with one another. And insofar as globalization represents the spread of modernity, its virtues, and its vices to nearly every corner and culture around the world, the forging of *global* civil society has in turn become as urgent as it is complex. What the Christian church has to offer to this project must in the first instance be its own life, a life that spans centuries but also continents and cultures. So while the practices of stability that allow the church to sustain its life together as a community are in the foreground of this book, the hope that Christians can yet model and offer practices of stability and the patience we need to live, work, and forge peaceably with our Others is one that never recedes entirely into the background.

To acknowledge those whose witness, friendship, and help have made this book possible may be even more perilous than usual for an author. From concept to outline to research to manuscript, the book has taken more than a decade to emerge, and so I am surely forgetting some of the debts of gratitude I owe. Further, I would not even have conceived of this book without the quiet witness of stability by many unnamable others over a course of decades—underpaid church workers, long-suffering parishioners, and "good enough" Christians of all sorts. These are the hobbits who populate this book and the world it describes, largely unseen, but whose muted history preserves the church and constitutes its real story as surely as J. R. R. Tolkien's hobbits sustain his imagined world of Middle Earth.

Four groups of people to whom I already have alluded certainly deserve acknowledgment, however. Michael Cartwright, Mark Thiessen Nation, Gerald Mast, and Weldon Nisly are the Protestant (or at least Anabaptist) friends who encouraged me to proceed with this project despite the complications of having become Roman Catholic. Among the many Catholic colleagues in Central America in the 1980s whose combination of fidelity, radical critique, and authentic service so intrigued me are our dear friends Don and Celine Woznica. Especially significant among the professors at Notre Dame who demonstrated nuanced ways of being Catholic are John Cavadini; Jean Porter; Todd Whitmore; Fr. David Burrell, CSC; the late Catherine Mowry LaCugna; Fr. Thomas O'Meara, OP (though I know this recognition will surprise him); and the late Fr. Richard McCormick (though he never convinced me of his ethical theory).

At the University of St. Thomas in Minnesota, I am privileged to work in a theology department that exemplifies the themes of this book through its collegiality and civility despite a spread of theological perspectives. Colleagues who deserve special mention for their encouragement or input into this specific project are Michael Hollerich, John Boyle, Paul Wojda, William Cavanaugh, Fr. J. Michael Joncas, Terence Nichols, and Catherine Cory. Special thanks to Isaac Alderman, who served as my research assistant through a crucial phase of this project. I am also grateful to the institution itself for the research and sabbatical leaves I used to write much of this book.

One other set of friends and mentors has accompanied me in discerning and carrying out my vocation in the last decade. Father Kevin McDonough, pastor of St. Peter Claver Catholic Church and longtime vicar general of the Archdiocese of St. Paul and Minneapolis, has been a guide, confessor, and friend without whose wisdom my

18

journey might have been far more convoluted. And as always I must mention my companions in Bridgefolk. Here the peril of beginning to name any while leaving off others grows especially acute, for by "proceeding in friendship" Bridgefolk has become a home where I have formed so many rich relationships. Clearly though I must thank a few especially: Lois Kauffman; Abbot John Klassen, OSB; Fr. William Skudlarek, OSB; Marlene Kropf; Weldon Nisly again; Darrin Snyder Belousek; Mary Schertz; and Regina Wilson.

Finally, my deepest gratitude goes to the three persons to whom I dedicate this book—Ivan Kauffman, also of Bridgefolk; Stanley Hauerwas, foil for setting up my argument but certainly much more; and of course Joetta, companion in sorrow and joy, faith and fidelity.

1

The Protestant Dilemma

In short, Protestantism helped to create, but even more, to legitimate, a form of social life that undermined its ability to maintain the kind of disciplined communities necessary to sustain the church's social witness.

Stanley Hauerwas[1]

O
F ALL OF Jesus' teachings, perhaps none is more enigmatic than the parable of the shrewd manager (Luke 16:1–13). The manager's boss is about to lay him off for squandering the boss's property and gives him a few days to settle his accounts. Wanting neither to beg nor to do manual labor, the manager must find a way to prompt the care and hospitality of the community. So he calls in the boss's clients and reduces their debts by 20 to 50 percent. Even as the boss shows the manager to the door, therefore, he congratulates him for his cleverness. Not only does Jesus let the boss's judgment stand, but he also goes on to hold the manager up for modeling the kind of faithful use of "dishonest wealth" that we need to practice on our way to more stable homes. What has puzzled interpreters of this text is that the story would seem to offer a counsel of embezzlement.

But Jesus is the one telling the story, and at the end he commends the manager for both his shrewdness *and* his faithfulness. How can this be?

Christians embedded in modern cultures face some formidable puzzles of their own. Whatever else Jesus' parable meant or means, it suggests a clue: sometimes we find ourselves forced to move beyond one set of cultural trends and social realities in order to sustain our lives, or even to survive. To do so, however, we find that we may have to use those very trends and realities in order to transcend them.

At its most basic level, this book is about what Protestants can learn from Roman Catholics concerning the practices and virtues they need to stick together faithfully and to sustain Christian community. But immediately a puzzle lurks. To learn from Catholics how to *unlearn* Protestantism well enough to sustain our communities could be to retain a fairly Protestant impulse, that of solving one's problems by shopping around for resources beyond one's own tradition. Jesus' parable does provide a precedent. But paradoxes are at work here, every which way.

On the one hand, much about the social and religious scene that makes it possible to work at the interface between Catholic and Protestant church life is exciting and promising. What some call the "postmodern" situation encourages a crossing of boundaries in hopes of mutual enrichment among communities and traditions. Striking about the phenomenon is how evident it is far beyond the trendy academics who might call themselves "postmodernist" and who associate most often with the cultural left. For years Catholics and Protestants have collaborated in groups working for peace and social justice, but so too in pro-life coalitions opposing abortion and euthanasia. Evangelicals and Catholics read and write for *Sojourners* magazine on the Christian left (for want of a better term), but likewise for *First Things* magazine, which tends toward the Christian right (for want of a better term). Still more intriguing are groups that defy easy right/left categorization—such as the Ekklesia Project, which seeks to restore the church to its place of primary identity for Christians, both Catholic and Protestant.[2] And these are merely a few American examples. Globally, the Pentecostal and Charismatic movement crosses all kinds of ecclesiological, racial, economic, and class boundaries, extending even into Catholic circles.

Meanwhile, the Vatican has been encouraging a variety of ecclesial movements that embrace some of the dynamics of participatory lay leadership and community formation often associated with radical Protestantism.

One longtime religious journalist and friend suggests that we might better name this "postmodern" situation the Ecumenical Age. His point is that more and more people recognize their need for insights and practices that other traditions embody. Whatever we call it, the postmodern or ecumenical situation offers individuals and communities the freedom to appropriate the wisdom of others, to enrich their identities, or even to reinvent their identities altogether.

On the other hand, much about this social and religious scene—and many versions of the borrowing, reforming, and re-forming it makes possible—also has a tendency to corrode community and commitment, rather than to enrich them. In 1985 sociologist Robert Bellah and a group of colleagues published a book that drew immediate acclaim and soon became a classic: *Habits of the Heart: Individualism and Commitment in American Life.* Twenty years later and counting, its warnings are hardly out of date. American individualism, its authors warned, works at cross-purposes with the American impulse to create new forms of community. The culture of the United States certainly has deep traditions of community formation, which continue to have some of their strongest roots in religious soil. American individualism itself has historically offered creative space and freedom to form all kinds of voluntary associations. Yet it also tends to corrode the very commitments needed to sustain community, stripping us of the language we need to articulate the common good that underwrites such commitment. What then passes as communities are often merely "lifestyle enclaves" of the like-minded, from Internet chat rooms to gated suburbs. Community commitment, such as it is, often lasts only so long as relationships meet the individual's therapeutic needs. One extreme expression of these dynamics is a religion of one—what Bellah and associates labeled "Sheilaism," after the interviewee who admitted she had made up her own religion.[3]

Protestantism is surely not the only historical force at work in such habits of heart and social interaction, but it has played a critical role in American culture generally and is obviously of special importance

23

for Christian theology and practice.[4] The Protestant Reformers supplied some of the best arguments both for individualism *and* for attempts to start over at community. Prominent twentieth-century theologian Paul Tillich summed these up as the Protestant Principle: *because all human institutions fall short of God's standard, they are always subject to "prophetic" critique and reform.*[5]

True as that is, the Protestant Principle creates a dilemma, especially for its adherents. To make this the very principle of community life, after all, is to invite the perpetual *un*making of community life. Individuals invent their own religions, and churches continue to divide. Less dramatic (but perhaps all the more corrosive because so many of us take them for granted) are the phenomena reflected in the language of "church shopping." When churches happily grow by marketing themselves and when believers commit only in the way of consumers, we are in danger of trivializing even the legitimate impulse toward reform and discarding commitments almost as quickly as consumer items. Still, like the shrewd manager seeking a more sustainable home (Luke 16), we may have to shop around just a little longer, at least for ideas and models.

Without necessarily abandoning their denominations, some influential Protestant thinkers are recognizing the need to do a better job of inculcating the practices and virtues Christians need to sustain community. Prominent and provocative among them is the Methodist theologian and ethicist Stanley Hauerwas. In this Ecumenical Age, he is but one Protestant who is looking to Roman Catholic traditions for help in sustaining Christian community. One way to summarize the problem Hauerwas and others identify is this: Protestantism tends to undo itself.

The Permanent Principle of Reform

Historically and continually, it has been necessary for Christians to reform the church, critique their leaders, defend individual conscience, and protest both moral and doctrinal corruption. Though Tillich named and explained the Protestant Principle from a rather airy pinnacle of mid-twentieth-century liberal Protestantism, Protestants far more grounded in orthodox Christianity concur just as

24

surely. In a way, so too do Roman Catholic historians as they look back on the sixteenth-century Reformation era that split the church in the West. In the tactful language of the Second Vatican Council, the Catholic Church has officially agreed.

Tillich had no illusions that the actual Protestant churches of either the sixteenth or the twentieth century fully embodied the "universally significant principle" that was foundational for Protestant Christianity.[6] That, in a way, was his point. Every institution, every culture, every church, including any church that claims to be reformed, continues to be subject to "prophetic judgment against religious pride, ecclesiastical arrogance, and secular self-sufficiency and their destructive consequences."[7] The criterion for such judgment stands permanently over against even its best temporal embodiments because it is eternal: "the power of the New Being that is manifest in Jesus the Christ."[8] Since the Protestant Principle transcends Protestant churches themselves, "The Protestant principle may be proclaimed by movements that are neither ecclesiastical nor secular but belong to both spheres, by groups and individuals who, with or without Christian and Protestant symbols, express the true human situation in the face of the ultimate and unconditional."[9] Not surprisingly, Tillich suggested that we must sometimes look outside the churches to find people who express the dynamic of Protestantism "better and with more authority than the official churches."[10]

Already we can begin to sense why the Protestant Principle, at least as Tillich explained it, might have a tendency to undo Protestant Christianity. Tillich was defining what is essential to Protestantism in a way that makes Protestant churches themselves superfluous. To be sure, Jesus Christ plays a leading role in Tillich's theology; Tillich called Christ the fullest revelation of the "New Being" that God intended for human beings. Yet it would surely surprise the Reformers to learn that "the sole foundation of the churches of the Reformation" is an ahistorical abstract philosophical principle, even if it is a "universally significant principle,"[11] rather than the person and work of Jesus Christ, in whom we must trust as our sole hope for salvation, *sola fide*.

Still, a dilemma is a two-sided creature that is doubly hard to extricate because it bites even as it comforts. Whatever our worries, Tillich was on to something. He was actually in good company when

25

he insisted that the task of reformation is never done. He rightly identified a dynamic that runs all the way back through classical Protestantism—and beyond. His most irrefutable arguments for a Protestant Principle draw on the prophetic traditions of Israel and on Christianity's judgment against every form of self-righteousness.

Honest reflection will add to Tillich's case with examples stretching from the New Testament through church history. The New Testament records the apostle Paul challenging none less than the apostle Peter on some of the most decisive questions that faced the young church as it sought to discern what was essential to the gospel in light of moral conflicts dividing Jewish and Gentile Christians (Gal. 2). Already in the early second century, one of the earliest texts to be included in the corpus of recognized Church Fathers shows that church officials in the Christian community of Rome were growing wealthy, pastorally complacent, petty in their bickering, hypocritical in their teaching, and in need of warnings from a charismatic but unordained layperson.[12] In the early fifth century, Augustine of Hippo carried on a prickly dispute with his respected elder Jerome; he cited Paul's rebuke of Peter as a thinly veiled assertion of his right to do so.[13] In the high medieval period, the rise of the Franciscan and Dominican orders, with their radical vows of poverty and itinerate ministries among the populace, represented a protest against the growing wealth of the church in general and the increasing luxury within landowning Benedictine monasteries in particular. So before conservative Protestants dismiss Tillich's point, or Roman Catholics dismiss Protestants, all would do well to recognize the reformation dynamic at work in the broad pre-Reformation Catholic tradition itself.

When Martin Luther, John Calvin, and other sixteenth-century Reformers broke with the Roman Catholic Church, they certainly felt a keen need to justify their actions—but in doing so they appealed to a broad consensus that the late medieval church was desperately in need of reform. In addressing his signal treatise *On the Freedom of a Christian* to Pope Leo X in 1520, Martin Luther could write with rhetorical certainty that none less than the pope would see himself sitting "as a lamb in the midst of wolves," prevented from leading a reform of his own by a despicable Roman Curia (the Vatican bureaucracy), which "neither you nor anyone else can deny is more corrupt than any Babylon or Sodom ever was, . . . characterized by a completely depraved, hopeless, and notorious godlessness."[14] Luther was quite wrong about Leo's good but stifled pastoral intentions, and probably he suspected that. But Leo's successor, Pope Adrian VI, would largely concur with Luther's assessment of the Curia.[15] In any case, Luther could appeal to the view of many other readers, or at least to their desperate hope for reform, as it had been growing among conscientious Christians throughout Europe for centuries. Precipitated by the Protestant Reformation, but gathering up centuries of authentic impulses for reform, that hope would belatedly bear fruit two decades later when another pope consolidated the Catholic Reformation by calling the Council of Trent. At one level, then, what divided Catholic and Protestant Reformers was only the question of how thoroughgoing was the need for reform and how to proceed.

This was the question that John Calvin took up in 1544 as he wrote explicitly on *The Necessity of Reforming the Church*. Calvin addressed his treatise to the pious Catholic emperor Charles V. Here again, Calvin could assume that the question was not whether the church needed reform, but how much and how it was to be accomplished. All "moderate judges," wrote Calvin, admitted that "the Church labours under diseases both numerous and grievous"; what they contested was "whether the diseases are of a kind the cure of which admits not of longer delay, and as to which, therefore, it is neither useful nor becoming to await the result of slow remedies."[16] Against the accusation that the Reformers had promoted innovations that were impious or at least rash, Calvin argued that the Roman Church had demonstrated the need for thoroughgoing reform by resisting even obvious and reasonable reforms: "When Luther at first appeared, he merely touched, with a gentle hand, a few abuses of the grossest description, now grown intolerable"; he did not so much seek to correct them himself as to call upon the proper authorities to do so.[17] Yet by its "inflamed" reaction, Calvin argued, the papacy discredited its own authority, deeming that "the best and shortest method to suppress the truth [was] by cruelty and violence" rather than "friendly discussion" and "calm arguments."[18] Centuries later the disagreement that continues to divide Protestants from Catholics[19] remains at one level over largely the same issue: it is not so much over whether the church has needed or sometimes needs reform, but whether the need for reform has been so fundamental that Protestants should continue to disclaim Catholic structures for sustaining the global life of the church altogether.

Writing like Calvin in Geneva, but now at mid-twentieth century and just a few years after Tillich, Jacques de Senarclens articulated Tillich's Protestant Principle in a way that the classical Reformers would more likely recognize as their own. His term for it instead was "The Evangelical Starting Point."[20] Influencing de Senarclens was the neo-orthodox theology of fellow Swiss Calvinist Karl Barth rather than the romantic liberal theology of Tillich. *Heirs of the Reformation*, by de Senarclens, seeks to answer a key question: on what basis can contemporary Protestant churches claim continuity with the Reformers? What, in other words, makes Protestants Protestant?

The Protestant Reformation itself rules out any claim of authenticity simply on the basis of ecclesiological continuity through institution and tradition, observed de Senarclens. Concurring in his own way with Tillich, de Senarclens insisted that according to the Reformers, "the faith of the Reformers can never be for us a final norm of truth." Rather, the starting point for their acts of reformation is not only a question that they put to Christians of their age but also one that Christians of every generation must face anew: "In your faith, teaching and activity, are you really a witness and therefore an heir of the Gospel of the prophets and apostles?"[21]

However right and valuable the decisions of the sixteenth century, according to de Senarclens, Protestants thus "are Protestants in virtue of the single fact that we understand the permanent need for this kind of examination." The question that the Reformers and all true heirs of the Reformation permanently pose "expresses at once a disquietude, a desire to obey, a demand for authenticity and the resolve not to be held by traditions which, venerable though they are, cannot offer any guarantee of agreement with the message of the living God." The church that preaches and poses this question does so because its faith is a "vigilant faith." In keeping with the "first instruction" and very life of its Lord, the church that holds such a faith is continually urged to submit truly to Jesus Christ and to make itself vulnerable to correction from the Word of God. The church recognizing that this is its raison d'être is one that also recognizes its own tendency to deviate.[22]

This permanent and self-critical posing of the question of fidelity to Jesus Christ is clearly another version of the Protestant Principle, but for de Senarclens its ultimate basis could not simply be the impulse to protest corruption or otherwise to resist sin. Rather, it lies in God's grace alone. De Senarclens found a formative reminder of this in one of Calvin's earliest catechisms, in which the Reformer had led his readers through a search for a reliable source of saving knowledge of God. Though human beings have a natural inclination to seek God, which God's self-revelation in creation evokes, sin has so twisted this embryonic religious sensibility that instead it consistently results in false images of God. Knowledge of ourselves as sinful is a somewhat more reliable source of salvation, therefore, since it prompts us to turn to God rather than construct illusions that suit us. Yet knowledge of sin itself is possible only through the revelation of Jesus Christ, and that comes through grace. It is because "the only truly solid ground for an instructed and obedient faith is where grace alone rules" that "the Evangelical Church can and should proclaim, even against itself and its own failings, that its own basis alone is the authentically Christian basis."[23]

De Senarclens clearly meant his arguments to contrast with some of the ways that the Roman Catholic Church has claimed authenticity on the basis of either historical continuity through tradition or sacramental connectivity between the natural and the divine.[24] Yet he actually supplied compelling reasons for Roman Catholics to stick with their church. De Senarclens's Christocentric arguments, tracing the Protestant Principle back to grace alone, should strike a loyal and well-formed Catholic as far more solid than Tillich's, and thus all the more likely to evoke second thoughts. His very emphasis on God's grace, however, prompted de Senarclens to affirm that "in [God's] faithfulness God never leaves the Church wholly destitute of his help"; thus despite all the church's "human hesitation and confusion, the Lord himself has always been at work."[25] Church history may well "give us a sorry picture of . . . perpetual alienation" from the Word of God, as believers themselves resist God's will, and unsurprisingly the church itself "succumbs to the many temptations which threaten it"; still, "the faithfulness of the Lord is stronger than our opposition."[26]

In any case, Catholic historians looking back on the sixteenth-century Protestant Reformation have concurred that thoroughgoing reformation was historically necessary at that time. The Second Vatican Council too has certainly recognized that the church must always be receptive to God's transformative work. These affirmations are what is at stake in the Protestant Principle, whatever else a Catholic might wish to call it.

Leading Catholic historians of sixteenth-century church history are prepared to recognize not only that the church of the late medieval period needed serious reform but also that the division in the Western Church prompted by the Reformers' efforts owed as much to Roman intransigence as to Protestant impetuousness. Decades before Vatican II, the German historian Joseph Lortz was arguing that while a Catholic such as himself could not say that the Reformation was an *absolute* necessity—since that would imply that God's very intention for the church was that it be divided—the Reformation was surely a *historical* necessity.[27] Historical forces, in other words, had made the Reformation all but inevitable.

Lortz listed various causes. Among them are the abuses that had become standard complaints among medieval Christians well before the Reformation: bad popes, decades of divided papacy, a lack of sanctity among the clergy, aristocratic control of monasteries, simony (the buying and selling of church posts), along with the arbitrariness and hedonism of the Curia.[28] Other causes provoking the Protestant Reformation might not be so obvious to the medieval populace but ensured that when controversy over indulgences broke out in Luther's Germany, the response from Rome would be utterly devoid of pastoral concern: the diplomacy of papal diplomats was almost purely political, without regard for religious matters; even on Good Friday (according to Erasmus) the pope's own homily was all humanistic oratory based on learning from antiquity, with no mention of Christ or his passion.[29]

Behind these causes were deeper ones still: the papacy itself was weakening the medieval unity of the church as it fought for political independence by playing one political power off against another.[30] Developing theological thought concerned itself less and less with the lived experience or sacramental life of the church; theological confusion thus originated not with heretical groups, nor did attacks on church doctrine originate with the Reformers, but both came from within the church itself.[31] The Reformation would come to express a far-reaching discontent arising from within the medieval Catholic Church; as early as 1200 this discontent was finding voice in a wide "call for a return to the simplicity of apostolic times."[32] Lortz was thus willing to speak of a "Catholic" Luther who, in his advocacy of "justification by faith alone," had rediscovered an old Catholic doctrine and only became less Catholic as his animosity toward the papacy began to harden.[33]

So Catholics must recognize the lesson that the very upheaval of the sixteenth-century Protestant Reformation represents and that Protestant churches continue to embody through their very existence. Thus the life of the church in human history requires continual openness to reformation, at least at some level. This modest restatement of the Protestant Principle is actually less bold than what the Second Vatican Council has affirmed with all the authority of an ecumenical council—"ecumenical" referring here to a solemn gathering of Catholic bishops from throughout the entire world:

> Christ summons the Church, as she goes her pilgrim way, to that continual reformation of which she always has need, insofar as she is an institution of men here on earth. Consequently, if, in various times and circumstances, there have been deficiencies in moral conduct or in Church discipline, or even in the way that Church teaching has been formulated—to be carefully distinguished from the deposit of faith itself—these should be set right at the opportune moment and in the proper way.[34]

But what is the opportune moment? What ways of setting right are themselves opportune? That is the question that initially divided conscientious Catholics from reluctant Protestants. By hardened implication, it continues to do so. After so many writers have spilled so much ink so polemically over so many centuries, I can hardly hope to settle this tired question here, especially by addressing it frontally one more tiring time. If any fresh insight may be possible, to say

31

nothing of fresh movement toward reconciliation, perhaps we can find it through an indirect approach.

Or perhaps we are already finding it as we grope ecumenically and stumble through the postmodern era. Consider this: Catholics have come to recognize the church's permanent need for reformation—and thus a version of the Protestant Principle. But as we now shall see, Protestants themselves must notice how that very principle also poses a Protestant Dilemma. What *all* of us need are the practices and virtues that make it possible to reform, protest, and even dissent out of love for one's Christian community—even while sustaining a doggedly loyal commitment to "hang in there" with those among whom we disagree. To develop these practices and grow in those virtues within our respective Protestant and Catholic communities may yet mean to find ourselves growing together. Whether or not official church unity eventually results, and however it may happen, all Christian communities need such virtues to sustain their lives together.

The Nagging Dilemma of Undoing

Faithful Christian life and practice must always be open and indeed vulnerable to the challenge of prophets, to the voice of conscience, to the work of reform—to protest. So we have seen. Admittedly, the term "Protestant" is a bit of a historical accident; it applied first to twenty Lutheran princes and leaders of free cities in Germany after they sent a letter protesting their treatment at an imperial assembly in 1529. Protestant thinkers have often objected that their tradition is not just negative and reactive. They stress its positive witness to the preeminent and all-sufficient work of Jesus Christ in human salvation, along with doctrinal affirmations that help believers remain clear about this, beginning with the authority of the Bible. Still, the permanent impulse to reform does run deep within the historic Protestant movement, while the fundamental need to reform has consistently justified its very existence. Consensus between otherwise divergent thinkers like Tillich and de Senarclens suggests that while the Protestant Principle of permanent vulnerability to critique may not be *sufficient* for authentic Protestantism, it is *necessary* and even essential.

The problem with the Protestant Principle is this: however right and proper are the corrective reflexes it names, once we elevate impulses to "protest" into identity markers for entire Christian communities, those impulses tend to undermine the very bonds of Christian community. If the Protestant Principle is not just one principle among many—though quite near to the core of Protestant identity itself—then Protestantism will tend to undo itself. This is not a broadside in the service of some triumphalistic old-fashioned Roman Catholic apologetic. It is heartfelt fraternal counsel I bear as one who has sojourned with Protestant brothers and sisters all my life. Precisely those who carry the deepest commitment to Protestant forms of Christianity must grapple most poignantly with how the Protestant Principle becomes the Protestant Dilemma.

Especially as Tillich worked it out, the Protestant Principle tends to render Protestant churches superfluous. His reading of Protestantism actually goes quite far to explain the languishing state of mainline Protestant denominations in the second half of the twentieth century and on into the twenty-first. This may be less because of his influence than the way he expressed the spirit of his time and class location.[35] Identifying with Bohemian German culture in his youth and hip New York culture as a middle-age émigré, Tillich gave voice to that class of cultural leaders and consumers in modern society that is at once resentful of *and* dependent on the technicians who actually manage society and produce its material goods.[36] His theology is famously abstract, philosophical, and averse to doctrine. At its most well intentioned, what guides it is a desire to articulate the Christian faith in broadly universal categories of human experience.[37] But at its most dubious, it constitutes a nostalgic and parasitic attempt to retain the cultural power of Christian symbols without accountable participation in real Christian communities.[38]

While Tillich continues to insist that the finality of revelation is in Christ, his affirmation that Jesus "manifests the power of the New Being" is finally a rather vague abstraction.[39] Turning Christian attention away from the concrete particularities by which the very life of God is incarnate in the fleshy life, jarring teachings, bloody death, and unexpected resurrection of Jesus of Nazareth, Tillich's *manifestation* nearly verges into gnosticism insofar as it risks obfuscating the *incarnation*. Still less does such a disembodied gospel invite us

33

to linger over the possibility that the life of that people called church might, in its very messiness and earthy imperfection, nonetheless constitute nothing short of what the apostle Paul affirms: "the *body of Christ*." After all, at any moment other social movements might seem to be doing better than the church at speaking to "the human situation." We can actually fill up "the New Being" with any and all good we perceive in our latest, favorite, most cutting-edge causes, and easily judge their efforts to be more promising than the church's. So why bother with church life at all?[40]

Yet the Protestant Principle characterizes far more than Tillich's liberal version alone. That raises a question: does the dilemma by which Tillich's liberal Protestantism tends to undo itself hold also for other forms? Though other forms of Protestantism may well have resources to offset the tendency that his version has fostered, unfortunately they too share the Protestant Dilemma.

The tendency of Protestantism to undo Protestant churches surfaced almost immediately in the sixteenth-century Reformation. Many have pointed out that doctrinal disputes quickly dashed early Reformation hope in the principle of *sola scriptura*—that if only the Bible were available for all believers, accretions of tradition and human teaching would lose their force and the renewal of authentic Christianity could proceed unfettered. The Bible did not turn out to be quite so self-interpreting; even learned Reformers with the best interpretive skills of the day soon found themselves disagreeing with one another over doctrine. The problem was not simply with the rich complexity of the biblical canon, however, but with the individualistic impulses that Protestantism itself had unleashed.

Wolfgang Faber Capito recognized this problem by 1538. This was scarcely twenty years into the Reformation. Capito was an early associate of Luther who became a leader in the Strasbourg reform. Based on both his desire to avoid further church division and his reluctance to use the coercive force of civil authority in matters of faith and conscience, for much of his career Capito was among the most tolerant of the mainstream Reformers when still-more-radical reformers in the Anabaptist movement dissented not only from Catholicism but also from the mainstream Reformation itself.[41] In any case, the anxiety he voiced seems directed not simply toward potentially schismatic teachings but also toward a general subjectivism in his own church:

34

The Lord is showing us now how much harm we have done with our overzealous attack against the Papacy. Since we have eliminated the Pope, the ministry of the Word, the sacraments, and pastoral care have come to naught. The people cry out, "I understand the Gospel well enough; I can read it myself. Why do I need your help? Preach to those who want to listen to you and let them accept what they want."[42]

This is precisely the dilemma that prompts a sympathetic Catholic interpreter such as Lortz to draw back, despite his deep respect for figures such as Luther. Protestantism, Lortz wrote, makes the individual Christian "subject to no authority but that of his own conscience." While it might be salutary for each Christian to "grapple with the words of Scripture on his own," on that basis it is not clear that the larger community can offer any guidance weightier than one more opinion, much less warn the believer away from outright error. As Lortz observes, "Even where the authority of the Church is recognized to the extent admitted by Luther, the basic Protestant attitude leads of necessity to an ultimate rejection of that authority."[43]

It is one thing to say that every human institution and tradition must be continually vulnerable to prophetic critique and correction. It is another thing to hold all tradition suspect as a matter of principle. A church then must either face the unstable prospect of perpetually starting over or pass along its convictions through traditions that go covertly by some other name. Illustrating both tendencies are Protestant groups that frankly call themselves "Restorationist" and try to return to a purer and more original form of Christianity, as they envision it.

In the context of early nineteenth-century American revivalism, for example, the followers of Alexander Campbell sought to reform the Reformed. One could tell a rich and ironic story right there about continuing cycles of institutionalization and dissent.[44] After all, the objections of antirevivalist Presbyterians were that the movement was subverting ecclesiastical authority and violating the dignity of traditional forms of worship.[45] The irony is that this was akin to what Catholics might have said about their Calvinist forebears!

What is even more telling is how the Campbellite Disciples of Christ immediately faced the impossibility of jettisoning tradition without starting a new one. Their goal was to unite all divided Christians around the essentials of the faith, not divide them further by founding one more denomination. Campbell urged his followers to promote a "simple, evangelical Christianity, free from all mixture of human opinions and inventions of men," and to do this by holding to "the professions and practice of the primitive Church." Adherents should not need to assent to any additional articles of faith or terms of communion. Yet it soon became necessary to structure the movement in *some* way; at the earliest organizational meetings there was already a strong impulse to write at least a catechism that would lay out a "complete system of faith and duty contained in the sacred oracles, respecting doctrine, worship, discipline, and government of the church."[46] The decades that followed brought new versions of the problem. Changing times brought new challenges that might require innovation—but every "innovation" was suspect because the movement was supposed to do no more than restore the ancient gospel.[47]

This might simply seem to be a quaint story of American frontier Christianity. Yet in a far more sophisticated and compelling theologian such as de Senarclens, the need for a perpetual starting over not only surfaces as well but also turns out to become a kind of metaphysical necessity. Even God's grace, it seems, can leave no traces in human history but must always be creating ex nihilo, out of nothing, as on the first day of creation.[48]

De Senarclen's case was eloquent and his concern legitimate. Not only did he seek to call us to trust in God's grace alone and to keep Christianity rooted in no other hope, but he also insisted that the church find its sustenance not in "a continuing life owed to organization" but in the "continuing vitality" of Pentecost. The very "doctrine of the Holy Spirit challenges the Church and its authority," he wrote. "In itself the Church is no more lasting than manna." If manna or church lives on, it is because Jesus Christ in his faithfulness constantly gives anew, and thus renews. The church is but "the effect of a living, actual, personal revelation of God by the Holy Spirit." Whenever we blur this truth, according to de Senarclen, the result is institutionalism. "Whether in its Roman, neo-Protestant or Orthodox form, institutionalism sins at this point. It finds truth in duration or tradition, not in the direct action of grace. It ascribes grace to an influence rather than a direct communication." Catholic and Orthodox sacramentalism misses the mark here, according to de Senarclens, and so does pietistic Protestantism, for these all rely on the ongoing influence either of a sacramental institution or an emotional experience to mediate grace—in place of a direct encounter with God's Word through Spirit-enlivened preaching. The result is religion rather than faith. Thus "the persistence of religion as an ecclesiastical or human phenomenon" substitutes for "the lasting faithfulness of God."[49]

Now, in what de Senarclen sought to *affirm* about our ultimate dependence on the work of God through Jesus Christ and the Holy Spirit, his argument should surely persuade. Still, it is unpersuasive in what it *denies*—paradoxically, at precisely the same point—for his argument would actually limit the power of grace and circumscribe the purview of God's incarnation. Though it is surely right that God in God's great faithfulness and steadfast love renews creation every morning with new mercies, the biblical passage that affirms this so eloquently also proclaims that those mercies "never come to an end" (Lam. 3:22–23). Thus the work of God abides. That God must daily create manna to sustain God's people does not mean that God leaves them utterly famished already before dawn the next day. Still less does it mean that God creates *only* manna but nothing else. And if something of God's old creation abides into each new day, surely God's new creation in the church has some durability as well—or more.

Certainly the church would be idolatrous to claim that it embodies the very life and presence of God so faithfully, perfectly, or infallibly as God incarnate in Jesus Christ. Yet one may join de Senarclens (and Calvin before him) in affirming that true Christian faith and theology must "rest on the basis of revelation alone, i.e., of the incarnation and reconciliation, of the covenant which God has concluded with [humanity] in Jesus Christ"[50]—and still say more. For if God in Christ has entered into human history and culture and then entrusted the gospel to sinful human messengers, God has deemed imperfect human ways good enough to carry revelation forward. If Christ has dwelt among us and shared our flesh over time, then God's own work has revealed that our limited fleshly lives through time are good enough to bear the imprint of grace, however imperfectly. If God can reconcile human beings, then human social relationships can enjoy a durability that participates in eternity. And if the covenant-making

37

God has disclosed the fullness of divine character in Jesus Christ, then as de Senarclens has so eloquently said, our God is one who never gives up on God's people. But to be a people at all—a human and not an angelic people—we must live together through those structured social relationships we call institutions. No more than manna ought we to think of institutions as ends in themselves, as self-sustaining or as incorruptible—yet we do need them too in order to sustain our reconciled life together. And no less than manna ought we to disqualify them as possible means of grace, simply because they last longer than a day, though not for eternity.

The Puzzle of Protestant Identity

I want to make it clear, one more time: some moments and some situations in the life of the church do require protest, dissent, and perhaps even prophetic departure for a time. If someone like Tillich had to chart the possibility of looking outside the churches of his day for humanizing social movements, one may lament how his influence helped to make churches superfluous, yet still sympathize, in light of what lay behind and before him. The German churches of his youth had generally been captive to nationalist fervor in World War I and to Nazi fascism in the lead-up to World War II. Before the 1950s and 1960s, the churches of his American readers were largely complacent about the suffering of African-Americans.

Anyone who forgets the mix of anguish and hope that can force conscientious Christians to find "church" somewhere beyond the church should read *God's Long Summer: Stories of Faith and Civil Rights*, by Charles Marsh. When white churches in Mississippi not only refused to admit black Christians but also ignored or supported Ku Klux Klan terrorism, one readily joins loyal church folks like the eloquent former sharecropper Fannie Lou Hamer and the Reverend Ed King, a Methodist minister, in seeing "the movement" as the true carrier of God's kingdom.[51]

Yet such situations result in part because Christians have *already* found church somewhere other than the church. Also among the stories of faith and civil rights that Marsh recounts is the proper Southern Baptist preacher Douglas Hudgins, who was less an apologist for segregation than a defender of what Marsh called "the piety of the pure soul."[52] Intended to strip away all that might keep individual souls from encountering God and their need for eternal salvation, Hudgins's preaching easily accommodated theologies of racial purity as well, since it had no need for corporately mediated salvation and no place for social engagement.

Well, that is not quite right. The radical individualism of his Baptist theology of salvation still needed some community life to aid the believer and provide a launching pad for evangelism. In Hudgins's Baptist ecclesiology, as Marsh put it, "the autonomous, local church thus becomes an extension of individual souls and their interior walks with Christ."[53] Such a congregation is not even accountable to a wider Baptist body pronouncing in favor of racial equality—much less a global "catholic" body reconciling many races and embodying witness to the kingdom by which God offers salvation to all humanity.[54] (To either impose external authority or mediate salvation in any way would begin to make Roman Catholic "mistakes.") In the end, however, Hudgins's Christianity still needed not just congregational life but also cultural expression. The wider "church" with which it identified was thus the anti-Communist "Christian" America as lived most faithfully through the Southern way of life. When Rev. Ed King organized a series of church visits in 1963–64, seeking to integrate Mississippi churches—most poignantly on Easter and World Communion Sunday—he was not only engaging in a savvy nonviolent campaign but also trying to counter this heretical church by reinstituting a thoroughgoing politics of baptism and Eucharist.[55]

Douglas Hudgins is admittedly an extreme example.[56] Still, such an example throws into relief a larger-if-subtler pattern that spans Protestant Christianity from right to left. Making the Protestant Principle an essential identity marker for Protestantism not only delegitimizes the continuity of tradition and accountability to a global catholic body but also destabilizes and corrodes Protestant churches themselves—the Protestant Dilemma, for Protestants also need community. They may not have a particularly strong ecclesiology—tending mainly to name the church's instrumental value as a launching pad for personal evangelism or for buttressing civilization or for social transformation or for therapeutic comfort and guidance. Yet they still need the church for more than that.

Each of these instrumental benefits, after all, reflects the deeper fact that human life is impoverished and outright impossible without others. Christians who think they can live good Christian lives apart from the church are simply but woefully self-deceived. Even "individual salvation" requires a messenger and forms an identity, which one must surely own personally and intimately, but which no one invents whole cloth apart from relationships and role models. And anyway, what is someone who has encountered God in a fresh and saving way to do next? If the gospel is to transform the shape of a life in a Christian way, it must take *shape* in a community. To name that shape is to name a culture. But with Protestantism's ambivalence about the role that church itself plays in salvation, and with the Protestant Principle as a self-corroding identity marker, Protestantism vacillates between undermining community and finding it somewhere besides the church itself. Civil religion—where the nation forms one's primary community or quasi-church—is one option. Liberalism—which seems less nationalistic but demands just as much loyalty to itself by requiring that every other communal attachment become a strictly private affair—is another option. Somewhere in between these lies denominationalism, in which every tradition may enjoy its identity as long as it accepts a subsidiary role in service to the social order or nation.

So we face a puzzle. Every human institution and tradition must be subject to prophetic critique, but to make that insight central to the identity of a Christian community is to undermine that community. Continuity for its own sake is surely idolatrous, and tradition for its own sake is often oppressive, but to delegitimate the continuity of tradition as a matter of principle is to limit God's grace to what God can do for a passing moment. If we cannot parse this puzzle, it may turn into nothing short of tragic. If we *can* parse it, however, it may prove fruitful.

Hauerwas's Hunch

Whatever else he is, Stanley Hauerwas is a controversialist. Named "America's Best Theologian" by *Time* magazine just a few days before the events of September 11, 2001, heightened patriotic fervor in the

United States, Hauerwas has long taken pains to identify himself with the people called church and not to belong to America at all. Or if he must name the place and culture that has formed him—as his approach to theology and philosophy says he must do—he is likely to name not America but Texas. A dogged opponent of liberal individualism in the modern world, Hauerwas is a unique and colorful individual.[57] Brash and provocative, he nonetheless exposes a surprisingly pastoral heart when he chides fellow academicians for writing mainly to one another rather than to ordinary Christians. A lifelong Methodist, Hauerwas advocates positions more closely identified both with the Roman Catholic tradition and with the Anabaptist-Mennonite tradition than with Protestantism. He signaled this years ago by calling himself a "high-church Mennonite," but his self-designation begs for further explanation since many would associate Catholicism with hierarchical authority, but Anabaptism with grassroots dissent.[58]

Yet here is the hunch we need. For decades, Hauerwas has intuited what I am calling the Protestant Dilemma. One of his most abiding concerns has been to help Christians recover from the very success of Protestantism. He has identified the Protestant Dilemma in his own way when he has said things like this: "Protestantism helped to create, but even more, to legitimate, a form of social life that undermined its ability to maintain the kind of disciplined communities necessary to sustain the church's social witness."[59] Hauerwas's bluster, his seeming inconsistencies, and the puzzling way in which he has advocated for both Anabaptism and Catholicism (without joining either in a conventional way) all snap into coherence once we recognize him as trying to unlearn Protestant vices that may at another time have been Protestant virtues.

That the character traits or habits of mind and practice we call virtues in one situation might turn into vices in another is something that the Greek philosopher Aristotle noticed long ago. This is not because right and wrong have no fixed tether, as situation ethics and moral relativism claim.[60] Rather, it is because our lives inevitably take the rich and complex shape of stories. Through time, we must grow into our very ability to name or recognize or do what is right. The naming, recognizing, and doing in turn happen at the intersections of other lives and stories. Virtuous parents, for example, will always—absolutely—seek to provide their children with nourishing food, but what kind and amount of food will actually nourish their children varies from child to child and sometimes depends on what they ate in a previous meal. Merely to choose the fitting meal is to live into and through a small but irreducibly storied story; that is just one decision so ordinary that we may recognize it as a moral decision only if something goes wrong and the parent instead neglects the child.

All the more so, then, with the intertwined practices, personal and social, that constitute the moral life as a whole. As the Aristotelian philosopher Alasdair MacIntyre taught Hauerwas early in his career, a virtue will turn into a vice most quickly when it is extracted from a rich and narratable social practice in the attempt to distill it into an abstract principle.[61] Part of the problem with the Protestant Principle, therefore, is precisely that it became *a principle*. When the Reformation willingness to protest has actually been a *virtue* rather than a principle, that is because the courage of conscience has operated in tandem with the virtues of justice, temperance, prudence, and above all Christlike love. These other virtues help the courageous person to avoid the vices of cowardice on one extreme and rashness on the other, between which courage must negotiate in order to be courage at all. Throughout the story of its development, true courage of conscience will not only have been shaped by participation in the very community whose unfaithfulness it protests, but will also remain embedded within that community if it is being practiced in life-giving love rather than out of dysfunctional anger.

Over the course of church history, the turning of virtues into vices is exactly what has happened to Protestantism, or so implies the sum total of Hauerwas's arguments. Hauerwas has been quite willing to recognize legitimate reasons for "prophetic challenge" against the power structures of Christendom in the sixteenth century.[62] Indeed, despite his respect for many Roman Catholic traditions, despite his admiration for figures such as Pope John Paul II, and despite his ambivalence about Protestantism, "he remains Protestant as long as Protestant churches are necessary to remind the Catholic Church that it is not yet what it is called to be."[63] Hauerwas argues, however, that sixteenth-century Protestantism in all its major forms could "work" and create cohesive forms of Christian community only because it owed a far greater debt than its leaders recognized to the formative habits and communal practices that had been forged in previous centuries.[64] The modern world, which the Protestant appeal to individual conscience helped to create, consistently corrodes such habits.[65] With the struggle for religious liberty won and secular culture celebrating individual autonomy above all other values, Christians who base their community life primarily on principles of voluntary choice may even start to become indistinguishable from "pagans." What is certain is that they have ever fewer resources for forming lives of Christian discipleship or communities of Christian witness.[66]

It was precisely this concern for the formation of authentically Christian lives that launched Hauerwas's theological project and led him to take positions he did not initially anticipate.[67] Recall de Senarclen's defense of a view of the Christian life that implies a perpetual starting over, with God's grace apparently leaving no traces that might help the believer to respond to God's call next time. De Senarclen reflects a far wider tendency in Protestantism. Accordingly, Protestant ethics has often stressed God's commands (one after another) and focused on decisions that the believer must make to respond to God in trust (on one occasion after another) without any apparent connection between these moments of existential crisis and decision.[68] Dissatisfaction with such a view of the Christian life is precisely what initially agitated Hauerwas and prompted him to attend to the place of character, virtue, and "sanctification" in the Christian life.[69] Though even his critics now recognize the helpful and leading role he has played in returning the attention of Christian ethicists to "virtue ethics," that was never his primary objective. Looking back, Hauerwas has commented that the church, not the theoretical question of virtue or character development, is the proper starting point for an adequately Christian ethic.[70]

After all, the formation of authentically Christian lives is unimaginable apart from communities of Christian character. If one is being formed, then one is not simply making discrete decisions but is developing habits that extend the character of one action into later ones. Habits require training, as one internalizes moral motor skills that one can only clumsily imitate at first, based on the example of others. If those habits are to be good rather than bad, however, practitioners must apprentice with those more advanced in the craft—in this case

43

the craftlike practice of Christian discipleship. The Christian life is already proving to be something more than a solitary endeavor here, but mentors and role models are trustworthy precisely because they embody convictions and practices that both emerge from and build up a wider community. To be sure, the interlocking components that make up *any* virtue ethic could just as easily form quite different tables of virtue—Greek warrior culture, a racist "Southern way of life," or a works-righteousness Christianity accessible only to those whom the apostle Paul chided for calling themselves "the strong"— except that the ultimate master to whom we apprentice in this craft is Jesus Christ. Christ thoroughly transforms the very meaning of virtue by making it available to sinners and all who know themselves to be "the weak." He has done so through the unexpected paradox of one who is our master precisely through nonviolent servanthood. Christ thus discloses both the very character of God and the very fullness of humanity that God intended us to "image."

A community being transformed according to the character of Christ must be rejecting violent patterns of oppression and inhospitality, yet the freedom that Christianity thus offers is hardly compatible with modern notions of autonomy as Immanuel Kant classically proposed them, at the height of the Enlightenment. As Hauerwas once succinctly explained:

> (1) The Christian thinks it important to live in recognition that life is a gift rather than to live autonomously; (2) Christian ethics involves learning to imitate another before it involves acting on principles (though principles are not excluded); and (3) the Christian moral life is finally not one of "development" but of conversion.[71]

Hospitality, mutual dependence, and dependence on the gifts of God mean, as Hauerwas once remarked, that "the last thing the church wants is a bunch of autonomous, free individuals."[72]

Now, how exactly Christian communities are to do all this will be an unfinished matter for discernment. Such discernment must respond to a working conception of the good of community life that God is in one sense imposing on its members through the lordship of Christ over the community, for it is not theirs to perpetually reinvent. This discerning response may rightly be called *obedience*—

even *submission* to the wider wisdom of the community as it in turn seeks to respond to the truth for which God has created us—yet it will invite rather than suppress the voice of the weakest in the community. However we are to hold all this together, it will be through virtuous practice, not through formulaic principle. What is clear is this: somehow the way the church holds all this together must disallow the tyranny of individual autonomy as surely as it disallows tyrannical leadership of the community.[73]

The challenge of later chapters (esp. 3 and 4) will be to explore how such a community life might be possible. The point for now is simply that in ways Hauerwas might see only in retrospect, his entire project represents an unfolding hunch about why we find ourselves trying to survive the very success of Protestantism. Although he may never have named this as his own driving intuition, he has left clues. One way or another, through what can hold together only as a richly complex practice that coheres in the way of a good story (not as an abstract set of principles or rules), we must hold together *both* a proper respect for authority in our Christian communities and a proper vulnerability to dissenting voices. Furthermore, through the naming of virtues and the narrating of lives that exemplify and embody those virtues, we will be able to identify this "one way or another" that is the glue holding together an intertwined practice of authority and dissent in Christian communities.

That practice, in good times, I will call by the Benedictine name of "stability." In hard times, it may have to go by the tenser name of "loyal dissent." Either way, the virtue it inculcates is fidelity. If "fidelity" sounds a bit sappy and pious to some ears, let me offer an irreverent definition: whatever else fidelity may be, on ordinary days in ordinary parishes, colleges, marriages, religious communities, and so on, *fidelity is the virtue that keeps us together even when we're pissed off at each other.* If Protestants would do well to learn models of stability, fidelity, and loyal dissent from Catholics, it is not because Catholics are inherently more virtuous. It is simply that Catholics have had to develop this virtue (like it or not) because their faith requires them to stick together (like one another or not) at those very sorts of junctures where Protestantism would allow or even propose the easier route of splitting and starting over. For Catholics to do that is, simply by definition, to become a Protestant. So they can't.

To practice stability, to learn the virtue of fidelity and unlearn the formerly virtuous vices of Protestantism, we may have to follow the maddeningly unruly and still-quite-Protestant example of Hauerwas—like him or not! Somehow, Hauerwas "wants Catholics to be more Anabaptist, and Anabaptists to be more Catholic, and Protestants to be both."[74] Yes, maddening! And yet consistent. Or at least commendable—in just the way that Jesus commended the shrewd manager, the righteous survivor, for using the remaining resources of an increasingly untenable situation precisely in order to move beyond it.

2

The Matter of Continuity

Renewal vision has been less than fully successful in maintaining first-generation devotion in the second and third generation in the life of a restored community. That proves that there are yet unsolved theological and practical problems involved in understanding how the life of the church is supposed to continue.

John Howard Yoder[1]

STANLEY HAUERWAS HAS taken to Mennonites for what might be contradictory reasons. Successors to the Anabaptist, or Radical, wing of the sixteenth-century Reformation, they constitute a tradition of *dissent*. But they also constitute a *tradition* of dissent. Here lies a tension, at the very least.

As a longtime colleague and close reader of John Howard Yoder, Hauerwas in his thought encountered the best and most trenchant Mennonite argument for principled *dissent*. Probably the most renowned Mennonite thinker of the twentieth century, Yoder was

An earlier version of this chapter, titled "Continuity and Sacrament, or Not: Hauerwas, Yoder, and Their Deep Difference," appeared in the *Journal of the Society of Christian Ethics* 27, no. 2 (Fall–Winter 2007): 171–207. I am grateful to the society for permission to reprint.

Hauerwas's colleague at the University of Notre Dame for many years and convinced him to swallow the bitter pill of Christian pacifism.[2] In one of Yoder's earliest essays, written in 1952 and published in 1954, he had labeled the very logic of Anabaptist ways of following Jesus as that of dissent.[3] What Anabaptist-Mennonite disciples most of all dissent *from*, according to Yoder, are violent ways of ordering the world, along with the pattern of sanctifying such worldly violence that has characterized so much of Western Christianity. To be sure, Hauerwas probably did not need much inspiration to dissent. He was already beginning to goad mainline Protestants and Roman Catholics into unmuting a distinctive yet public voice shaped by specifically Christian convictions. Christians should be no more concerned that those convictions mesh with dominant assumptions of the day—liberal, conservative, or whatever—than Hauerwas was in using working-class Texan profanities in polite company.

Hauerwas found Yoder's theology convincing too, and it gave him greater access to a living *tradition* that exemplified how all Christian churches ought to constitute "communities of character."[4] Much to his initial surprise, he wrote, "Yoder's account of the church fit almost exactly the kind of community I was beginning to think was required by an ethics of virtue."[5] Besides that, sinced he lived in northern Indiana, Hauerwas's interest was piqued in actual Mennonite communities; one of the leading centers of ethnic and intellectual Mennonite life was in Goshen just a few miles east of Notre Dame. Mennonites demonstrated concretely why Christians needed more than abstract principles to live faithful Christian lives. To be a truthful but peaceable people required concrete practices of mutual admonition, forgiveness, and reconciliation.[6] To maintain something like the "oddness of [Mennonite] pacifism" required at least a lingering memory of community discipline.[7] Above all, a thoroughgoing critique of the illusions of this age (or any age) required a community that holds and embodies an alternative narrative, in turn shaped by the narrative of Jesus of Nazareth, the Christ, over the long haul.[8]

So what's the problem? The tension between dissent and tradition may be a contradictory, uneasy, or creative one—but a tension it is. Hauerwas has recognized the longitude in that Mennonite "long haul" to be far more crucial than Anabaptist-Mennonite theology has known how to name, or than Yoder especially has wanted to do.[9]

As we shall see, that foundational 1952 essay by Yoder on Anabaptist dissent did not simply aim to place Mennonites in a dissenting posture vis-à-vis society at large or vis-à-vis mainstream churches cozy with society's sources of power. The essay was also part of a radical program of church renewal challenging the very Mennonite leaders and institutions that had trained and shaped Yoder's generation. It relied on theological assumptions far deeper and more abiding than the youthful zeal that helped to embolden it. It was deeply suspicious of settled community based on the continuities of family, ethnicity, and tradition—to say nothing of priestly office, apostolic and episcopal succession, or sacramentality. And it was equally suspicious of those formal church structures and institutions that might turn Mennonites into one more Protestant denomination.

Yet all these communities, at least in their particularly Christian shapes, are integral to the formative and sustaining practices that Hauerwas sees as necessary to constitute those Christian "communities of character" that we call the church. Craftlike training at the hands of masters who have internalized a community's moral standards and purposes, apprentices who cannot really know that moral craft until they learn it first by habit, ancient narratives retold across generations, saints and other mentors who are a bridge to Jesus across time, sacraments that reenact and re-present the fullness of his very life, moral disciplines learned through patient accountability both to the weakest in a community *and* to its authorities—all this is the stuff of continuity, character formation, and *tradition*. Dissenters almost always owe more to tradition than they know. And Hauerwas has noticed the debt that has made Mennonite dissent possible in the first place, even when dissenters have been relying on tradition far more parasitically than they dared to admit.

A tradition of dissent, then, is nothing to take for granted. To trace the seam that makes it possible for courageous dissenters to form a tradition at all—and that then keeps such a tradition from tearing itself apart with the bad habits of dissent by which its virtue may turn to vice—is to begin freeing ourselves from the Protestant Dilemma. This is not to say that Mennonites have any great track record at avoiding their own successive rounds of schism. Therein lies an implicit warning. Still, in the story that follows, Mennonite movements and leaders did manage to stay together, sometimes

49

despite themselves. They did not altogether avoid that more subtle form of schism that is modern individualism. But then, the case of Mennonites is instructive both for the unique resources with which they have faced the corrosive acids of modernity *and* for the way their difficulties reveal how formidable is the challenge they share with other Christian communities.

Mennonites amid the Acids of Modernity

Modernity, Hauerwas once remarked, "names the time of the loss of Christian habits." The Protestant Reformation in all of its branches—Lutheran, Calvinist, or Anabaptist, "established or radical"—maintained greater continuity with popular practices of piety and charity among ordinary Christians in the "Roman Catholic" Church of the medieval period than we usually recognize. That continuity, Hauerwas has argued, is why Protestantism continued to "work":

> It could continue to rely on habits—habits as basic as the assumption that marriage means life-long monogamous fidelity—developed over the centuries. Once those habits are lost—and modernity names the time of the loss of Christian habits—Protestantism has often found it lacks even the resources to know how to form those that wish to be Christian.[10]

Modernity certainly names much else as well. Because the modern world is the ocean we live in, a formidable navy of sociologists, historians, theologians, and other social cartographers has produced a vast literature in trying to chart its waters.[11] They have marked modernity in what may at first seem quite different ways. One polemicist has simply called modernity the ideology or worship of "nowness," by which individuals and cultures throw down any attachment to the inheritance from their past.[12] The German theologian Ernst Troeltsch, founder of what has been called Christian sociology, characterized the modern age as he knew it in the early twentieth century by pointing to the culture and society of mechanization, which treats the entire natural world as machines, including human beings.[13] What could link such disparate definitions?

One finds links between these and other characteristics of modernity in an explanation by sociologist Robert Bellah. Modernity may actually be a kind of punishment, he wrote in the 1970s, for being "the most developed, progressive and modern society in the world"—punishment for breaking covenants with one another and with our forebears:

> What those adjectives point to is utter devastation—of the natural world in which we live, of the ties that bind us to others, of the innerness of spiritually sensitive personality. . . . Our punishment, ironically, lies in our "success," and that too not for the first time in history. . . . Our economic and technological advance has placed power in the hands of those who are not answerable to any democratic process; weakened our families and neighborhoods as it turned individuals into mobile, competitive achievers; undermined our morality and stripped us of tradition.[14]

The apparent link then is this: the same assertiveness that would throw off any accountability to continuity and wisdom from the past (the ideology of "nowness") does so by claiming a more universal reason than that of any particular tradition, and then uses such reason to manipulate both nature and other human beings (the culture of mechanization).[15]

Whether or not this produces the perpetual "progress" of which modernity is also markedly confident, modernity's "universal" and instrumental reason is what has produced the "economic and technological advance" of which Bellah wrote, with all its promise *and* its alienation. That in turn alludes to a still longer series of phenomena associated with modernity, the -ations that all reinforce the -ism of individualism: specialization, industrialization, secularization, organizational complexity, and fragmentation of life into public, private, and many other pieces besides. In any case, what all these definitions of modernity have generally united in doing is to mark the distance that much of the West (and now the globe) has traveled away from another, more ecological kind of complexity—that tradition-shaped life of intimate, familial, and organic relationships apparently found in the village or *Gemeinde*, as the Germans have called it.

Now, almost any commentator who thinks out loud about the problems of modernity faces a common charge and perhaps some real danger of romanticizing premodern, village, or small-town life. I have lived in areas of the world that have exposed me to other cultures and enmeshed me in neighborhoods that retain a living memory of village life even amid modernizing third-world cities; from that experience, I remain convinced that there are qualitative differences between "traditional" and "modern" societies, however difficult to name. Against the accusation of sentimentalist nostalgia, I argue that there should be such a thing as hardheaded nostalgia. Picture it this way: the genetic pool of the Amazon and Northern Pacific rain forests slips away, taking along precious codes that might have provided new medicines or ways to convert solar energy. The layperson bemoans the burning forest, but only ignorance prevents that person from reacting with something more profound than sentiment at the loss of more pretty scenery. Nonetheless, something really, concretely, *is* disappearing forever—something that could have made life more sane and sustainable, something worth conserving for reasons that have little to do with the varying conservatisms of either an Edmund Burke or a Jerry Falwell. So too with the pool of knowledge and wisdom that family farms, small towns, *and* presuburban city neighborhoods have encoded. If we are condemned to sentimentality, it is only because we are so ignorant of how much, concretely, we may already have lost.

Amid such real-yet-elusive trends, Mennonite communities in the United States and Canada have sometimes looked like proverbial canaries in the coal mine of modern life. After breaking with some forms of European village and canton life, Anabaptist-Mennonites have re-created it in their own European church communities and then transplanted it into North America. Though pacifist, Mennonites have hardly been so passive as caged canaries. Nor have they been nonresistant before the spiritual and sociological forces they have occasionally cited as the "principalities, . . . powers, [and] rulers of the darkness of this world" (Eph. 6:12 KJV). Even Mennonites who have been ready to modernize have generally been more sensitive than most groups to the implications of modernity and keener to make sure they were adapting carefully and self-consciously.[16] What makes them the proverbial canaries, therefore, is that if even they cannot survive unscathed, then others are surely vulnerable to the acids of modernity too.

Against many of the markers of modernity, North American Mennonites actually seemed for many generations to do remarkably well at sustaining their communal identity. Most Mennonite groups have participated in the general movement from farm to small town to city that the wider population experienced in the latter half of the twentieth century. According to extensive sociological surveys of five Mennonite denominations done in 1972 and 1989,[17] however, this was not by that time having a decisive impact on their adherence to sixteenth-century Anabaptist principles, including matters such as adult baptism and nonparticipation in war or government office.[18] "Contrary to what some have predicted, the move to cities has not made Mennonites more secular, individualistic, and materialistic," wrote the sociologists who compiled the 1989 survey, J. Howard Kauffman and Leo Driedger.[19] Urbanization had only a negligible effect on church participation or the practices of prayer and Bible reading that the surveyors called "devotionalism."[20] It made them no less likely to support evangelism or community service and a bit more likely to support the peacemaking and international development ministries of their church.[21] Not decisive either, on any of these counts, was a general rise in socioeconomic status—as indicated by education, income, and occupational rank—or geographical mobility.[22] Mobility and rising socioeconomic status actually appeared to have a positive impact both on church participation and wider community involvement.[23]

Predictably, all these "forces of modernization" did decrease the adherence of Mennonites to "general religious orthodoxy" a bit, lessened "fundamentalist beliefs" even more (though they actually increased "Bible knowledge"), and left a clear "trend toward theological pluralism" among Mennonites.[24] The 1989 survey of Mennonites suggests that they were being pulled in those contrary directions that North Americans now know as the "culture wars"— over moral issues such as abortion, homosexuality, and the role of women on the one hand, and over the moral priority of poverty, racism, and social justice on the other.[25] Just as the sociologist Robert Wuthnow famously noticed among all American denominations at about this same time, Mennonites were often diverging more within a given denomination than they were between denominations.[26] Still, if sexuality, gender roles, and marriage have often seemed to define the front lines in the culture wars, Mennonite marriages in 1989 were staying together at a far higher rate than were marriages in wider

North American societies, even as patriarchal patterns gave way to somewhat greater egalitarianism.[27]

Data on the sociology of modern Mennonites in North America has its limits, though. At the time of this writing, nearly two more decades have passed since the 1989 survey. And even in 1989, its compilers admitted that their study did not account for community members who had been lost to their churches altogether, and they wondered, "Have the more secularized individuals dropped their Mennonite affiliation, leaving only the more highly educated members whose Mennonite identities are stronger?"[28] Conclusions concerning the negligible impact of various forces of modernization on Mennonites might have showed only that urban Mennonites were changing no faster than rural ones, therefore, or that those with higher socioeconomic status were changing no faster than those with lower status. Though comparisons between 1972 and 1989 surveys allowed Kauffman and Driedger to chart longitudinal changes, seventeen years is hardly long enough to trace the massive yet subtle effects of modernization.[29] The survey could only begin to scratch the surface of an underlying question: as modernity spreads to every corner of the culture—rural and urban, rich and poor—how might it be changing all segments of the community at once and together?[30] Now, in the early twenty-first century, anecdotal evidence leaves many Mennonite leaders and educators discouraged.[31]

Researchers Kauffman and Driedger did not seem altogether confident that what they called "the concomitants of modernization" would keep from corroding Mennonite communal identity over the long run. Going into the study, they had been skeptical enough that they not only followed other sociologists in formulating measures of secularization, urbanization, and materialism but also constructed an innovative "individualism index."[32] Even if these -isms and -ations had impacted Mennonites equally across urban-rural and socioeconomic scales, those who were most secularized, individualistic, or materialistic clearly did show signs of diminished religious belief, practice, and commitment to Anabaptism.[33] They also tended to identify less with the Mennonite community.[34]

To be sure, the researchers' conclusion as of 1989 was this: "While modernization tends to seduce people toward secularization, individualism, and materialism, this tendency is, for the most part, counteracted by strong religious, family, community, and institutional identity that provides a sense of peoplehood."[35] Yet still they seemed to worry. Might Mennonites not be spending down the capital of communal cohesion they had accumulated over generations? "The first generation of higher status, urban Mennonites may have sufficient religious commitment and community supports to combat countervailing forces," wrote Kauffman and Driedger. "Will this also be the case several generations later?"[36]

Four Strategies: The Debate That Was "the Goshen School"

Worrying about modernity *more* may well have given Mennonite leaders in the twentieth century *less* to worry about, even as they modernized.[37] In other words, if Mennonites have survived modernity relatively well to date, that may be precisely because they have worried about it long and hard. Kauffman and Driedger have hardly been the only ones.

One center—perhaps the North American epicenter—for Mennonite reflection about how to navigate the shoals of modern life and sustain authentic Christian community has been Goshen College, in northern Indiana. Since soon after its founding at the turn of the twentieth century, the college's very motto has hinted at the project it has carried forward. "Culture for Service" is emblematic of the attempt by many Mennonite leaders to engage their surrounding society and its best cultural resources in fresh but faithful ways—to modernize carefully, critically, and self-consciously for the cause of Christ and Christlike service in the world.[38]

The middle decades of the twentieth century were a time of especially creative ferment at Goshen College, as leading thinkers there forged an approach to Mennonite identity, history, theology, and peaceable alternative witness in society that would later come to be known as "the Goshen School." That term has most often applied to an approach to sixteenth-century Anabaptist historical studies led by Goshen's academic dean and commanding presence, Harold S. Bender, which he summarized in his 1943 presidential address to the Society of Church History. Titled simply "The Anabaptist Vision,"[39] Bender's paper not only won the respect of his fellow church

55

historians but also provided many Mennonites with a sense of self-respect, communal identity, and programmatic purpose.[40] Given the communal and programmatic function of the Goshen School even in its strictly historical sense, one may apply the term more broadly to the wider intellectual climate centered at midcentury Goshen College. Any lively school of thought, however, is really a conversation and sometimes even a bitter debate. We would do well to recognize that the Goshen School was actually a conversation and eventually a debate among at least four interlocking strategies for how Mennonites ought to relate faithfully to the modern world.

The four major strategies that took shape in the creative debate that constituted the Goshen School were not mutually exclusive—although the last of the four turned one of the first three (Bender's very definition of "the Anabaptist vision") against the other two.[41] Nor were they the only strategic options available to twentieth-century Mennonites. All four emerged against the background of two additional strategies, between which they all tried to navigate. On one side was the theoretical possibility, at least, of frankly attempting to maintain Mennonite versions of village life with only the barest minimum of modernization.[42] On the other side was an option that stopped just short of outright assimilation by trying to find a comfortable Mennonite niche within a larger mainstream religious culture.[43] Finally, the creative debate that constituted the Goshen School would spawn additional strategies, most notably one that sought to sustain the vitality of community life by directing it outward in mission.[44] Still, as we lay out these four strategies and the creative debate among them, the seam of "loyal dissent," the practice of stability, and a way out of the Protestant Dilemma will open up for us to explore. In any case, before we can figure out why Hauerwas would want Protestants and Anabaptists to be more Catholic, we must first unpack why he wants Protestants and Catholics to be more Anabaptist.

Strategy #1: Intentional Gemeinde

The setting for all the creative ferment among Mennonites at midcentury, and the background to all four of the strategies whose debate constituted the Goshen School, was two world wars. World War I was a shock to all kinds of intellectual systems and social movements; yet the lack of any provision for conscientious objectors created an especially bracing pastoral crisis among Mennonites. Some young men endured persecution and torture in prisons and military camps, while others defected from their church to join the military; either way, church leaders hoped to better prepare for a future war that soon was all too imaginable. As World War II loomed, pressure both to negotiate legal options of conscientious objection for young Mennonite men and to demonstrate that the church as a whole was not impervious to the needs of society met with a still more sophisticated version of a standard charge—that military nonparticipants were "shirkers."[45]

Reinhold Niebuhr, a rising American Protestant theologian, was glad to concede that groups like Mennonites were right to read Jesus as having renounced all violence and taught his disciples to do the same. But, he said, Jesus also never intended this ethic as a guide for politics and government. Christians could approximate Jesus' ethic in face-to-face relationships or a small community—in a *Gemeinde*!— but their very attempt to be faithful to Jesus rendered them politically irrelevant in more complex and impersonal institutions, which increasingly characterized modern life, to say nothing of the state.[46] So if military conscription prompted a practical need for Mennonites to offer "alternative service," young Mennonites and their leaders felt a deep and piercing existential need to demonstrate that their community offered an alternative way to serve their neighbors and society in socially responsible but Christlike ways.

Leading both the intellectual and practical response to this challenge was an unassuming yet tenacious professor of sociology and American history at Goshen College, Guy F. Hershberger.[47] In a paper published in 1935, and elsewhere, Hershberger laid out the rationale for what would become Civilian Public Service: an "alternative service" system that grew out of provisions that the historic peace churches—Brethren, Mennonite, and Quaker—got written into draft law in 1940 so that conscientious objectors could serve in various nonmilitary settings in World War II. War was not the only kind of violence or coercion to which Mennonites objected, however; as an increasing number of Mennonites moved from farm to factory, Hershberger also guided negotiations with labor unions so that Mennonites would be released from union membership as long as they donated funds to charity that were equivalent to union dues[48]—another kind of alternative service.[49] Meanwhile, though Hershberger was not a theologian per se, he consolidated biblical and ethical arguments for the Mennonite "peace position" first in numerous articles and then in a now-classic 1944 book, *War, Peace, and Nonresistance.*[50]

But there was more. The developing model of alternative service that Hershberger was formulating both required and provided a rationale for alternative community itself. In this respect Hershberger was like another more famous leader of another stream of nonviolence, Mahatma Gandhi. The Hindu leader of India's independence movement, Gandhi is best known for his formulation of nonviolent thought and strategy, but he actually put more of his time into human-scale economics and village-level community development in order to build and sustain the kind of social life that corresponded with his philosophy of nonviolence. So too with Hershberger, whose vision of a sustainable peace church, capable of holding forth a recognizable social witness to Christ's way of peace in the world, required not just a set of ideals or principles but a flesh-and-blood community that is living its life according to a self-conscious or intentional sociology.[51]

Influenced by the same Weberian sociology that Reinhold Niebuhr took for granted, Hershberger was ready to agree with one of Niebuhr's central premises, even as he took it to an opposite conclusion. Hershberger agreed that the ethic of Jesus is most practicable— perhaps *only* practicable—in the *Gemeinde*. The implication for him was surely not that he or his church must abandon Jesus' ethic of nonresistant love, but that precisely in order to stay faithful to it, they must also sustain community life at a small-enough scale that employers and employees, for example, knew each other personally. This did not mean that all Mennonites must be farmers. Nor did it mean that Mennonites should shun their neighbors and relate only to one another in "separatist" communities. But it did mean that Mennonites had a long-term stake in the economic and cultural viability of the small towns in which, or around which, most Mennonites still lived.

Above all it meant that church membership should not simply bring Christians together in the pews, on Sunday morning, but should also tie them together through all kinds of economic practices and social bonds. Hershberger was the leading thinker behind a cluster of conferences, publications, and initiatives known as the Mennonite Community Movement that was parallel to efforts of such groups as the Catholic Rural Life Movement and that shared a confidence that such efforts could claim the eminent "social responsibility" of contributing to Jeffersonian democracy. In the postwar boom of the late 1940s and 1950s, Mennonites had gained newfound self-confidence and administrative skills by administering alternative service programs and postwar relief efforts. They were thus in a period of institution building anyway. The Mennonite Community Movement directed some of this energy into creating new institutional mechanisms to provide mutual aid throughout "the brotherhood." For example, it facilitated the investment of better-off members via church institutions so that young families could acquire the credit they needed for land and businesses, rather than seeking employment at greater remove from their congregations.

In the face of modernizing forces—Mennonite urbanization in particular—the efforts of Hershberger and the Mennonite Community Movement were not a striking success. (Here too, Hershberger may parallel Gandhi.) Mennonites—Mennonite intellectuals especially—have criticized Hershberger for tying Mennonite social ethics too closely to a rural sociology. That charge is probably accurate, though in fairness Hershberger never saw the preservation of rural and small-town life as a quaint end in itself. The end was communal witness to the cause of Christ.

In service of that end, the strategy of intentionally using the rational tools of modernity—both intellectual and management tools—to strengthen the *Gemeinde* may actually have been savvier than the three other strategies we will shortly review.[52] It was keen to the relationship between what a Marxist would call superstructure and structure— the way in which whole worlds of culture and ideas rest on concrete economic and productive relationships. And it was keen to the truth of what many theologians now refer to as embodiment: in a faith where the incarnation of God in Jesus Christ is central, Christianity must take shape in social practices and community structures extended over time. Mennonites have named some of these practices "discipleship," but if this is not simply to bespeak an individual following Christ, it must necessarily issue in a culture. And then—despite all the ways in which faithful Christianity must undermine rigid, hateful, and exclusivist forms of ethnic division—it may also mean the creation of some qualitatively new and permeable *ethnos*, or people.

Strategy #2: Denomination Building

Though the pace of Mennonite institution building picked up in response to the challenge of two world wars, it hardly began then. Since the latter half of the nineteenth century, Mennonites had been building the structures that would make them into a denomination—or rather a number of denominations eventually linked together loosely through cooperative projects such as the relief and development agency known simply as Mennonite Central Committee, or through ecumenical bodies such as Mennonite World Conference. Some sooner and some later, all but the most conservative Mennonite groups were forging the denominational apparatus of constitutions and official minutes, mission agencies and paid professional pastorates, as well as educational programs from Sunday schools to colleges and eventually seminaries.

In his generation and throughout the midcentury decades of ferment, none was more involved in building either denominational or inter-Mennonite structures than Goshen's academic dean, Harold S. Bender. By the end of his career, Bender was holding fourteen administrative positions in Mennonite institutions and boards simultaneously.[53] Of special concern to Bender was the training of pastors who would be biblically and historically well educated and professional, yet orthodox and attuned to congregations that only a few years before had called out leaders from their own ranks, sometimes by lot, expecting them to support themselves. Bender was the driving force behind his denomination's first seminary, also founded in Goshen in 1944, whereupon he became its first dean. In whatever his official role at Goshen, meanwhile, Bender was well known for tapping promising young men on the shoulder, anticipating future positions in the church that would fit their intellectual or administrative talents, and insisting on the field and location of their graduate studies. When shoulder-tapping felt more like arm-twisting to some of the church's best and brightest, their resentment earned him the title of "the Mennonite pope."

Even Bender's work as a historian, however, served the project of denomination building in another way. By defending the legitimacy of their Anabaptist forebears against old charges that they were nothing but heretical rabble-rousers, Bender made a place for them on the denominational map of Protestantism. His articulation of the "Anabaptist vision" did this in at least two ways. First, it offered a path through fundamentalist/modernist controversies such as Bender had experienced in his youth. Anabaptism, after all, offered a third way that was biblical, orthodox, and evangelical yet also socially minded. Second, it gave young Mennonites a sense of identity and self-respect—inward-looking self-respect but also outward-facing respectability.[54]

Some of Bender's most conscientious students would eventually argue that the desire for denominational respectability and institutional growth had actually betrayed the witness of the Anabaptists and Bender's very "vision." So we will soon see. But simply to accept the denominational map carried with it a subtle danger. Particularly in culturally Protestant America, a working understanding had developed that each denomination had its place in expressing some essential truth of Christianity in its partial way.[55] The place of each tradition was all the more secure if it could trace itself back to one of the logical possibilities that the sixteenth-century Reformation had created. All this implied some kind of overarching ecclesiology (or theology of the church) that took the functional place of Roman Catholicism's claim to catholicity. Just what is that Protestant ecclesiology of the larger church, of which denominations are a part? Protestant ecclesiology is generally quite vague. As a result, the whole of which Protestant denominations are a part has too often become Western civilization, American civil religion, or the nation-state itself.[56] To be sure, Bender's Anabaptist vision of a church of disciples who have made a voluntary commitment to follow Christ in the way of nonviolent love and reconciling peace carried with it many checks against the seductions of nationalism. Denominationalism alone, however, had few such checks and might even be a seduction itself.

Strategy #3: Historical Identity Made Portable

Though supportive, Bender was never so involved in the Mennonite Community Movement as was Hershberger, or so convinced as his colleague seemed to be that the survival of Mennonite faith and practice depended on a rural or small-town sociology.[57] If anything, Bender promoted worldwide Mennonite community through an emerging Mennonite World Conference with the same visionary persistence by which Hershberger promoted local Mennonite community. Appropriately, Bender's definition of that "Anabaptist vision," which ought also to be the core of Mennonite faith and practice, was more sociologically portable than Hershberger's strategy of intentional *Gemeinde*. In other words, it was capable of extraction, transport, and reinsertion into disparate cultures and social locales.

Inevitably if not intentionally, therefore, Bender's Anabaptist vision was also more abstract. Bender summarized the "central teachings" of "genuine Anabaptism in its Reformation setting" with a succinct three-point outline of what he alternately called emphases, elements, and principles:

> The Anabaptist vision included three major points of emphasis; first, a new conception of the essence of Christianity as discipleship; second, a new conception of the church as a brotherhood; and third, a new ethic of love and nonresistance.[58]

As he elaborated, all three principles certainly had practical implications. Bender was quite aware of the danger of reducing the life and faith of his tradition to principles so abstract that they might apply equally well to the democratic development of Western civilization as to the church. Thus he was ready to agree with other historians that "the great principles of freedom of conscience, separation of church and state, and voluntarism in religion, so basic to American Protestantism, and so essential to democracy, ultimately are derived from the Anabaptists of the Reformation period"; yet he also insisted that "in the last analysis" a concept such as freedom of religion "is a purely formal concept, barren of content; it says nothing about the faith or the way of life of those who advocate it, nor does it reveal their goals or program of action."[59] Whatever the Anabaptists had contributed to the West's "development of religious liberty," such a concept "not only does not exhaust but actually fails to define the true essence of Anabaptism."[60]

Yet Bender's phrasing here is symptomatic of a paradoxical ab-straction.[61] Discipleship *itself* was an essence, if that is possible—the very essence of Christianity according to the Anabaptists, Bender claimed. Even while advocating a vision of Christianity that must be performed and acted out as one's "whole life [is] brought liter-ally under the Lordship of Christ in a covenant of discipleship,"[62] Bender turned often to the language of "principle," "concept," "es-sence," and "vision" to make his case. "First and fundamental in the Anabaptist *vision* was the *conception* of the *essence* of Christianity as discipleship" (emphasis added).[63] Practice was a principle that required actual practice, he argued circuitously at one point.[64] One might write off Bender's vocabulary of essence to the intellectual climate of his day or attribute the lapses in his generally eloquent essay to the hasty redaction that his overworked administrative du-ties required[65]—except that in hindsight this terminology hints so tellingly at precisely the role Bender was playing. Still quite grounded in the concrete practices of traditional Mennonite community life, Bender *was* attempting to distill their essence in order to give new generations of Mennonites the guidance and self-understanding they needed to be faithful but versatile witnesses in the world.[66]

There can be no doubt that in many ways this greater portability was the strength of Bender's Anabaptist vision. It was able to excite the imaginations and mobilize the service of successive generations of Mennonites. They could take it into cities and universities; they could apply it within new vocations. In the decades since Bender's death in 1962, Bender's essay has appealed to new Mennonites of other races and cultures around the globe. Meanwhile, at home, Bender's vision was soon inspiring fresh experiments in house-church-based church renewal, while also calling tradition-bound Mennonite com-munities beyond a merely ethnic identity.

Still, the capacity of a succinct three-point Anabaptist vision to pull up roots from the communal soil of Mennonite traditions and ethnicity would come to haunt Bender's final years.

Strategy #4: Heroic Pneumatology

In April 1952, seven young Mennonite intellectuals from America gathered for a two-week theological retreat in Amsterdam.[67] Some were graduate students; others were serving with Mennonite Central Committee or their church's mission agencies. Their purpose in gathering was to analyze the devastating cultural, intellectual, and economic crises they were observing firsthand in postwar Europe, and to do so in light of Anabaptist sources, which some of them had been studying afresh. When they turned to apply their conclusions to their home church in North America, however, those conclusions surprised them. And as they disseminated their findings first through correspondence and then in *Concern: A Pamphlet Series*, those conclusions not only shocked but also troubled their friends and mentors back home. For the lesson—at once devastating and invigorating—was that Mennonite reality fell far short of the Anabaptist vision and called for a radical movement of the Spirit to renew the church.[68] Mennonites could claim the Anabaptist legacy through their ethnic heritage but not through their own heroic discipleship. And for a church formed by martyrs killed for living out their believers baptism and its implication that every generation of the church must find and confess its faith anew, an ethnic claim to the Anabaptist legacy was no claim at all.

The eighteen *Concern* pamphlets that this new generation of promising young church leaders published sporadically from 1954 through 1971 were, by intention, virtually their only quasi-institutional expression. The series thus gave them their unofficial name—the Concern Group, or Concern Movement.[69] Reticent to create a formal structure and thus repeat one of the very mistakes they saw their elders committing, the Concern Group was nonetheless deeply indebted to their church's institutions.

After all, the first three Goshen School strategies for navigating Mennonite faith and practice through the modern world had shaped all the men who met in Amsterdam in 1952, and also those who would soon join their loose circle back in North America. The postwar relief efforts that had taken some of the seven in the original Concern Group to Europe were in direct continuity with the alternative service programs that historic peace church leaders had forged for conscientious objectors. The critique they refined in Amsterdam relied on training they had received from professors in the Mennonite Community Movement, which helped them to critically examine their church's sociology in order to intentionally shape and sustain an alternative community. All were either working in denominational institutions or were among the students whom Bender was grooming for denominational leadership. Those who could do so were conducting their own historical research into Anabaptist sources; most were students of Bender at Goshen, and all seven were deeply shaped by his theological "vision."

Yet the Concern Movement was nothing if not an effort to turn the Anabaptist vision back upon both Mennonite ethnicity and Mennonite denominationalism. While movement leaders looked back to sixteenth-century Anabaptists for precedents, they were deeply suspicious of all tradition, even the traditions that connected them with the Anabaptists. If John Howard Yoder was the intellectual leader of the Concern Movement, Paul Peachey was its publicist, and in this role he could sometimes exercise nearly as much influence as Yoder. Peachey's preface to the second *Concern* pamphlet stated the views of the group bluntly: in the context of the social crises in recent decades, of a divided Christendom, and of an often "spineless" ecumenical movement that hardly improved upon the situation,

> denominational structures present themselves ever more clearly as a distortion of the Gospel. . . . If the supernatural redemptive reality of the Christian Church is again to break forth, if the "church" is to become the Church anew, it is clear that we must emerge from the strictures of dead traditions where we are bound by them. . . . Renewal will come only if the corn of wheat is ready to fall into the ground and die. The Church of Christ will break forth anew if we are ready to receive her. This is *the* issue as we see it.[70]

Tradition, in either its denominational and ethnic ways of passing down faith and practice—or worse, in the combined form of ethnic denominationalism[71]—must always stifle the very freshness, spiritual renewal, critical edge, and vibrant church life by which Christianity engages the problems and crises of any age, they believed.

This spiritually fresh but socially critical edge is what the Concern Group saw in both sixteenth-century Anabaptist and first-century Christian communities and also sought to recover from them.[72] Among themselves they sometimes debated whether and in what sense they wanted to claim a frankly "sectarian" posture.[73] But they

65

had no doubt that even when the church stands most boldly "over against" the world, it must do so in service to the world. The opening paper both at Amsterdam and in the first *Concern* pamphlet was Peachey's ambitious analytical survey, "Toward an Understanding of the Decline of the West."[74] Mennonite historian Paul Toews has commented on the original Concern Group in Amsterdam: "After their nurture in parochial Mennonite environments, their European experience brought them into direct conversation with the ideological debates of a Western culture darkened by the shadows of Auschwitz and Hiroshima."[75] The wrenching failures of Western civilization, they believed, owed much to the compromised position of the church of Christendom. The Anabaptists had been a prophetic voice in the sixteenth century, heroically offering an alternative until persecution quenched that voice. What was especially tragic, though, was that the survivors of persecution had settled for and settled into quiescent ethnic enclaves that reproduced the patterns of Christendom, only on a smaller scale.

In Concern Group theology, pacifism, voluntary community, believers baptism, a missionary impulse that bursts through ethnic bonds, and thoroughgoing social critique—these were all of a piece. In an early encapsulation of arguments he would make throughout his career, Yoder wrote, "Much of what is characteristic of western society results from the Constantinian liaison of church and world," by which Christians since the time of fourth-century Roman emperor Constantine had assumed that all of society could become Christian and thus had began cooperating with the state and its violence. "The church by her acceptance of the system became, not an autonomous moral force representing [in] the midst of the world the demands of God's righteousness, but simply the moral backbone, the moralegiver, the sanctifier of the society she was tied to."[76] For the church to maintain the moral autonomy it needs if it is actually to offer society a qualitatively new witness or service, the church must ever constitute itself in a way different from the way in which society sustains or reproduces itself. Not only must the church reject "the sword" by which the state governs and protects itself; infant baptism also is a subtle form of coercion, since the child becomes a member of the community involuntarily. But then, so too are the organic patterns of family and tribal life by which an ethnic group passes on its culture or faith to its children, even if it has eschewed infant baptism. Perhaps the most telling sign of how radical was the Concern Group's rejection of tradition, therefore, was its critique of Mennonite church schools, at least at elementary or secondary levels.[77]

In all this, the Concern Movement itself was seeking to recover a kind of *Gemeinde*, but here the trend in Bender's theology toward abstraction gathered momentum. As Concern Group members read the "crucial words of Christ in Matthew 18:20"[78] about the gathering of as few as two or three in Christ's name, they believed they were discerning the very definition of the church, or *ekklēsia*. A congregation did not always have to be that small, but it dare not stifle the authenticity and intimacy of true Christian relationship among those "two or three" who gather for sharing, fellowship, mutual admonition, and mutual forgiveness. If congregations grew too large or if supracongregational structures grew so overbearing that the essential quality of face-to-face New Testament *koinōnia* suffered, the church was already ceasing to be church.[79] Advocating the formation of house churches and small-group gatherings within congregations, the Concern Movement recommended simple leadership patterns, warned against the professionalization of ministry, and emphasized "informality and naturalness."[80] All this reflected a Concern Group consensus, but some members admitted to even more radically anti-institutional sentiments that in hindsight look rather romantic: "I am for a true gathering together of the saints," John W. Miller wrote, "and I am for it to that extent that nothing else matters until and unless this again happens. . . . As it turns out, the institutions that are meant to promote the kingdom, all too often serve to crush such a true gathering."[81]

The stated ecclesiology of the Concern Group was almost entirely "pneumatic" from the beginning—understanding the church to be dependent on the renewing work of the Holy Spirit and sometimes, it seemed, on little if anything else. They certainly did not want to repeat mistakes of the spiritualist wing of the Anabaptists by departing from the authority of the New Testament. Reporting on the 1952 meeting in Amsterdam, however, the introduction to the first *Concern* pamphlet placed the group's thinking entirely on one side of a series of dialectical oppositions. Over against "a church which becomes traditional or justifies the process of assimilation,"

67

therefore, was "the renewal and perpetuation of the true Christian community." And how might such a church be renewed and perpetuated? Not through "conformity and organization in the institutional church" but through "freedom and necessity as expressed in the pneumatic church."[82]

Interlude: Heroic Pneumatology in the Later Yoder

To be sure, John Howard Yoder's later writings would temper his early views somewhat, and even in those early years of Concern, he was never quite so radical as his colleague Paul Peachey.[83] Still, even when Yoder affirmed a certain role for church structures as he wrote to clarify "our concerns" in the fourth *Concern* pamphlet, he continued to deny that institutions ever had any ecclesial status except as ad hoc tools in the service of local congregations, which were the only sure place in which to identify the presence of the church universal.[84] Resonating with Peachey, Yoder was certain that American Mennonite churches "would be differently organized if they were more 'pneumatic.'" Prefiguring a pattern that would continue, even when Yoder acknowledged a role for church institutions, his caveats kept his position quite guarded; here, for example, he continued by observing that although "the growth of conference and other machinery [was] not bad in itself," it was a "poor substitute for the Spirit."[85] A certain youthful idealism surely animated the anti-institutionalism of the entire Concern Group. Yet too many of Yoder's lifelong arguments are present in that first paper from Amsterdam in 1952, "The Anabaptist Dissent," for interpreters to isolate any of them without evidence to the contrary.[86] Evidence that Concern Group presuppositions continued as the bedrock of Yoder's thought actually resurfaces mid to late in his career, despite a more nuanced attitude toward tradition and the community-sustaining stuff of continuity, as well as attempts to come to terms with sacramentality.

Yoder's mature nuances did lead him to state the role of tradition in relatively positive ways. He sometimes described the role of the Christian scholar as an "agent of memory" by appealing to Matthew 13:52, where Jesus described the proper role of a "scribe who has been trained for the kingdom of heaven" as that of "the master of a household who brings out of his treasure what is new *and what is old.*"[87] He firmly rejected a naive restorationism that would try to restructure church life by jumping backward over centuries of development and mimic earlier forms.[88] Likewise, he explicitly disavowed the option of a formless "spiritualism" that imagined the church getting along without any structures at all.[89] More affirmatively, in the keynote to a conference at Bluffton College where some voices were calling for an altogether distinctive approach to theology on the part of believers-church groups, Yoder insisted on accountability to wider Christian traditions.[90] Perhaps most strongly and eloquently, in one 1990 essay Yoder appealed to the principle of incarnation to insist that "God is the kind of God who takes on the risks of enfleshment. God takes on the available human shapes of community." Even in Old Testament eras when tribalism, holy war, and monarchy limited God's alternatives, the fact that it "*is* the *nature* of Jesus and of JHWH" to "take on the risks of history" means that God is not "diluted or denatured."[91]

Even as the mature Yoder cited God's ability to risk enfleshment in human institutions, however, Yoder carried forward early Concern Group themes. For another author, a reminder of God's risky enfleshment might have abetted an argument for stable persistence within catholic Christianity—even of the Roman sort, even despite the fallible vicissitudes of medieval institutions that Yoder sometimes disparaged. Yoder took the lesson in a different direction. The "human story of Jesus" meant that "God has entered historical relativity in a way that women and men everywhere are called and enabled to replicate by repenting, and by joining concretely accessible human communities of celebration, edification, service and proclamation."[92] But note the word "replicate" here. Continuity for Yoder was the steady beat of repetition and recurrence, not a line of transmission that might proceed unbroken even for a while. Closer to Yoder's midcareer, a 1967 speech to Mennonite World Conference required him to address the problem of valid change and continuity in the ongoing development of Christian theology. But the punctuosity of congregationalism was Yoder's answer at every point; only the local body could discern what was valid change and what was required continuity with tradition; supracongregational structures remained of purely instrumental value.[93] Twenty-five years later, Yoder's profound skepticism toward hierarchical priesthood, office, and classical understandings of sacrament could prove as sharp as ever—even or especially when he tried, in the final decade of his career, to state his own understanding of the sacraments in his 1992 book *Body Politics*.[94]

The argument here is not that Yoder was necessarily wrong, a priori, at those points where he maintained a distance from Catholicism, much less where he differed from Hauerwas. What drove Concern at the beginning and continued to animate Yoder throughout his career was something quite right: a passionate concern for thoroughgoing church renewal issuing in authentic Christian discipleship and the active participation of all believers through manifold charisms of ministry. Free-church theologians will surely do well to carry forward Yoder's arguments, and Christians of any tradition who share a like passion for church renewal will benefit. Yoder was also surely right when he cut through old Protestant and Catholic formulas of self-definition by insisting that the issue "is not tradition versus Scripture but faithful tradition versus irresponsible tradition."[95] Thus even those for whom continuity with tradition is a preeminent value, such as leading Eastern Orthodox ethicist Vigen Guroian, have been able to appropriate Yoder's suggestion that "the wholesome growth of a tradition" is more like a vine than an ever-growing tree, insofar as a vine needs regular pruning and new roots in order to extend fruitfully.[96] Here, after all, is a considered approach to change and continuity that gives place to the dissent that would correct a tradition precisely through respectful accountability to it.[97]

No, the argument here is simply that Yoder's mature nuances were precisely that: qualifiers, not major premises. They qualified arguments that almost always continued to accent the need for dissent, critique, and corrective. The result, surely, was a version of the Protestant Principle that purged Tillich's version of its naive romanticism and filled it in with a far richer account of social practices.[98] "It cannot or should not be argued that *any old* revisionism is better than tradition," Yoder remarked in a 1993 essay, "or that rebellion is in itself always morally imperative."[99] The balanced assessment by which he concluded his essay on "The Authority of Tradition" in his 1984 collection *The Priestly Kingdom* was that "we reconstruct [faithful tradition both] by critiquing and by remembering."[100]

Nonetheless, when Yoder framed this and other essays in his introduction to *The Priestly Kingdom*, he took pains to distinguish his position from many other views of how God carries forward God's project through time and history: "To be both more hopeful and more critical means finding more clear lines within the (particular, historical) orientation of the Christian movement and thereby being equipped to doubt (especially) those answers which have claimed a hearing because they were official."[101]

Yet again we must insist that the point is not to deny that in many times and places suspicion and dissent from official positions may be necessary or morally imperative. Rather, the problem is that to continually stress such occasions and their exigencies will leave us with inadequate resources for discerning other moral imperatives, those of continuity, stability, and sustainability. An unpublished essay Yoder wrote in 1988 includes a tacit admission that his own theology had too little to say about these problematics. Over the years, many people committed to Yoder's vision of church life had written to him in moments of disillusionment, in effect asking, "Really now, have you ever seen a true church?" Yoder was thinking through his response to this continuing challenge.[102] Reviewing ways in which he had in fact experienced the grace of Christian community beyond anything that he or his family had merited, Yoder insisted both that the truth of the gospel does not depend on a given person's experience of it anywhere, anytime, and that phenomena of church renewal do recur constantly through history. Still, he admitted:

> Renewal vision has been less than fully successful in maintaining first-generation devotion in the second and third generation in the life of a restored community. That proves that there are yet unsolved theological and practical problems involved in understanding how the life of the church is supposed to continue.[103]

The heroic pneumatology of the early Concern Group, then, continued to supply Yoder's ecclesiological bottom line throughout his career. In his private memo to himself, he put it this way: if any kind of proof from history can be expected to authenticate the true church, it is obviously not that any church is perfect; instead, "the proof that matters most must rather be that, where there is no such church at all, the idea of renewal can be seen to sprout again, and the reality of renewal can be seen to develop again in all its frailty and tentativeness."[104] Or as he said in print near the end of his life, "The continuity that counts is that the same Gospel witness again and again evokes the same community-forming response, *even without* institutional connections."[105] In other words, authentic Christianity and the true church were reliably present only in the pure gift of manna, the fresh start from the Holy Spirit that Christians need every day and that cannot be counted on to leave traces in human lives, practices, or institutions that last into other days.

Freedom and Discipline: Lessons from an Unruly Synthesis

As with any story or case study, much about Mennonite debates in the middle decades of the twentieth century is particular to them— particular in fact to one contentious "school" of thought centered in one particularly influential locale. Tracing that story in detail, however, exposes us to challenges that characteristically face other Christian communities as they seek to sustain their life and witness within modernity:

- How might a community maintain its identity in a pluralistic world without relying on a vicious and impermeable exclusivity—tribal, racist, nationalistic, or ethnic?
- What is the proper relationship between structured institutions and the organic life of the communities they claim to serve?
- How best shall the church use the modern tools of rational social organization in order to sustain both tradition *and* community?
- Can the shared life of a community ever really be distilled into mere principles or a disembodied "essence" in order to transport them into other communities, cultures, and social locations?
- What is the creatively constructive role that dissent should play in calling communal traditions, authority structures, and church institutions back to their vocation to serve God's still wider

purposes—yet do so without delegitimizing them altogether in the process?

Because this final challenge is so crucial for discerning our way through all the others, it will continue to receive our focus in this chapter and in this book.

The role of dissent is obviously inseparable from the place of authority in our lives and communities. One sign of modern confusion about authority, however, is this: we modern folks tend to see the question of authority as simply "To obey or not to obey?" Or else we conflate the question of authority with the question of hierarchy. We then ignore the possibility that those around us, or those preceding or following us in time—and not just those "above" us—might exercise some guiding authority in our lives and rightly impinge on our individual autonomy as surely as any king or pope. We are then all the less prepared even to consider the possibility that those "above" us might properly play a role in gathering and representing the authority of those around, before, and after us. As our Mennonite case study discloses, the issue of authority is really a cluster of issues. Whether and how we think authority has a proper role to play in our lives, as opposed to one that we but grudgingly concede, will really depend on our attitudes toward mentors, social practices, institutions, and tradition. If ideals, principles, or the very work of the Holy Spirit are to be embodied in matter at all, over time and not just in spontaneity, these must arguably play a role. This is the stuff of continuity.

As we have recognized, Stanley Hauerwas has famously taken to Mennonites because they constitute what might seem to be an oxymoron—a *tradition* of *dissent*. If he is right, they combine virtues needed to take a clear and courageous stand against the violence and conceit of the age, cultivating virtues needed to do so as a community enjoying sufficient discipline and cohesion to offer a collective witness sustainably over time. What Hauerwas has seen in Mennonites, however, is something about which they themselves have been deeply ambivalent.

One way to arbitrate among the four strategies proposed within the Goshen School and to evaluate the Concern Movement's most contentious strategy is to use one of Paul Peachey's own claims as a test. Peachey once observed favorably that sixteenth-century Anabaptism

> can be viewed as a synthesis between Christian freedom and discipline rare in history. The fact that one and the same group could be variously accused of legalism and libertinism, as was the case in the sixteenth century, would illustrate the pronounced presence of both impulses. . . . Actually, as has been so well said recently: "In the Anabaptist tradition, the freedom of the Christian is combined with the utmost discipline in community."[106]

This suggests a standard by which to assess Mennonite strategies for exercising faithful discipleship and community life amid modernity. If Peachey and the Concern Movement were right to argue that Mennonites could be more faithful by jettisoning ethnic, institutional, and tradition-bound ways of sustaining faithful practice, then the legacy of Concern should include a stronger "synthesis between Christian freedom and discipline." In other words, we should find Mennonites sustaining high ethical standards and consensus without relying on the stuff of continuity. Otherwise we will have reason to suspect that Hauerwas instead has been right to see something about Mennonite community that prominent Mennonites themselves have hesitated to recognize: the moral vigor of the Concern Movement's heroic pneumatology actually depends on both communal folkways and formal institutions for sustenance.

Now, it is obviously impossible for anyone other than God to judge faithfulness definitively. After all, I do not even have the resources to design or conduct a comprehensive sociological survey, such as the 1989 study by Kauffman and Driedger, to amass quantifiable indicators for or against a "synthesis between Christian freedom and discipline." What I can do is collect some signs and markers.

The first marker is that leaders of the Concern Movement sought to avoid schism and to their credit did avoid it. Too often in their past, Mennonite internal dissent and renewal movements had issued in church splits, both congregational and denominational. From its beginning, the Concern Group took pains to avoid such a fate.[107] Participants reminded one another that the Anabaptists of the sixteenth century had not wanted to separate themselves but had left only when established churches forced them to do so.[108] They reflected on historical precedents and models by which other renewal movements had formed groups within their own churches.[109] They continued their service within formal church programs and determined not to take a "precipitous or sectarian action."[110] When a house church began to form right under the noses of Hershberger and Bender in Goshen, Concern participants maintained a tense but patient dialogue with the elders of the Goshen College Mennonite Church until the congregation commissioned them to form a new mission congregation in a low-income area of the city.[111]

Less happily, a second marker is that Concern Movement ideas and models have hardly spared Mennonites from another kind of division: the "culture wars" that have buffeted other denominations in North America. Their challenge, we may recall, has been to project the Anabaptist vision beyond the strictures of the organic village *Gemeinde* while seeking to maintain cohesive moral communities amid modern, individualistic, and increasingly urban life. One way the Concern Movement tried to hold "freedom" and "discipline" together in the process was to promote quite intentional processes of moral discernment and discipline within small groups, house churches, and congregations.[112] These models have actually proved influential among North American Mennonites. Yet it is not altogether clear whether this has helped or hurt the prospects for churchwide consensus or moral clarity.

In the last decade of the twentieth century and the first decade of the twenty-first, the two largest Mennonite denominations in North America were completing a historic merger. The process became significantly more complicated and painful as it coincided with conflicts over the status of homosexuals in the church and over the status of congregations that accepted them as full members. Previously the two merging denominations had tended to locate ultimate decision-making authority at different places—congregations in one case, and regional conferences of congregations in the other case. Mennonites thus found themselves trying to decide the moral issues surrounding homosexuality while also deciding on new structures for deciding. In some congregations, the ongoing influence of the Concern Movement inspired careful processes of communal discernment. Results could sometimes be models of healing and community building.

Yet other congregations and regional conferences who undertook such processes experienced standoffs and outright division. On the churchwide scene, meanwhile, Concern Movement influence had been strengthening congregationalism in both denominations over previous decades. As merging Mennonites grew tired of their debates, and as leaders pressed to complete the denominational process they called "integration," congregationalism increasingly provided a rationale for conferences and the new denomination simply deciding not to decide. That resolution may have kept the peace in this historic peace church. But it would be hard to argue confidently that the process offered a marked demonstration of Spirit-guided moral discernment when just what Mennonites were actually discerning remained so uncertain.[113]

However one assesses that question, a third marker for tracking whether the Concern Group legacy has held together freedom and discipline does indicate success—but only through a most telling irony.

Kauffman and Driedger have provided evidence that the Anabaptist theological vision has done much to sustain a sense of Mennonite communal identity. The researchers correlated adherence to distinctive Anabaptist-Mennonite convictions concerning baptism, war, discipleship, and a Christian's relationship to the state with other indexes.[114] Mennonites who were strong on this index of "Anabaptism" did just as well at resisting secularism as those who were strong on either orthodoxy or fundamentalism; they resisted individualism more strongly, and materialism even more strongly.[115] Not surprisingly, these respondents were also stronger on "peacemaking, service to others, and support for the work of Mennonite Central Committee."[116] Furthermore, "Mennonites strongly committed to Anabaptism attended church and Sunday school more regularly, were more involved in church leadership, and showed stronger interest in serving their congregations."[117] Alluding to Peter Berger's notion of a "sacred canopy" that once enveloped traditional societies with worldviews integrating all of life, Kauffman and Driedger concluded that "because of the greater capacity of Anabaptist Mennonites to integrate their faith under the influences of modernization, Anabaptism appears to be the most viable engine for fueling the reconstruction of the Mennonite canopy, in a holistic way, amidst modern complexities."[118]

Neither the sociologists nor their data distinguish the role of Bender from the role of his Concern Movement students in promoting Anabaptist thought; the decades since the 1950s have actually tended to merge their influence on the church, and so we must credit both. What Kauffman and Driedger's work did make clear is the crucial role that ordained church leadership had played in spreading this influence: "In our examination of leadership we found considerable differences between the laity and leaders," they wrote. Some of these differences were hardly surprising: credentialed leaders probably cannot practice their ministries at all without being "more involved in religious practices, such as stewardship, devotionalism, and church participation." As compared to other members, ordained leaders "more strongly favored outreach through peacemaking, evangelism, MCC work, and service to the poor." And while clergy and laity did not differ much on personal morality, "the laity tended to be more independent, secular, individualistic, and materialistic," while the clergy's "Mennonite identity was stronger."[119] "Lay members reflect the dominant spirit of the modern world more fully than do the clergy," the researchers wrote in summary, while "Mennonite leaders tend to spearhead efforts to foster Anabaptist identity and outreach, and to serve as a brake on excessive secularization, individualism, and materialism."[120]

The irony here may not be obvious until we recall the Concern Movement's critique of the professional pastorate. Here is where Yoder played a longer and larger role than did other Concern Group leaders. Yoder may never have been *quite* as anti-institutional as was Peachey, but this was only a matter of accent. For Yoder, "supercongregational bodies" like denominations and other institutions for Christian collaboration were useful as tools but no more than that; they were not churches or the church itself and could claim no sociological or ontological continuity once they had outlived their ad hoc instrumental value.[121] Over the years, Yoder thus became the group's most prominent advocate for congregationalism and for a conception of Christian ministry that erased distinctions between lay and ordained leadership, tending to delegitimize the latter. Yoder's laudable intention was to release the "fullness of Christ" (Eph. 4:13 KJV) by returning to what he considered to be the Pauline vision of ministry; in such a vision *all* members of the body of Christ are called to specific ministries, and the ordination of certain offices does not create the "heretical" "use of the word 'lay' to mean 'non-minister'" or "uninvolved."[122]

Yoder's hope was to push discernment, decision making, and ministry downward until it resolved at the proper "unit of action and authority in the church [which] is the local congregation."[123] His arguments, however, had the effect of pushing authority and agency even farther downward—to the level of individual and increasingly individualistic believers. To be sure, this was not his intention. Writing with greater nuance in the early 1980s on "The Hermeneutics of Peoplehood," Yoder presented congregationally based discernment as an alternative both to authoritarianism *and* to individualism.[124] Recognizing the force of Catholic accusations that Protestantism was "incorrigibly individualistic," he observed that this was not the Reformers' intention "when they argued the perspicuity of Scripture and the priesthood of all believers." Still, he insisted, "openness to unaccountable individuality was potentially present in their logic."[125] But then it is fair to ask whether the logic of Yoder's congregationalism might not have overridden his intention to avoid both authoritarianism and individualism therewith. After all, what logic prevented unaccountable congregationalism at best, and unaccountable cadres of "two or three" or even one individual within a congregation at worst?

Despite Yoder's hope, many Mennonite pastors and church leaders now believe that his arguments have had exactly this effect: pushing authority and agency downward to the level of individual and increasingly individualistic believers. In this regard, Yoder's critics are among those same leaders whom Kauffman and Driedger have credited with "spearhead[ing] efforts to foster Anabaptist identity and outreach." Yet they report hearing church members repeatedly citing "the priesthood of all believers" as a rationale for resisting the very leadership of their pastors.[126] By the 1980s and 1990s some Mennonites were citing "the priesthood of all believers" to claim an Anabaptist mantle for their individual "authority," as though they were invoking papal authority.[127] Influences that these assessing leaders cited could range from the egalitarian impulses of 1960s' student movements, to business management models implying that church members are consumerist clients, to the individualistic assumptions of the therapeutic culture that increasingly dominated North American religious life and ministry.[128] But as one experienced pastor and seminary professor put it, general secularism or business models or precarious faith experiences cobbled together from the "religious supermarket" were only part of why Mennonite pastors were struggling to exercise legitimate leadership:

> An equal threat to our ministry, I believe, has come from an overinter-pretation of selected biblical texts like Ephesians 4, Acts 4, Romans 12, and Titus 1 and an overinterpretation of selected Anabaptist themes like servanthood, community, and priesthood of all believers, to the point where meaningful leadership, pastoral identity, and yes, pastoral functioning has been difficult if not impossible for many.[129]

It was Concern Group's ecclesiology and Yoder's book on *The Fullness of Christ* that this writer and others had in mind.

Some took a second look at the Concern theology of ministry and argued that it grew less from New Testament models than from the very process of cultural assimilation that the Concern Movement thought it was countering: "What amazed me," wrote another Mennonite pastor turned seminary professor, "was the realization that the great theological shift in understanding ministry which we had defined as 'Anabaptist recovery' was in fact more rooted in the political, cultural, and sociological realities of the modern era." One clear indication came as he surveyed debates in other Christian traditions over how to discard older authoritarian models of clerical authority without inviting the dysfunctional patterns of a misguided egalitarianism: "The debates were the same; even the language was the same."[130]

Still, some of the ironies that surround the Concern Movement are more welcome.

Continuity Anyway (or, Why Hauerwas Really Is Not Yoder but Nonetheless Is Right about Mennonite Community)

Concern Movement thinkers have undoubtedly made a vigorous contribution to church renewal—but in some ways they have done so *despite themselves*. Or better, they have contributed so much despite

79

the more radical and one-sided tendencies of their very ecclesiology. After all, they have done so in part by internalizing virtues *within themselves* of the very sort that Hershberger's Mennonite Community Movement and Bender's institution building were far more likely to celebrate. These virtues include (1) patience to continue working within the very church structures about which the Concern Group had such deep misgivings; (2) rootedness in communities that continue to need all kinds of organic bonds in order to survive the corrosiveness of modernity while struggling together amid the tensions of North American culture wars; and (3) formative practices capable of producing leaders who represent their traditions in themselves even when they doubt the priestly legitimacy of representational ministry. Among other things, this suggests that Hauerwas has rightly perceived something that may not have been obvious to Mennonites caught up in their own internal debates: the dissenting witness of a John Howard Yoder is unintelligible apart from the communal and institutional practices of continuity that he and his Concern Movement peers were dismissing as mere ethnicity and stifling traditionalism.

In its principled dissent and even in its case for a principle *of* dissent, the Concern Movement was obviously articulating a Mennonite version of the Protestant Principle, though disciplined and strengthened by the (Mennonite) tradition that was subject to their critique. Its most influential thinkers represented the Protestant Principle quite pointedly—though most problematically—through an anti-institutionalism that was almost metaphysical.

Recall the view of Jacques de Senarclens: "In itself the Church is no more lasting than manna" and must rely on the continual replication of Pentecost, or else institutionalism immediately begins to set in.[131] The problem with this view, I argued in chapter 1, is not that it trusts the work of Christ through the Holy Spirit too much, but that it actually trusts the Spirit too little, for such a view determines in advance that the Holy Spirit cannot leave any trace in human habits, practices, social structures, or institutions.

In what is perhaps the most polished statement of the Concern Movement agenda, published in 1957,[132] Paul Peachey articulated precisely the view of de Senarclens. No truly Anabaptist missionary movement could ever break forth as long as Mennonites were "tied existentially to their culture as supposedly infused with a spiritual quality (and the same must be said of any other denomination or tradition)." Their prophetic impact and creativity had waned as soon as "their genius" had "crystallized into cultural tradition" when they developed "externally transmissible sub-culture systems." Those who said that a truly committed church of believers could maintain its distinct character only in the first generation were correct, Peachey concluded. Only unmediated existential authenticity seemed to count as Christian at all: "Even one's personal experience of yesterday may militate, as tradition does in the group, against the decision of today!"[133]

No infusion, crystallization, or transmission. Peachey certainly bore a deep commitment both to Christian community and to the work of the Holy Spirit. But he consistently rejected any metaphor that might have given him language to describe how God's work could abide in human affairs and thus survive to shape those affairs another day—even the very next day!

Peachey always articulated the heroic pneumatology and pneumatic ecclesiology of the Concern Group most starkly, yet this was the logic that all their writings shared. The only power on which the church may properly rely is prophetic, not programmatic or institutional at all, Peachey had earlier insisted; it is thus a mistake for denominations to sustain themselves through "rational social organization."[134] The "universal people of God" does not become visible, nor is the "real presence of Christ" realized, except in the fellowship of the local church.[135] Though Abraham's response to God was "an act of faith which had nothing to do with human institutions," all bodily, ethnic, or territorial bonds have continually put the spiritual reality of the people of God "in constant jeopardy."[136] This was not to say that the church of the New Testament is "'merely' spiritual" and thus invisible, Peachey acknowledged, for "the believers are gathered together visibly, engage in observable activity, and live in visible discipleship, mutually submissive to one another."[137] Yet "precisely because the Church is visible, men confuse the visible expression with the reality itself," Peachey wrote.[138]

Clearly Peachey was struggling here to express the relationship between "Spirit and Form in the Church of Christ," as the title of one of his essays announces.[139] Tellingly, "form" mainly evoked for him dead "formality," not the shaping or formation of human clay by which grace might perfect nature, thus imbuing "nature" (in some purely materialistic sense) with the supernatural. What he and others in the Concern Movement desperately needed was a *tertium datur*, a third option or category, for naming the possibility that the earthy stuff of human continuity—institutions, structures, offices, social practices, families, organic communities, and not just intentional communities sustained through pure intentionality alone—might be capable of embodying the charismatic work of God.

No doubt there were some historical reasons why Concern Group thinkers failed to discover such a category: neither Peachey nor his Mennonite peers denied the doctrine of Christ's incarnation, but theologians of their era had not yet made the notion of embodiment available in fresh ways. Likewise, writing as they were before the Second Vatican Council, which opened new theological exchanges with Catholicism that no Mennonite could imagine at the time, Concern Group writers had dismissed the category of sacrament out of hand.[140] If it had been available, the category of sacramental practices might have offered a third way, transcending both an exclusionary, nonportable, and strictly ethnic form of embodiment on the one hand, and an Anabaptism so strictly *visionary* as to become intellectualist and abstract on the other. The Concern Movement acutely needed some such category.

Peachey, after all, was most sure of this: confusion about the church's visible expressions results especially when Christians "believe that these expressions can be 'inherited from one generation to another' by external means and that the Spirit must adjust . . . to these 'cultural' structures."[141] In a telling lament near the end of his 1957 statement of the Concern agenda, Peachey observed that Christian parents inevitably "seek to throw a Christian influence about their children." Yes, it is a *lament*, for the result that Peachey bemoaned is that these well-meaning parents "may well limit the 'chances' that theirs [the faith of their children] will be a daring, heroic faith." Alas, Peachey admitted, these are "fundamental facts of life." But realism concerning such facts dare not lead to any reevaluation of Anabaptist ecclesiology as the Concern Movement understood it. No, those fundamental facts did not "justify our transformation of the church of Christ into something which she essentially cannot be and was never intended to be."[142]

Peachey was not simply speaking for himself. At about this same time, *Concern* editors were trying to gather enough essays for a pamphlet on Mennonite "parochial" schools and colleges. Though they were unsuccessful, Yoder did write a major essay on Christian education that went unpublished. Every claim or assumption in Peachey's paragraph of lament finds fuller elaboration here. Just as Peachey resisted "fundamental facts of life," Yoder affirmed early Anabaptists not just for resisting the sociological "sect cycle," which tends to alter every Christian renewal movement after two or three generations; rather, he praised them for condemning it entirely, as though one could wish it away or overcome it through sheer will-power.[143] Though Yoder's tone was less of a lament, the challenge he articulated for Mennonite education was likewise a dilemma: how can we transmit the vision but not the sociology of previous generations?[144] Yoder was just as certain as Peachey that well-meaning parental attempts to transmit Christian faith to children could often backfire:

> The possibility of exerting such pedagogical and psychological influences as to reproduce quite faithfully a desired behavior pattern is in fact not an aid to the propagation of true faith but often a hindrance, for those pedagogical and psychological influences can get in the way of faith.[145]

No starker statements could be found of the Concern Movement's radical rejection of the possibility that God's Spirit might use the earthy stuff of human continuity to embody the gospel. And with it could be paired no more striking an admission: such an ecclesiology is probably unworkable except perhaps for a few heroic and extraordinary Christians. Yet such a view was far less uniquely "Anabaptist" than the Concern Movement assumed; in many ways it was the logical implication of the Protestant Principle turned into Protestant Dilemma.

In the years following Yoder's death in late 1997, a small cottage industry has begun among scholars delineating the differences between Hauerwas and Yoder.[146] Since Hauerwas did much to bring Yoder's thought to prominence far beyond Mennonite circles, some readers have equated the two. Scholars correcting the impression

83

of unanimity have generally focused on the tone of their respective social ethics. Both have certainly been prominent spokespersons for Christian pacifism. But despite Yoder's call for Christian churches to adopt a posture of such frank and countercultural dissent that by some definitions of the word "sectarian" might apply, he was consistently at pains to demonstrate that ultimately this posture offered Christianity's distinctive service to society and not simply a critique. As the title of the last book that Yoder himself prepared for publication, he deliberately chose *For the Nations*, in contrast to Hauerwas's more contrarian *Against the Nations*.[147] Yoder was also always more interested in politically engaged forms of Gandhian nonviolence than Hauerwas has been, and he wrote more favorably of liberal democracy and Enlightenment ideals. All of these points are valid, and on most of them I tend to side with Yoder. Yet none of them delves into the fundamental distinction that separates these two brilliant thinkers like the chasm of a hidden ravine.

It is the matter of continuity. As we observed in chapter 1, Hauerwas launched his career by endeavoring to restore the stuff of continuity to the Christian moral life: character development, habit and virtue, formative Christian social practices, and anything else that would help Christians sustain traditions of community. Thus would he help them reconnect the dots of discrete moral decisions and atomized lives within modernity. In contrast, Yoder launched his career as the intellectual leader of a movement arguing systematically against the assumption that traditions and organic communal life could carry practices of authentic discipleship forward across time and generations, or that institutions ever had any ecclesial status except as ad hoc tools in the service of local congregations, which were the only sure place to identify the presence of the church universal.[148]

Though Yoder was never as radical as Peachey was, his strongest affirmations for a principle of continuity tended to be intellectualist. Not long before his death, Yoder made a statement that could well mark his ultimate distance from the way that Peachey had sought to speak for the Concern Movement in 1957, when Peachey called into question the value of both tradition and yesterday's personal experience for today's discipleship decisions. "Without some thread through the past," Yoder wrote in 1995, "any faith community is stranded in the present."[149] Yet even here, the thread of continuity that Yoder could most readily affirm was "the recovery of history"—the work of those he had elsewhere called the church's "agents of memory." For Yoder, it was the intellect and not the organic habits of social practice that carries the burden of such continuity.[150]

While Hauerwas's first allegiance is to Jesus, not to Aristotle, he has welcomed all the help that Christians living amid the acids of modernity can find for sustaining practices across time that will continue markedly Christian communities. Hence has come his far greater attention than Yoder's to welcoming and forming children.[151] Hence he has not joined Mennonites in rejecting infant baptism but has recognized it as a practice that incorporates children into Christian communities from the beginning.[152] Hence, and with even more certitude, he has insisted that liturgy and especially the Eucharist do not distract Christians from discipleship but actually ground and form discipleship.[153] Hence he has rejected the assumptions of Weberian sociology and argued that office can be the bearer of charismatic authority rather than its antithesis.[154] Hence he has even been willing to reconsider ways that some ethnic traditions on the one hand and some practices associated with Christendom on the other might help to sustain a Christian witness within modernity.[155] Hence his sympathy for Catholic authority structures and his provocative pairing of Pope John Paul II with John Howard Yoder as two of the greatest witnesses to Christian truth and practice in the late twentieth century.[156]

Still, if in so many crucial ways Hauerwas is not Yoder, it is thanks precisely to these differences that he has seen something about Mennonite communities and practices that Yoder, his peers, and too many of Yoder's students were taking for granted and thought they could dismiss.[157] Thus he has highlighted the lines of continuity that show why the insights and impulses of Hershberger's Mennonite Community Movement, Bender's institution building as well as his theological vision, and the Concern Group's dynamism have needed each other all along. This has been a service to a church tradition that has stressed Christ's call to be reconcilers but needed some reconciliation itself. And it should be a service to other church traditions that might read inter-Mennonite debates only as a curious case study if it were not for their own need to hold together loyalty and dissent.

Mennonites can thus be glad that the Concern Movement did not entirely live up to its theological ideal. The ecclesiology that in so many ways was the movement's strength was strong in part because it was parasitic: drawing strength from traditions, intergenerational practices, and church institutions whose very legitimacy the Concern Group tended to deny. Participants were influential not just because they offered a cogent dissent at a critical juncture in the Mennonite Church. They were also influential because they stuck with their tradition even as they delegitimated traditions, stayed rooted in their church even though they disallowed ethnic means of continuity, and worked within its institutions even though their theology and ecclesiology discredited institutional forms of continuity.

If Hauerwas has urged Protestants and Catholics to be more Anabaptist, it is because the Concern Movement Mennonites who had such an impact on him stood in greater continuity than they themselves acknowledged with the Mennonite communities that formed them, thus constituting a tradition of dissent capable of maintaining a recognizably Christian witness amid the violent delusions of their age. If Hauerwas has nonetheless urged Anabaptist-Mennonites along with more mainstream Protestants to be more Catholic, it is because the traditions and virtues needed to sustain their witness are nothing to take for granted. To think otherwise is nothing short of delusional.

3

The Practice of Stability

By making a vow of stability the monk renounces the vain hope of wandering off to find a "perfect monastery." This implies a deep act of faith: the recognition that it does not much matter where we are or whom we live with, provided we can devote ourselves to prayer, enjoy a certain amount of silence, poverty, and solitude, work with our hands, read and study the things of God, and above all love one another as Christ has loved us.

Thomas Merton[1]

I WAS TRAVELING AN on-ramp to the Ohio Turnpike one weekend in 1997 just as an old Carole King song came up on my tape deck. Brash orange cones flashed by, for the interstate highway needed a third lane to accommodate more and more traffic in our mobile society. Just at this moment, however, Carole King voiced the unease of

Earlier versions of this chapter have appeared in two places: as "The Vow of Stability: A Premodern Way through a Hypermodern World," in *Anabaptists and Postmodernity*, ed. Susan Biesecker-Mast and Gerald Biesecker-Mast, foreword by J. Denny Weaver, The C. Henry Smith Series 1 (Telford, PA: Pandora Books, 2000), 301–24; and as "Stability amid Mobility: The Oblate's Challenge and Witness," *American Benedictine Review* 52, no. 1 (2001): 3–23. I am grateful to both publishers for permission to use this material here.

our hypermodern world with lines that have nagged for some thirty years. Does anyone "stay in one place anymore?" she wondered in the song, hoping that the road won't "come to own me" too.[2]

On this particular day, however, the road was taking my family to an abbey of Benedictine monks in Cleveland, where—after more than a year of reflection—I was to commit myself to a much older, premodern road by becoming a Benedictine oblate. Oblation simply means offering. Benedictine oblates are people who are not monks but who dedicate themselves, in communion with a particular monastic community, to the service of God and neighbor according to the Rule of St. Benedict, insofar as their state in life permits.[3] Specific commitments include the practice of *lectio divina* (meditative reading of Scripture), praying the Psalms through some portion of the daily liturgy of hours, and working in the world as unto God.

I learned about this quickly enough once I discovered that it is possible for someone who is not Roman Catholic to become an oblate.[4] Some lessons take longer to learn, however. Reflecting on what the Rule of St. Benedict might mean for one's busy nonmonastic juggling of family, career, service, and solitude in the midst of a highly mobile society amounts to looking at juggling and mobility in the mirror, for although there is nothing inherently place bound about monastic life generally, Benedict's Rule requires a "vow of stability"—a uniquely Benedictine commitment to live in a particular monastic community for life. At first, this may seem to be the monastic vow that is least likely to apply amid other ways of life. Yet precisely because it contrasts so sharply with the fragility of most commitments in our highly mobile society, the Benedictine vow of stability may speak more directly to our hypermodern age, and to our churches' challenge within that age, than does anything else in the Rule.

Application must be by analogy. And one cannot understand the vow of stability apart from the Benedictines' two other vows of conversion of life and of obedience. That in turn requires attention to the Rule's conception of authority. Still, what I wish to argue is this: To live *any* kind of serious Christian life in our age may require the subtle but stubborn form of countercultural resistance that Benedictines know as stability. By its very existence, monasticism already constitutes such countercultural resistance.[5] But as Benedictines give a gift to the church and to the world through the formation of oblates, those oblates and other Christians who appropriate the Rule of St. Benedict by struggling prayerfully to apply it to their own lives have the opportunity to mediate analogues to stability and other vows in both fresh and ordinary ways. In an obsessively mobile society, one wonders whether Christians can be the body of Christ together at all if we will not *slow down and stay longer*, even if we cannot stay put indefinitely, and practice something like *a vow of stability*. Slow down: because what many call postmodernism may really be hypermodernism. Stay longer: because there is no way to discern God's will together without commitment to sit long with one another in the first place. A vow of stability: because it is no use discerning appropriate ways to be Christian disciples in our age if we do not embody those ways through time, testing, and the patience with one another that transform good ideas and intentions into communal practices. As one Christian leader remarked to me concerning the impact of constant mobility on our parishes and congregations, "It's getting so the Abrahamic thing to do is to stay put."[6]

Mobility in Question

Postmodernism, however, seems to thrive on the problem of instability rather than confronting it—*if* there is any such thing as postmodernism. Frankly, I have yet to hear a convincing case that the phenomena bearing the name "postmodern" are distinct enough from modernity to deserve the name. My argument in this chapter is simply agnostic on the matter, for to the noncommitted observer, the difference between late modernity and postmodernity often seems to be more a matter of pace and presumption than of kind.

Consider the following: Much "postmodern" thought proceeds through "deconstruction" or a "hermeneutic of suspicion." Yet long ago, René Descartes's method of reasoning was to doubt everything, see what remained, and proceed from there—which the Enlightenment did by trying to reject the authority of all traditions. "Postmodernism" has now lost confidence in that very reason by which Descartes went on to seek certain foundations. Yet the Enlightenment arguably reached its high-water mark precisely when Immanuel Kant turned

Enlightenment reason on itself with his own *Critique of Pure Reason*. In reacting against Enlightenment reason, some "postmodernists" instead celebrate the nonrational and explore affective knowing. Yet so did nineteenth-century romanticism and twentieth-century existentialism.

All this has purportedly led to postmodernist "decentering" of all authority and knowing, but American individualism, at least, has always thrived by urging movement out to frontiers. "Postmodernism" sometimes seems to celebrate the individual and sometimes community, so here things become confusing. At the extremes of modernist and "postmodernist" thought lie ontological individualism[7] and the possibility of solipsism,[8] respectively. Some postmodernists do locate distinct ways of knowing in particular communities, but modernists have hardly been naive about this, since it is precisely what they have feared about older traditions. In any case, it will not be clear that "postmodernism" has shaken the modernist bias against traditions as long as every commitment to any particular tradition can be deconstructed and exposed as irrational assertion of will.

"Postmodernism" seems to announce the end of every "master story" of human progress. Although the "post" in "postmodernism" still hints at a lingering addiction to notions of progress, we are sensing the limits of human progress in a way that is distinct from the proud self-confidence of modernity. Still, if we had listened to Augustine of Hippo, we would have renounced proud illusions of limitless human progress long ago!

(Have I forgotten something? Well, one really *nice* thing about postmodernism is that I do not have to cite an encyclopedic list, since according to postmodern thought, there can be no such thing!)

So maybe there is such a phenomenon as postmodernity, and more astute observers than I will show a way of responding to it that we may call postmodern*ism*. But they will have to forgive the skeptical for wondering a while longer whether postmodern phenomena and thought are not simply modern *phenomena* proceeding at a more frantic pace—and modern *thought* both gaining and losing confidence in itself more intensely. In other words, they will have to forgive us for punting and simply calling it all hypermodern, until we are convinced otherwise. And if they want to convince us that they are listening to multiple voices and "Others," they will have to show themselves vulnerable to the wisdom of premodern voices such as St. Benedict's.[9]

Actually, though, one does not even have to stretch backward that far, for at least a few of the most incisive voices on the contemporary scene are calling us to decompress, slow down, stay in place, and commit ourselves *to* places for the long haul, precisely so that the planet can provide a human home *over* a long haul. Wendell Berry and Scott Russell Sanders come to mind.

Throughout his many essays, the farmer-poet-environmentalist Wendell Berry has been arguing tenaciously that our very humanity may depend on sustaining or rediscovering the link between culture and agriculture, through local communities that recognize and nurture their relationship with the land. In "The Work of Local Culture," for example, Berry argued that a healthy local community will imitate the work of forests by improving the land and storing rather than depleting energy, while holding local memories in place like topsoil. Our national culture, Berry lamented, is doing exactly the opposite. We have come to accept as a norm that our resources and our children will move away and never return home. The succession of generations tied to a place, and intrinsically learning to care for it, has been broken. Educational systems prepare youth for an indeterminate career anywhere (and probably elsewhere) rather than to return home and be of use to a place and community. Berry recognized that cycles of adolescent rebellion are necessary, but unless adolescents have viable economic opportunities for returning to their parents and meeting them as fellow sufferers and friends, whole generations become locked into the permanent adolescence of rebellion and mere critique, untethered from a corresponding responsibility for *re*construction. Contemporary scholarship itself reflects this permanent adolescence. Local cultures die because they cannot be stored in books, but only in living communities. And without local cultures, we are all the more vulnerable to exploitation. Can all this be changed? Only through local communities themselves. Berry has disdained every "global" solution—even from fellow environmentalists, to say nothing of governments and corporations—as the kind of abstraction that is our problem. A single revived local community, he once suggested provocatively, could do more through its example than all the government and university programs of the last fifty years.[10]

If Berry's plea for a return to rural community seems too much of a stretch for many of us, then perhaps we can hear the arguments of academic city-dweller Scott Russell Sanders, of Indiana University in Bloomington. In an essay in a book that is only ostensibly about home ownership, Sanders challenged the voices in his own head, in American culture, and from the admittedly eloquent emigrant writer Salman Rushdie—all of which urge us "to deal with difficulties by pulling up stakes and heading for new territory."[11] The culture of the United States is wrong when it tells us that "the worst fate is to be trapped on a farm, in a village, in the sticks, in some dead-end job or unglamourous marriage or played-out game," and Rushdie is wrong to tell us that uprooted "migrant sensibility" brings tolerance while rootedness breeds intolerance.[12] "People who root themselves in places are likelier to know and care for those places," insisted Sanders, "than are people who root themselves in ideas," as Rushdie would have his permanent migrants do.[13] In our hemisphere, people rooted in ideas rather than places have been the ones who have committed the worst abuses against land, forests, animals, and human communities—and hardly without shedding their bigotry. "To become intimate with your home region, to know the territory as well as you can, to understand your life as woven into the local life does not prevent you from recognizing and honoring the diversity of other places, cultures, ways." After all, those who do not value their own places are unlikely to value others'. Unless one is "placed," one merely collects sensations as a sightseer, lacking the local knowledge that grounds and measures global knowledge. "Those who care about nothing beyond the confines of their parish are in truth parochial, and are at least mildly dangerous to their parish; on the other hand, those who *have* no parish, those who navigate ceaselessly among postal zones and area codes, those for whom the world is only a smear of highways and bank accounts and stores, are a danger not just to their parish but [also] to the planet."[14]

Stability in the Rule of St. Benedict

One does not have to speculate about what St. Benedict would have thought of the hypermodern propensity to move on, try to reinvent ourselves, and keep trying to construct lifestyle enclaves to our liking—without sticking to any one project long enough to create authentic community. Following St. Benedict's prologue, the first chapter in his Rule proper describes four kinds of monks. The first two are cenobites or monks living in community (RB 1.1–2)[15] and anchorites or hermits living alone (RB 1.3–5). During the third and fourth centuries, cenobitic monasticism had developed out of anchoritic (solitary) monasticism in the deserts of Egypt, the mountains of Syria, and beyond. At first, new or prospective monks simply sought out experienced ones to guide them and then attached themselves as apprentices to these spiritual masters they called "father" or "mother," *abba* or *ama*. The historical process that turned clusters of hermits—who already constituted small communities in spite of themselves—into large and ordered communities during the fourth and fifth centuries need not detain us. Suffice to say that Benedict knew this history well enough that he commended anchorites as well as cenobites, even though he seemed to prefer and obviously wrote for cenobitic communities.[16]

The third and fourth categories of monks in his typology are another matter. "Sarabaites" (RB 1.6–9) were "the most detestable kind of monks," who thought they could form small communities of two or three without the aid of either experience (i.e., an experienced master or abbot) or a rule to order their life over time.[17] Without the aid of a shepherd, they were sheep trying to construct their own sheepfolds rather than being part of the Lord's sheepfold.[18] Their law was their own fancy: "Anything they believe in and choose, they call holy; anything they dislike, they consider forbidden." Yet a fourth kind of monk was even worse, the "gyrovagues" (RB 1.10–11), who drifted all their lives from monastery to monastery, staying only a few days. "Always on the move, they never settled down, and were slaves to their own wills and gross appetites." Though the sarabaites were "the most detestable," the gyrovagues were "in every way . . . worse," if that is possible. We might say that the sarabaites were trying to form "intentional communities" on the strength of intention alone, without accepting the need for some structure based on time-tested experience to even out the peaks and troughs of whim, passion, and mere enthusiasm for the *idea* of community. If the gyrovagues were worse, it was precisely because they were even more hyper. Think monks on MTV!

So what Benedict meant by stability, along with the other Benedictine vows of obedience and conversion of life, is quite clear already in chapter 1, even though he initially said little about the cenobites themselves except that they "serve under a rule and an abbot" (RB 1.2). There may have been good historical reasons for insisting on stability in the early sixth century, and not all those reasons may apply to our own. For centuries, Christian communities had tried to find the proper way to take in itinerant Christians hospitably, without being *taken* in—as the *Didache* demonstrated already in the late first century. As monastic communities matured, they had both to recognize their debt to initial forms of hermetic asceticism and to recognize the danger in some of their more extravagant practices. And the political instability of the sixth century promised even more immediate dangers.[19] When Benedict associated life in the monastery with salvation itself (RB Prol. 42–44, 48), he was not necessarily pronouncing judgment on the status of Christians in ordinary parishes, but he certainly was warning that the prospects for thoroughgoing conversion of life are not so good out where bishops are getting caught up in shifting political alliances and thus failing as shepherds.[20]

But maybe such reasons for stability pertain more to our own century than we like to recognize. In the closing paragraph of the first edition of his book *After Virtue*, philosopher Alasdair MacIntyre baited his readers famously by suggesting that we await "another—doubtless very different—St. Benedict."[21] According to MacIntyre, "the barbarians are not waiting beyond the frontiers, they have already been governing us for quite some time"—polling, managing, manipulating, and creating our consumer preferences through corporate and governmental bureaucracies alike. Meanwhile, theorists of modern democracy fail to account for the moral life as anything more than emotivism, thus reducing moral action itself to consumeristic choice. For MacIntyre, our hope then is in new and localized forms of community life, constituting traditions of virtue wherein Aristotelian apprenticeship (not Kantian autonomy) shapes the moral life. Such communities must divest their hope in empire and shape their lives through narratives capable of countering its illusions in ways that discrete and intermittent *decision* making fails to do. Only within such communities and traditions—which pass on their virtues through narratives and the heroes or mentors who embody them—will intellectual, civil, and moral life survive the competing wills-to-power that are preying on us.

If MacIntyre's implication is that we require a "doubtless very different" St. Benedict because we have exhausted the wisdom of the first, he has hardly convinced me. But he has pointed to ways that our own hypermodern age is more like Benedict's early medieval one than we may like to admit. Television preachers afflict conservative Christians, and theological fads afflict liberal ones; in other words, itinerant "gyrovague" Christianity cycles all around us, without the discipline of sustained community life. Further, as Stanley Hauerwas has observed, the "voluntary community" for which Anabaptists once died has degenerated—in this liberal society where most organizations are voluntary anyway—into the marketing of churches and church shopping among all sectors, within all traditions.[22] Thus, even if these groups have far more than the two or three members that Benedict imagines, they are still "sarabaite" in their desire for community only on their own terms. And all this occurs in a larger socioeconomic context where most days are far too much like the sixth century insofar as marauding bands of advertisers, pollsters, and other well-groomed MacIntyrean "barbarians" comprise a global danger to Christian faithfulness that is far more subtle and ubiquitous than either the Roman Empire or the modern nation-state.

Some will no doubt find this MacIntyrean cultural diagnosis extreme.[23] For my purposes, what matters is not that the reader should find it altogether convincing but that one should find it sufficiently worrisome. Sufficient for what? Sufficient to prick the pretense of modern Western faith that tyranny lies mainly in the past and only elsewhere, in "backward" or totalitarian societies. Sufficient at least to notice subtle tyrannies of our own age. Sufficient, therefore, to begin reappropriating the wisdom of the famous opening paragraph of Benedict's prologue, which to modern ears can often sound irretrievably authoritarian and hierarchical:

> Listen carefully, my son, to the master's instructions, and attend to them with the ear of your heart. This is advice from a father who loves you; welcome it, and faithfully put it into practice. The labor of obedience will bring you back to him [Christ] from whom you had

drifted through the sloth of disobedience. This message of mine is for you, then, if you are ready to give up your own will, once and for all, and armed with the strong and noble weapons of obedience do battle for the true King, Christ the Lord. (RB Prol. 1–3)

Benedict's stated intent for his Rule was to "establish a school [*schola*] for the Lord's service" (RB Prol. 45; cf. Prol. 14), or a "workshop" in which to learn to exercise the "tools of the spiritual craft" (RB 4.75–78) that are needed for Christian perfecting. As he concluded his Rule, he actually called it a "little rule . . . for beginners" (RB 73.8; cf. 73.1). In the trust that monks had entered the monastery out of a desire to grow into the likeness of Christ by conforming their habits and practices to community life,[24] the Rule conceives of their growing virtue as a paradoxical advancement in humility (RB 7); it also includes a worrisome number of calls for instant obedience to the commands of one's abbot and the renunciation of all self-will (RB Prol. 1–3; 4.61; 5; 7.19–21, 31–35; 33.4). Benedictines themselves have recognized the danger of absolutist authority here.[25] But skeptics must themselves recognize a simple fact: it was not supposed to be easy to enter a Benedictine monastery in the first place. "Do not grant newcomers to the monastic life an easy entry," wrote Benedict (RB 58.1). Turn them away three or four times to test their sincerity, he continued (RB 58.3–5); then read them the Rule at least three times over the course of their novice year and generally warn them of the "hardships and difficulties" they will encounter if they resolve to seek God through life in the community (RB 58.6–16).

The obedience to authority that Benedict called for, then, both requires and creates stability, but it is not coerced obedience. It is the obedience of an apprentice who has sought out someone who knows the life one longs to live better than one can yet know it oneself, at least without a master who has advanced in the craft of living this life and is in position to thwart one's favorite illusions. This is exactly what one has asked for by approaching an abbot in the first place, and the opening paragraph of Benedict's prologue is simply a reminder. The abbot is one's superior (*maior*), but the term is a play on words, for the one who has hierarchical authority is first of all to be one who is "better" or more advanced in the communal search for God to which one has committed oneself.[26] The "master" whom one must obey is a *magister*—not as in "slave master" but as in "master craftsperson" or "teacher."[27] No human system precludes every possibility of abuse, but the community that elects an abbot as its leader for life should be seeking someone who is already well-schooled in the virtues that *all* are seeking (RB 64.2–3). If, as Benedict hoped, they identify someone with abilities for administering temporal concerns even while keeping the call to be a shepherd primary (RB 2.30–34), the monks will be freed to dedicate themselves to their own primary calling to seek God.[28] If they themselves have entered the community for the right reasons, the power of position will not be something for which they themselves are competing; if anything, they will be trying to avoid it.[29]

Benedict countered some of the potential for abuse in the abbatial system, though probably only some of it.[30] Above all, he warned the abbot and would-be abbot that they do *not* have absolute power in the community. For one thing, the abbot is himself subject to the Rule (RB 3.10–11; 64.20),[31] which is in turn a distilled application of Scripture to community life.[32] All learn the Rule from the very beginning of their monastic lives (RB 58.9–16; 66.8), and they are to give every day to meditative reading of Scripture in rhythm with prayer and manual labor (RB 48; 4.55–56). A truly thriving monastery will thus be full of people whose consciences are being formed by the Rule and Scripture; such people will know that their abbot is subject to both and dare not guide or command them in ways that violate Scripture, Rule, *or* conscience (RB 2.4–5). For another thing, Benedict warned the abbot repeatedly: you will give account on judgment day; God is the owner of the sheepfold, not you, and you will be examined about those entrusted to you (RB 2.7, 11–15, 30, 39; 3.11; 64.7, 20; 65.22). If we dismiss the efficacy of this promise of transhistorical sanctions upon abbots who fail to live up to their calling to make Christ himself present in the community (RB 2.1–2), that may say more about us than about the Benedictine system of authority and accountability itself.

In any case, Benedict also required certain procedures that favor intracommunity accountability. In guiding the lives of the monks, an abbot's directions are not to come with legalistic one-size-fits-all rigidity; rather, he is to adapt them to the need, personality, and circumstance of each monk (RB 2.23–29; 27; 37; 64:7–19). This necessarily requires two-way communication. Benedict also made provision for monks to object to commands that seem impossibly burdensome to them, though the abbot still retains the last word (RB 68). On major community matters, Benedict also expected the abbot to make a final decision, but not before taking counsel from the entire community (RB 3). The justification he gave should warn us against caricaturing the system from the outside as crudely authoritarian: "The reason why we have said all should be called for counsel is that the Lord often reveals what is better to the younger" (RB 3.3). If this were not enough, Benedict also put aside the suspicions of itinerants he had expressed in denouncing gyrovague monasticism, when he not only encouraged hospitality toward visiting monks (RB 61; see also RB 53) but also insisted that the abbot receive their "reasonable criticisms or observations"—for "it is possible that the Lord guided [them] to the monastery for this very purpose" (RB 61.4).

So is this system democratic? Authoritarian? Participatory? Is it perhaps what "aristocracy"—the rule of the virtuous or excellent— would mean if that term took its meaning more often from Christian virtues of humility, compassion, and vulnerability to the presence of "the least" among us? Or is it something else that we will not be able to recognize, much less name, unless we have learned to look respectfully at traditional premodern societies (both ancient and contemporary) from within? John Paul Lederach, who has greatly advanced the field of conflict mediation by developing it for cross-cultural situations, once told me about the practices of a South American indigenous tribe. When a clan needs to make a decision, all the men in the group gather in a circle. (No, they do not include women; the point here is not that the procedure is utopian.) One by one, from youngest to oldest, each shares his counsel. No one loses face, since the words of those more elder are *expected* to supersede those who have already spoken. Yet all do speak and all do hear. At last the eldest speaks, having had time and opportunity to hear from all, and the word of the eldest constitutes the group's decision. End of meeting. It is an -ocracy for which we have no prefix—and modern conceptions of democracy will not supply one. To understand, interpret, and learn from these communal practices, we would do well to hear the admonition of Theron Schlabach, historian of nineteenth-century Mennonites,

concerning those quasi-monastic communities we more often call
Old Order Mennonite and Amish:

> To understand the Old Order outlook, people with modern and
> progressive outlooks must, at least for the moment, set aside some of
> their own ingrained assumptions. They must *not* assume: . . . That
> people who accept the ideas of the eighteenth century's so-called
> Age of Reason are the "enlightened" ones of the world. . . . That the
> individual is the supreme unit, individual rights the most sacred rights,
> and human life richest when individuals are most autonomous. . . .
> That a structure of rules and explicit expectations . . . is always le-
> galistic and at odds with the Christian idea of grace.[33]

In any case, Benedictines read their Rule within their community,
as their community's text. They do not treat it as a historical ar-
tifact, but neither do they read it like fundamentalists. What most
commends the model of stability in the text—together with its con-
comitant pattern of authority, obedience, and measured openings for
loyal dissent—is precisely that it has engendered a tradition in which
flexibility, adaptation, critique, and reform are possible within the
nurture of deep continuities. The Rule of St. Benedict itself calls for
flexibility at a number of points. In establishing his "school for the
Lord's service," Benedict said that he hoped "to set down nothing
harsh, nothing burdensome," even if "the good of all concerned"
requires "a little strictness in order to amend faults and to safeguard
love" (RB Prol. 45–47). At the end, he attached a chapter remind-
ing his monasteries that "this rule [is] only a beginning of perfection" (RB 73). Benedictines have taken this to authorize careful and
thoughtful adaptation as circumstances demand and communal
wisdom counsels.[34]

But the point is not really to create the perfect monastery. The
Cistercian contemplative Thomas Merton once commented on the
significance of the Benedictine vow of stability by stressing the realism
of St. Benedict and the hermits of the desert before him. Benedict,
he observed, "introduced this vow into his Rule precisely because he
knew that the limitations of the monk, and the limitations of the
community he lived in, formed a part of God's plan for the sanctification both of individuals and of communities." In making this
vow, "the monk renounces the vain hope of wandering off to find a

'perfect monastery.'" That requires deep faith and a recognition that finally "it does not much matter where we are or whom we live with, provided we can devote ourselves to prayer, enjoy a certain amount of silence, poverty, and solitude, work with our hands, read and study the things of God, and above all love one another as Christ has loved us."[35]

It is clear from Merton's biography that this recognition did not come easily. Nor am *I* quite ready to say that just *any* community will do. What I *am* saying is that any true and sustainable community will need the virtues of mutual patience and practices of mutual submission that the vow of stability requires and engenders. With or without a formal vow of stability, it will need the practice of stability. In their struggle against oppression, patriarchy, and abusive authority, some may imagine and promote radically egalitarian forms of community along liberationist, feminist, or putatively Anabaptist lines and assume that a premodern patriarch such as Benedict can offer little counsel. My response is simply this: *write to me when you get halfway to your utopia and tell me whether you do not need some vow of stability more than ever to see you through.*

That reply, however, requires unpacking.

Replies to Objections

The most obvious objection to any attempt to retrieve Benedictine stability for other communities is the one I have already had to anticipate: that the vow of stability comes linked so closely with that other vow of obedience to hierarchical authority that we had better steer clear. Let me summarize and extend my response to this objection with a chain of replies, some of which I have already hinted at:

1. Historical and textual studies indicate that Benedict significantly—even drastically—reduced the paternalistic language of the most important sources he used in redacting his own Rule, especially a much longer document known as The Rule of the Master. It is always too easy and inadequate to defend historical figures simply by calling them men or women of their times, precisely because it is always true. What counts here is that a contemporary commentator such as Terrance Kardong, OSB, has done careful textual criticism

showing that where Benedict pruned, he most often removed harsh legalisms and metaphors that would make monks into the "sons" of an abbot whose fatherhood over them was that of a Roman *paterfamilias*[36]—and where Benedict inserted his own original material, he most often showed great pastoral sensitivity or required abbots to be more collegial.[37] Benedict's sparing language of the abbot as a father exhorting a son thus reflects Hebrew Wisdom literature more than Roman politics,[38] and he retained language that makes the abbot a master because monastic life is unimaginable without the structure of apprenticeship that had first developed in the Egyptian desert.

2. What is arguably most important about democracy are the ways that it holds powerful leaders accountable.[39] But if we study premodern traditional cultures carefully and respectfully, we begin to notice that modern democracy does not have a monopoly on accountability. Christian polities should strive toward the accountability of all, but modern democratic processes actually do rather poorly at holding their *electorates* accountable. When congregationalist polities using modern democratic processes allow dysfunctional churches to run out one pastor after another, we have only exchanged one abuse of authority for another. And where congregational or parish participation is a matter of consumeristic taste, we gain the accountability of the marketplace but undermine growth in discipled Christian virtue. At minimum, then, patterns of accountability in premodern communities such as the indigenous people of Lederach's telling, the Old Order Mennonites and Amish, and the Benedictines—all deserve a second look if not a reappropriation.

3. Adding together points 1 and 2, then, we should begin to develop a critical distance from the paradoxically authoritarian hold that modern *anti*authoritarianism has on us. Whether or not the kind of counsel taking, fear of God, and vulnerability to "the least" of those in Benedictine monasteries convinces us that Benedict's abbot is adequately accountable, we should at least gain enough charity toward premodern texts, and enough humility about the limits of our own hypermodern sensibilities, to appropriate the wisdom in vows of stability in order to negotiate our way through a hypermodern world.

4. Before we pass over the wisdom of a vow of obedience, however, we might ask ourselves: do we really want to completely excise the

101

apprenticing shape of Christian life and community? Let us call our spiritual *magistri* "teachers" or "mentors" if that is more palatable than "masters." Let us remind them, as Benedict did, that the obedience of their apprentices is ultimately to Christ. Let us even spread them throughout Christian communities that are discerning God's will collectively rather than one to one. But let us remind *ourselves* that all learning in the Christian life involves *un*learning—that to put on Christ by growing more fully into our baptism involves a putting off of old habits and illusions that die hard. For that, we need guides with enough authority and integrity to confront us with lessons we so fear to learn that we may not learn those lessons at all unless we obey before we fully understand or desire.[40]

5. No such guides are themselves free from sin, and thus none should be exempt from accountability; furthermore, true authority bears no rightful power without the integrity that earns our trust. I certainly do not want to be led by unaccountable leadership, any more than does anyone else. But the ecclesiological and administrative agenda in all Christian churches should be to forge authority patterns in which leaders are properly accountable, rather than to delegitimize church authority per se. The vision that guides any call for a more participatory exercise of gifts by all church members should not have abstract equality as its goal but Christian maturity. The problem with authoritarian church rule is that it fails to call forth maturity throughout the laity, but the problem of strictly democratic church rule is that it too easily settles for the immaturity of the members. To work at either of these problems, however, we must grant the probability that some members of the community know and embody the Christian life in fuller and more trustworthy ways than do others. Otherwise there is hardly any point in speaking of Christian growth at all, much less yearning to grow, for we thereby give up on the possibility of our own growth in Christ.

6. In any case, here is the rub: the *more* egalitarian a Christian community is, the *more* it will actually need protracted processes of participatory discernment as they seek to discern God's will for them collectively. And for *that* they will require *more, not less*, of a vow of stability! Consensus takes much time to reach. Good intentions and the initial romance of community life wane. Patience frays, and righteous conviction turns to anger. The elusive option of

starting over with a group of one's like-minded is never absent from any Protestant church, is far too accessible in all Anabaptist ones, and is especially tempting in the modern milieu, where voluntarism is nothing we need to die for anymore. So it is actually going to be much *harder* for us to make a figurative vow of stability stick than to maintain stability in the technical Benedictine sense, *yet all the more crucial*! We are probably being far more modern or hypermodern if we think otherwise.[41]

7. So as I say, write to me when you get halfway to utopia, because there is good reason to think that you are going to need something like a vow of stability more than ever—to be patient and long-suffering enough with one another that God has the space to take you the other half of the way.

Stability beyond Monastic Walls

The real difficulty with Benedictine stability, then, would seem to be another issue. It is the challenge of translating stability into the world through forms of Christian life and community that are analogous to the monastic one that Benedict laid out, yet adapted in ways appropriate to nonmonastic lifestyles. Benedictine oblates provide one test case here, for the commitment of oblates—to live according to the Rule insofar as their station in life permits—already constitutes a commitment to discover analogies and make translations.

The best translations, however, turn out to be quite ordinary. That is an important clue, and just to learn to see it is already to begin practicing it. The baptismal vow in some Christian traditions requires those being baptized, and the Christian community that surrounds them with support, to "renounce the glamour of evil." It surely is the glamorous and exotic that lures human beings not primarily to what is patently evil but first of all to distraction from their basic callings, or to the false assumption that they must go somewhere else to fulfill those callings. The practice of stability begins as we learn to notice God's presence and work in the ordinary.

To become a Benedictine oblate is only exotic from a distance and for a while. For laypeople caught up in the hectic pace of hypermodern society, a retreat into the lush silence and ancient rhythms of a monastery can certainly offer solace and much-needed perspective. To commit formally to an ongoing relationship with a monastery, as oblates do, can then be one sign of deepening Christian commitment. But the perspective gained on a retreat, to say nothing of the ongoing work of practicing Benedictine values in the world, should actually turn a person into a more and more ordinary Christian. To be an ordinary Christian, after all, *ought* to mean being attentive to God's presence, to Christ's calling, and to the needs of others in all the ordinary places of life. The most important lessons from St. Benedict—whether passed on by his Rule, by monks, or by oblates—are lessons for all Christians, only a few of whom will ever take on the name "Benedictine."

The down-to-earth practicality of the Rule, therefore, should in every case call us beyond both merely sentimental piety and the "cafeteria" religion that too often passes for spirituality today, without fundamentally transforming lives. New and creative initiatives are certainly welcome. To appropriate the Rule concretely, oblates and others might need to create fresh models by which to gather together as lay Benedictine "base communities" dedicated to prayer, reflection, discernment, simplicity, peacemaking, and service. Likewise, they might be instrumental in helping to gather others within their parishes and churches for this purpose. But again: this really ought to be part of ordinary church life, if only we are attentive enough to the ordinary people in the pews around us and patient enough to discover how Christ is calling and equipping them where *they* are.

So even while welcoming fresh models for living out Benedictine values, we should expect that the practice of stability will always, also, take shape in quite ordinary ways. Marriage, local church life, neighborhood life, care for the earth, good work, "hanging in there" with our church traditions, and better kinds of mobility when God does call us to move—all are opportunities to live out the practices of stability, obedience, and conversion of life in the world.

Marriage

On my first reading of the Rule, as I first saw Benedict's call to accept "the labor of obedience" and abandon "the sloth of disobedience" by attending to a master's instructions, I sensed a problem. The note I wrote in the margin of the prologue went something like this: "But where to find an abbot? What if they've all been abdicating?" The answer that soon came to me was that in all of the most important ways, my wife—to whom I have made my most stable vow—*is* my abbess. I do not mean to suggest that this can or must be the case for every marriage.[42] In good marriages, however, and in marriages where spouses are struggling toward authentic mutuality, a case such as my own should be anything but exceptional.

After more than two decades of a marriage that we have dedicated to Christ's service, my wife is the one person in the world who is best positioned to confront my illusions, test my hopes, call me to hospitality, remind me to "regard all the utensils and goods of [our household] as sacred vessels of the altar, aware that nothing is to be neglected" (RB 31.10–11)—and generally, gently, nudge my life unto the Lord. To imagine any stability that neglects obedience to this relationship would invite self-deception, that most tenacious obstacle to conversion of life. And this suggests the larger pattern that oblate stability must take—probably not in formal obedience to one abbot or spiritual director, but in attentive, discerning obedience to the web of primary commitments one discovers through life in Christ.

Local Church

Since the publication of her book *Cloister Walk*, Kathleen Norris may have become one of the best-known oblates alive. In a later book, *Amazing Grace: A Vocabulary of Faith*, Norris made clear in a hundred ways, however, why she could not become a Christian by drawing cafeteria-style on Benedictine spirituality alone. "It is the people we live and work among who can teach us who God is, and who we really are," along with God's grace, and "what it means to . . . live in the real world." What she most needed was an ordinary small-town congregation that was decidedly not an enclave of the like-minded.

On the day Norris joined her Presbyterian congregation, an ill-tempered elder whom she did not really like was the one who muttered her welcome into the body of Christ—and thereby strengthened her "shaky legs." In turn, she now reminds herself that we do not go to church for ourselves but because someone might be there who needs us. Here is the mystery of the incarnation. Union of human and divine means that faith always must express itself in specific, local, particular ways.

Though incarnation has always been a "shaky proposition," Norris was discerning the unity of the body of Christ in the very turmoil of Christians who stick together despite years of bitter contention. Though "organized religion" is hardly as organized as its detractors say, Norris noted, ordinary Christians do manage to organize soup kitchens, AIDS support groups, domestic violence hotlines, and the Eucharist itself—even in places where few other institutions remain to serve others. Old women in churches who hold their ground, Norris the poet imagined, may even hold the world together.[43]

Place and Neighborhood

Gary Gunderson, a Baptist social activist, has also written of the unsung strengths of ordinary congregations and parishes. As believers join together in specific locales, one of these strengths is that—in a way that transcends "simplistic rationality" and defies "consumer choosing"—they commit themselves to be present in their neighborhoods through demographic changes and passing decades: "Against the tide of individualism and private spirituality, God calls people together into a physical place, on a real corner amid Sheetrock and lumber and plumbing."

Gunderson began to reflect on this when he found himself, despite his 1960s' idealism, on a congregational building committee. He needed a theology of place. "A congregation's building tends to slow down change like ballast slows a ship at sea," he eventually concluded. However much this may impose limits and restrict the flow of resources, there is a good side. After all, "once the congregation is committed to a particular corner of the universe, it should be difficult to leave, to change one's mind. Because it is hard to move, a congregation may be willing to deal with the homeless, the poor, immigrants, elders, those living with HIV whose needs they might otherwise overlook."[44]

106

St. Andrew's Abbey in Cleveland, where I first became an oblate, has done this by staying in place and adapting its ministry as the city grew around it. But whenever Christians combine Norris's stubborn commitment to live her faith in a jagged local church with the tenacity by which Gunderson's church has stayed in its neighborhood, they give a very Benedictine gift to the world—with or without the name.

Care for the Earth

Oblate or monastic, Benedictines who practice stability may also offer signs pointing toward the healing of the earth; though those signs may be small and local, it is the nature of the case that only such signs may count. Near the end of the essay that I cited earlier, Scott Russell Sanders told of the sound in the distance that had convinced him he could use no word short of "holocaust" to describe the damage that modern mobile society is doing to the earth. Even as he wrote, Sanders recounted, "I hear the snarl of earthmovers and chain saws a mile away destroying a farm to make way for another shopping strip."

The devastation was particularly tragic because the farm's most recent owners were two out-of-state sisters who had inherited it from their mother on the condition that they preserve it. "The machines work around the clock. . . . The earth is being pillaged, and every one of us, willingly or grudgingly, is taking part." Just as we now ask how seemingly upright people could tolerate slavery or the Jewish Holocaust, predicted Sanders, our descendents "will demand to know how we could have been party to such waste and ruin." In such an era, stability that is deliberate and not grudging, attentive and not lazy, can at least begin the process of healing the earth: "We can begin that work by learning how to abide in a place," Sanders wrote. "Strength comes, healing comes, from aligning yourself with the grain of your place and answering to its needs." And this must mean the needs of "the land itself, with its creeks and rivers, its weather, seasons, stone outcroppings, and all the plants and animals I share with it."

Sanders's confession could have been a Benedictine one: "I cannot have a spiritual center without having a geographical one; I cannot live a grounded life without being grounded in a *place*."[45]

Rightly Moving

Still, only in this age may staying put have become quite such an Abrahamic thing to do. Hebrew faith was born in flight from the stasis of ancient civilizations, while Christian faith grew out of and beyond even the Jewish Diaspora. Monastic communities themselves have often played a critical role in the migratory missionary spread of Christian faith and practice. No reflection on Benedictine stability, then, should imply that God never calls Christians to move.

Rather, we should expect authentic stability to nurture the virtues that allow Christians to become mobile in the best of ways: ready to hear an Abrahamic call, to live among the poor by both giving and receiving hospitality, and thus to nurture the newly deepened commitments by which God's people make Christ present in new communities and cultures. After all, the conversion of life that we learn through stability and obedience is still conversion to following Christ—this Jesus who was of Nazareth yet finally had no place to lay his head.

Good Work and the Common Good

Commitment to employers and workplace relationships is so tricky in our age that it may be best *not* to elevate workplace loyalty into a rubric for the practice of stability and obedience. One business ethicist, Michael Goldberg, has observed that corporate culture increasingly demands such quasi-religious devotion that we might do better to speak of corporate cults.[46] Joanne Ciulla, another business ethicist, has explained that many corporations have been using the mystique of team building and "empowerment" simply to manipulate employees in new ways—sometimes trying deliberately to erase the distinction between work and family.[47] Thus when Christians find the workplace demanding more and more of their time, defining their social life, and claiming to offer them "meaning," work may become an idolatrous competitor to discipleship rather than a stable site to heed the Benedictine call, *ora et labora* (pray and work), in service to God and neighbor.

The tragedy is that good work, ordered to the common good, *should* be a primary location for learning obedience to Christ in the web of commitments that together constitute an abbot-like word of guidance for Christians who gather to discern Christ's way for them in the world. Martin Luther recognized this when he corrected narrowly monastic notions of Christian vocation in order to make clear that every ordinary work in service of neighbor and the common good can, when done in grateful faith, be a good work that makes Christ present to others.[48]

The Continuing Witness of Monastics

In Luther's day, admittedly, talk like his emptied out monasteries and convents across Germany.[49] That may indicate only that too much late medieval monasticism had lost a sense of its own vocation to invigorate rather than to displace the faithfulness of all Christian people. Nonetheless, it should remind us even now of just how critical is the question at hand: how *shall* we offer fully Christian lives to God in the world?

One only need read the Shepherd of Hermas, from the turn of the second century, to realize how abiding this question has been. We find there the early anguish of a layman seeking to keep his loyalties straight and his family dedicated to God amid the pressures of society and commerce, while Christ tarries and time goes on. (The self-conscious discipline of Christian ethics virtually begins in that anguish.) In providing one kind of answer, monasticism has helped to keep the question alive, never solving it altogether. In their attention to the ordinary, oblates and other Christians who translate Benedict's biblical *lectio* into nonmonastic lifestyles must continue therefore to seek fresh models of Benedictine community for their age.

If Luther represents a careening between monastic and nonmonastic models of Christian faithfulness, let that stand as a warning, or better, a sign: one of the greatest gifts that monks can give to the larger church is a conversation between such models, or even their fusion. From the long view of Christian history and moral reflection, the contemporary oblate movement could have greater import than even Benedictines may recognize. If I have lingered over the implications of Benedictine stability and used oblates to illustrate its import beyond monastery walls, that is precisely because my concern extends far beyond oblates alone.

109

Staying Put in One's Church

The practice of stability could hardly shape our relationships in so much of life without profoundly shaping our relationships to the church itself, and reshaping the particular church traditions by which that church has in turn shaped us. A Christian who has not been disappointed by the church is either maintaining a courageous front, deceiving herself, or is still new enough to Christianity to be enjoying the honeymoon phase of church life. Whatever else is helpful or dilemma producing about the Protestant Principle as Paul Tillich and other theologians have articulated it, they have certainly given voice to that experience. However much one loves the church, therefore, every Christian will find something to dissent from, even if quietly. Whether it is a virtuous act to voice one's discontent, critique, "prophetic judgment," or dissent publicly will depend on whether that act has also been nurtured and guided by a loyal love for the church.

Loyal dissent, in other words, must be an expression of the very practice of stability that holds loyalty and dissent together. Whether loyalty is virtuous or instead is blind conformity will depend on whether it has the courage to contemplate dissent, however reluctantly. Dissent itself is an act, not a virtue, so it can either express a bad habit of discontent or express the virtue of courage in the face of injustice. By holding loyalty and dissent together, therefore, stability shapes both for the better. As a practice that keeps people involved constructively in their communities through good times and bad, stability ought *always* to be operative in our lives. Loyal dissent, however, is but one way to act conscientiously in hard times.

As a virtuous practice, stability is not a rule at all, much less a rule demanding that one should never under any circumstances depart from one's community or church of origin. My final chapter will draw further on the work of Alasdair MacIntyre to examine how traditions handle internal disagreement and debate among themselves as rivals. Disagreement and debate may constitute creative junctures that allow a tradition to grow and remain lively in the face of new challenges. Sometimes, however, a tradition in crisis may fail to negotiate such junctures and will survive (if at all) only through the deadening rigidity that distinguishes a living tradition from mere traditional*ism*, and slowly undermines its credibility. Tragically, some who once participated in a tradition will find at some point, amid such a crisis, that they may need to leave it, switch allegiances, or start over in another community. If they have cultivated the virtue of fidelity through the practice of stability, however, those who are morally mature and not simply resentful will do well to consider their departure a state of exile, not schism. Likewise, those who do not seek to depart, yet are expelled, will do well to call the bluff of their judges by narrating the purpose of the community they then must form not as rivalry but as service. In any of these cases, where the practice of stability does its work, the witness that a reconstituted community or tradition embodies will aim for the healing and the good of the whole.

The argument here is not therefore that those who cultivate the virtue of fidelity through the practice of stability will always be able to avoid such crises or tragic choices. Obviously the most relevant example at hand is the Protestant Reformation and the meaning of its continuing legacy. The lesson I wish to draw is not that Protestant churches lack legitimacy or purpose. It is that the state of a divided Christendom would be healthier even now if churches who separated from one another would have narrated their particular identities not over against one another but as reluctant postures taken for the sake of witness to the catholic whole. Such reluctance and such openness to a catholic future would itself be another expression of stability. And it may not be too late to renarrate Protestant identities accordingly. Such renarration would be fruitful even now. Not only might this allow for healthier relationships between separated churches, but it would also be healthier for the internal life of Protestant communities. It would, after all, staunch hemorrhaging cycles of division that come from making the Protestant Principle of endless critique into an identity marker for entire communities.

I do not know whether God will give the gift of restored Christian unity on this side of the eschaton; I can only imagine some next steps toward unity, not the conditions for its fulfillment. What I am certain of is this: even if restored unity in the body of Christ does *not* come fully into view, Protestants as surely as Catholics will need the practice of stability, inculcating the virtue of fidelity, in order to sustain their communities. And if unity *is* ever again to be found, that will in part be because Protestants and Catholics (among others) will have learned one another's best practices and strengths as they have grown toward Christ.

As reported in the introduction, none less than Walter Cardinal Kasper, president of the Pontifical Council for Promoting Church Unity, has made just this point. The aim of ecumenical dialogue is the renewal and conversion of all—a fuller conversion of all parties to Christ, not "a simple return of others into the fold of the Catholic Church, nor the conversion of individuals into the Catholic Church." Unity, in other words, is not to be found by moving toward one another as much as by moving together toward Christ: "As we move nearer to Jesus Christ, in him we move nearer to one another."[50] In such a movement toward Christ, I suspect, Catholics would become less jittery about dissent, in part because Protestants would learn to practice it more loyally. Meanwhile, Protestants would become less jittery about authority, in part because Catholics would have learned to practice it more accountably. Thus, perhaps, both may grow more stably in the practices that nurture fidelity to one another and to Christ.

A Not-So-Innovative Postscript

MacIntyre's call for a new and "doubtless very different St. Benedict"[51] missed one crucial point. At least as a writer, Benedict was not very original; most of his Rule is a thoughtful redaction from earlier and often longer documents on monastic life. His innovation was simply the wise and enduring balance that he struck between solitary and communal ways of searching for God, and between asceticism and realism, insularity and hospitality, rigor and flexibility. And if Benedict was rarely altogether original, he sensed no need to *claim* originality.

Now, someone might observe that the core message of the present chapter need not have referred to matters Benedictine at all, for what has long been called the "second baptism" of monastic vows coincides strikingly with the meaning of first baptism, as groups in the Radical Reformation believed themselves to be recovering it. My message might then have simply been: let us take seriously our baptism, our church commitment, and the "giving and receiving of counsel" that both are supposed to entail. And so it might have concluded: let us support these primary commitments by strengthening our secondary commitments to family, neighborhood, place, and the land. But that might not sound "glamorous" enough to deserve a new chapter, let alone a new book.

One lesson of premodern ways is that we might not need to say as many new things as we think. One reality of our hypermodern world, however, is we might need to hear old lessons from voices that are new and a bit exotic for us. Either way, though, the lesson is that what we need may not be a new theory or -ism at all but the virtue of patience, and the practice of hunkering down to stay together through the long haul, as we listen to God's voice.

The psalm that most often begins the daily cycle of prayer in Benedictine monasteries is Psalm 95: "Come, ring out our joy to the LORD; hail the rock who saves us." The Lord our God, it proclaims, is "a great King above all gods," and bears in hand the earth, mountains, seas, and dry land. Come, the psalm urges, let us bow down, for we belong to this very God as the people of God's pasture, the flock that God leads. And then, suddenly the psalm issues a warning: "O that today you would listen to his voice! 'Harden not your hearts as . . . in the desert when your forebears put me to the test. . . . For forty years I was wearied of these people and I said: "Their hearts are astray, these people do not know my ways." Then I took an oath in my anger: "Never shall they enter my rest.""'[52] And there the psalm abruptly ends.

The stability of the Benedictine way does not claim to be a stability written into the fabric of the universe. But for the enabling grace of God, it is a humanly made vow, and a postmodernist may well call the stability that issues from it a socially "constructed" order. But it renews itself each day by listening. And it listens from the living assumption that something is there beyond us to which we must listen—something beyond our every ability to construct reality. Thus it finds its stability not in the unreliable hardness of our own hearts but in the socially embodied conviction that God has a will to voice and a hand to lead.

God is the stable rock, the rock who saves. In the stability of God and God's purposes lies our deepest freedom. As the psalmist warns

113

and the Benedictines repeat, hardness and the kind of burden that allows no rest lie not in God but in hearts that go some other way. In praying and seeking to live out the stability of God, our saving rock, the Benedictines thus proclaim a freedom that the hypermodern world can barely know, a freedom *not* to change everything always, a freedom even to sustain premodern ways, a freedom to conserve, a freedom to obey, a freedom to stay.

4

Stability Writ Large

It is precisely in this combination of continuity and discontinuity at different levels that the very nature of true reform consists.

Pope Benedict XVI, reflecting on the fortieth anniversary of the close of the Second Vatican Council[1]

I N THE OPENING chapter of this book, I named a dilemma: Protestant churches have so often narrated their identities as heroic, prophetic struggles against error and injustice that they have elevated critique into their defining identity marker and guiding principle. As a guiding principle for community life, however, what Paul Tillich called the Protestant Principle becomes inherently unstable and corrosive.

Chapter 2 sought at least to wrestle this dilemma into a paradox: authentic and courageous dissent in fact requires a tradition to sustain it. Healthy traditions live and thrive not through the harsh and rigid imposition of obedience but through persuasive mentoring, stories retold and then embodied through community practice. In other words, traditions stay healthy through lived-out virtue. The case study of Mennonites suggested that for a Christian community to offer a tenacious countercultural critique over time—dissent at its best—it will need the continuity of tradition and virtue all the more, not less.

We need to hang with one another over time in order to allow such community life to thrive—this is the practice of stability. In chapter 3, therefore, we turned to the vow of stability in the Rule of St. Benedict and to some of the ways that Benedictine communities have practiced it for centuries. Our goal was to identify a model for finding our way through the increasingly mobile hypermodern society in which we live. The practice of stability encourages us to work for change precisely within a relationship of communion. I argued that even Christian communities with a strong commitment to egalitarian participation will require the practice of stability, and the virtue of fidelity that it engenders, in order to discern God's will for their life together and to change accordingly, faithfully.

Though I sought to meet likely objections, one quite crucial objection remains: can the practices and virtues that the Rule of St. Benedict represents apply more widely than a face-to-face monastery? We saw that it can and should apply in general ways to marriage, congregational and parish life, rooted engagement in our neighborhoods, and even the care of the earth. But can it operate in a global institution? Can it apply to a large, worldwide, highly structured church? If the practice of stability is something that Protestants would do well to learn from Catholics, then the obvious test case here is the Roman Catholic Church itself.

"Participatory Hierarchy"

Can a global church, which needs complex institutional structures in order to function, practice something like Benedictine stability? The impulses of those who are skeptical of institutions and critical of every form of hierarchy will be to answer this emerging question in two quite different ways. Some will say, "Yes, the Benedictine model has been applied to the wider church ever since the Middle Ages—and that's the problem!" Others will say, "No it hasn't—or if it has, only fitfully—and *that* is the problem." The first view points to the strong and central role of the abbot in the Rule of St. Benedict and sees that Rule as already having contributed all too much to top-down authoritarian patterns in the Roman Catholic Church.[2] A second view points to the corresponding spirit of community consultation that is also basic to the Rule of St. Benedict, along with a flexibility with' regard to local and pastoral circumstances. Holders of this view may not be altogether confident that such a model can operate within structures larger than the face-to-face community of a monastery—but they wish it could![3] The disparity between these two views is striking, however, and simply to account for that disparity may provide a prima facie argument that it is actually possible to practice stability as a global Christian community, even though such a community will inevitably require well-developed institutions to structure its life together.

Theologian Terence Nichols has, in effect, done both—accounted for the disparity and demonstrated the possibility of what he calls "participatory hierarchy." Much of Nichols's recent scholarly work has been on the relationship between faith and science. But his studies in that area have yielded unexpected side benefits for another of his areas of expertise: ecclesiology.

Nichols has argued that we go wrong in our attitudes, appropriation, and practice of church authority when we assume that our only available options are a purely top-down command hierarchy or pure egalitarianism.[4] If there were nothing other than these two options, the church could never be both democratic and hierarchical. The prevalent assumption that we must choose either/or, however, explains why some find it difficult to imagine an abbot-like figure leading the entire global church, while others despair of such a church incorporating participatory consultation into its structures at all.

In fact, participatory hierarchy is all around us—and actually also within us. Here is where the biological sciences help us to correct our faulty assumption that top-down chain-of-command hierarchies are the only kind available. As Nichols has noted, all biological systems involve complex ordering of many subsystems (and of other subsystems within these) from biosphere to ecosystem to organism to cell and on "down" to the molecular level. Less-complex "lower" subsystems contribute to the good of the whole yet operate with a measure of autonomy. They influence the development of the whole, even while they benefit from the regulating structure that the whole provides. Subsystems may be logically "lower" in one way. Yet subsystems are all in mutually dependent relationships, so there is always a sense in which "lower" subsystems also exercise power "over" the "higher" in other ways.[5] Just think of how a lowly infection in your respiratory track—a common cold—can exercise veto power over the agile functioning of neurons in your brain. A treatise on the superiority of the human animal over microbes, or of higher brain functioning over common mammalian respiration, will prove little if you are too listless to do more than watch mindless sitcoms from your couch!

Biological analogies are only one piece of Nichols's argument, to be sure, but they free him to recognize participatory hierarchy at work throughout the biblical narrative, as well as at key junctures in church history. Participatory hierarchy characterizes the covenant relationships between God and the people of Israel in the Old Testament; it operates in Jesus' gospel proclamation of a kingdom (hierarchical language) in which outcasts find new dignity (egalitarianism); it urges us toward models of community life in which leaders exercise authority through a servanthood that invites others to share in the exercise of authority more fully.[6] Nichols has also pointed out ways that participatory hierarchy works in large and complex social systems, particularly federated ones that recognize principles of inclusion and subsidiarity. The principle of subsidiarity, in particular, insists that those who are most *affected* by decisions can and should take responsibility for *making* those decisions whenever the scope of their impact makes this possible and appropriate.[7]

Nichols readily admitted that many centuries of Roman Catholic Church history have involved a struggle between participatory hierarchy, which would locate ultimate authority in churchwide councils, and command hierarchy, which would locate ultimate authority in a monarchical papacy. Although he conceded that command hierarchy may be appropriate to emergency situations, attempts to make it the norm for all churchwide ecclesial discernment is the source of what defenders and critics of papal authority widely concur to be a crisis of confidence and authority in much of the contemporary church.

Space does not permit me to recapitulate Nichols's arguments in all their biblical and historical detail; let it suffice to say this: the Second

Vatican Council has demonstrated that participatory hierarchy is possible on a global scale. The historian John W. O'Malley, SJ, has described the Second Vatican Council as "one huge committee" of over two thousand that inevitably left ambiguities in the documents it "hammered out" through compromise. Still, O'Malley concluded, "I know of no other such assembly in history that undertook such a bold reshaping of the institution it represented, and did it with more fairness, serenity, and courage."[8] The very experience of the council was one of debate and dialectic, not only within the college of bishops but also with theologians, non-Catholic official observers, and the non-Christian world; the documents of Vatican II were in turn a "thematizing" of this experience.[9] As the late Cardinal Joseph Bernardin of Chicago said of the council, "The recognition and highlighting of dialogue remain one of the glories of [the council] and of the papacies that nurtured and followed it."[10]

Nichols acknowledged shortcomings in Vatican II deliberations: "Lay persons were present but did not vote; women's voices were largely unheard"; and Pope Paul reserved two issues for himself, artificial birth control and clerical celibacy. Precisely around these two issues, and related issues such as the role of women in the church, nonparticipatory procedures have been the greatest sources of distrust in succeeding decades.[11]

Yet after four hundred years of momentum toward monarchical hierarchy, the council was "a signal advance." The bishops made the council and its documents their own, wresting its control from the Curia (Vatican bureaucracy). They consulted Catholic universities, religious orders, and even leaders of other Christian traditions as they prepared their agenda. They drew on the expertise of leading theologians. They thoroughly discussed views pro and con, yet achieved a degree of consensus that came as close to unanimity as a gathering of up to 2,400 leaders from around the globe could ever be expected to do. Nichols concluded that despite its imperfections, "Vatican II is one of the best examples of participatory hierarchy in action in church history."[12] To this I would add: the promise of the Second Vatican Council and the authoritative guidance that its texts offer the church as it struggles to fulfill that promise are unimaginable apart from practices of stability by bishops gathered from around the world.[13]

Toward a Stable Narrative of Vatican II

"Participatory hierarchy," Nichols has noted, "is not just a matter of structure. It is also a matter of style."[14] Before we proceed, the implications of that insight deserve reflection. "Style" may actually be too weak a word for what Nichols was getting at, but the clue he offered is this: participatory hierarchy in the manner of the Second Vatican Council requires not just certain kinds of procedures and structures but also a certain quality of communal life and relationship. Thus there are ways of appropriating Vatican II that run counter to its style, but more than that, undermine the very practices and virtues for which the council should stand before us as a model.

This is not to say that it is possible to renarrate Vatican II in an entirely neutral and disinterested fashion. Precisely because the genius of the council lay in the ability of the bishops to hold various forces and convictions together in creative tension, through the practice of stability, rival narratives concerning the council were bound to emerge. Catholic journalist Peter Steinfels has identified at least four such counternarratives: (1) an ultraconservative story line that sees the council as a betrayal; (2) a moderately conservative one that sees it as welcome but misrepresented and thus irresponsibly applied; (3) a liberal one that sees the council as a Spirit-led breakthrough that remains unfulfilled; and (4) a radical narrative that sees it as halfhearted at best and thus requiring still more sweeping changes.[15]

Steinfels confessed a certain sympathy with all four narratives (though only with a "whiff" of the ultraconservative view). Advocating, as I do, practices of stability that require Christians to listen to one another across what too often are ideological divides, it can be no surprise that I join Steinfels in expressing a measure of sympathy for all four of the rival narratives that he identified. Still, I can hardly feign neutrality concerning the council itself. Neither my own embrace of Roman Catholicism, nor a book on what Catholicism has to offer Protestants for the sustaining of their lives together, would be imaginable without the communal witness, the ecumenical breakthroughs, and the monumental hope that emerged from the Second Vatican Council.

Virtually all debates in the Roman Catholic Church since the early 1960s have in some way been debates over how to realize the promise and mandate of the twentieth century's great ecumenical council. Vatican II breakthroughs in ecclesiology made ancient questions urgently fresh, after all: what responsibility does the pope have to consult with bishops, theologians, or even the laity in making decisions? Vatican II reaffirmed papal infallibility, even while rooting the pope's authority in his role as the presiding bishop of bishops, who speaks most authoritatively when he voices a churchwide consensus. So is this responsibility to consult simply a desideratum, or is it an obligation and criterion for validating the full authority of any given papal pronouncement? And what will it mean to recognize the full dignity of the laity within the church, as Vatican II began to do?

Fierce controversies over contraception, liberation theology, the ordination of women, and now a scandalous cover-up of priestly sexual abuse have demonstrated the importance of all these procedural questions. How can the church draw simultaneously on multiple sources of wisdom and authority? How can the church ensure accountability and create fair procedures for administering this worldwide church? These are important matters awaiting resolution if Vatican II theology is to be structurally integrated in the church.

Yet the Second Vatican Council was as much an event as it is the set of documents that it produced, or the reforms it initiated. So argue the scholars who have produced the most definitive history of the council to date.[16] Nichols thus had good reason to observe that "participatory hierarchy" is as much a "matter of style" as it is a "matter of structure."

Nichols's remark offers us a salutary reminder and a crucial lead, for as theologian and council adviser John Courtney Murray, SJ, insisted amid the heady but anxiety-laden period immediately following the Second Vatican Council, we would do better to speak not of a "crisis of authority" in the church or of a "crisis of freedom," but of a "crisis of community."[17] As important as fair procedures are, and as helpful as the resolution of postconciliar debates would be for the witness of the church, no procedural clarity can substitute for charity, patience, and courage, as well as the community virtue that holds these together through difficult times: fidelity to one another engendered through the practice of stability. To carry on the conversation and debate that Catholics need in order to structure their life together according to the best insights of Vatican II, Catholics must already be drawing on this practice and this virtue.

Stability as a practice and fidelity as a virtue are both deeply engrained among Catholics—*but not always named and celebrated.* It is thus that I leave other theologians and historians to survey the more technical details of conciliar and postconciliar debates over authority and dissent, the ordinary and infallible magisterium, the relationship between local and universal church, and how bishops or popes ought best to seek the "sense of the faithful."[18] As Ann O'Hara Graff would remind us,

> We are a church because we want to respond to Jesus the Christ. It is that simple. No in-house squabble is more important than that central religious fact. And every issue we Catholics raise as a Christian people, without exception, must be responsible to the person and event of Jesus Christ. To say that so directly is to name the necessary center of our struggle with our Christian commitment.[19]

If Christians are to grow as a community into the fullness of Christ, just procedures and appropriate structures will surely have a role to play. But they must serve, reflect, and embody our growth in Christ's virtue. The alternative, and the temptation, is nothing less than inadvertently to replace Jesus Christ himself as our source of hope.

The upshot is this: too often conservative and progressive Catholics alike fall into the trap of proceduralism. In other words, they defend papal authority on the one hand, or quasi-democratic decision making on the other, as though getting church polity right will automatically ensure church renewal and Christian faithfulness either way. Arguing about procedures dare not become a way to defer the real work of listening and learning from one another. My suggestion is that God's people will forge better procedures anyway (when procedures are what we need) only through practices of stability that begin with patient attentiveness to one another as brothers and sisters in Christ.[20]

Stability under the Mantle of Aggiornamento

Critical to the entire Vatican II event was the word that Pope John XXIII chose to describe its central task: "aggiornamento."

"Aggiornamento" is a loanword from Italian that most often is taken to mean "updating." This is accurate, and it was a stroke of genius for Pope John to choose a word so rich in nuance and meaning. Still, any single word runs the risk of becoming a slogan. Precisely as a slogan, the word has sometimes seemed to imply that the only purpose of Vatican II was to catch up with the modern world, to get with the program, as it were.[21] To be sure, positive engagement with the modern world plays an important part in both the story of Vatican II and the meaning of aggiornamento, which should remain of great interest to twenty-first-century Christians as we continue seeking to chart a faithful course through the corrosions and gifts, challenges and opportunities, of modernity or postmodernity. Still, this is only half the story.[22] The other half is that updating also implies continuity. The task of updating is valuable only if there is something to update, after all—something worth conserving because it offers a richness to our present and a life-giving fecundity for our future.

After centuries of defensiveness following the Protestant Reformation and the Enlightenment, climaxing in the French Revolution but continuing in a series of feuds with "modernist" thought, the Catholic Church certainly did need to come to terms with modernity. Many Catholics felt themselves caught in what Giuseppe Alberigo, a leading historian of the council, has described as nothing less than "the psychosis of a siege-mentality." Such Catholics were "increasingly aware that they were lagging behind as 'modernity' continued to spread, at least in western culture."[23]

Pope John implicitly recognized the need for a new relationship with the modern world in his opening speech to the council. His confident trust, he said, was that the council would provide the church with those "spiritual riches" and "strength of new energies" that would allow it to "look to the future without fear." Famously—electrically—he even rebuked those of his own papal staff who did nothing but speak with nostalgia for the former glories of previous Christian eras, while despairing of the world beyond Vatican walls:

> In the daily exercise of our pastoral office, we sometimes have to listen, much to our regret, to voices of persons who, though burning with zeal, are not endowed with too much sense of discretion or measure.

In these modern times they can see nothing but prevarication and ruin. They say that our era, in comparison with past eras, is getting worse, and they behave as though they had learned nothing from history, which is, none the less, the teacher of life. . . . We feel we must disagree with those prophets of gloom, who are always forecasting disaster, as though the end of the world were at hand.[24]

If the church and its pastors would look more discerningly and attentively to the "new conditions of modern life" (a practice that Vatican II documents would soon call reading "the signs of the times"),[25] it would recognize newly favorable conditions for carrying out the work of the church. Specifically, observed John, the church no longer suffered so much from the obstacles, perils, and temptations that came from interference by civil authorities in the church's life; however sincerely the "princes of the world" had sought to protect the church of the past, their actions had often brought "spiritual damage and danger."[26]

Whether the now-passing era was the long period of alliances, mixed blessings, and entanglements that had begun sixteen centuries earlier with the emperor Constantine, or whether it was the era of siege and retrenchment beginning with the Council of Trent four centuries earlier, the church was at a historic juncture.

Pope John wanted a Council that would mark a transition between two eras, that is, that would bring the Church . . . into a new phase of witness and proclamation, and would also recover substantial and binding elements of the tradition considered able to nourish and insure fidelity to the gospel during so difficult a transition period.[27]

The *First* Vatican Council, nearly a century before, had left internal church business unfinished, and this was part of the agenda for the Second Vatican Council. But the world's agenda now was pressing the church to provide a positive outward-looking word of hope for *its* historic juncture too. As if the gathered bishops needed reminders of the dangers that the Cold War imposed on all humanity, the opening of the council turned out to coincide with the Cuban missile crisis, in which the United States and the Soviet Union came closer than ever to nuclear war. Meanwhile, colonialism was coming to an end, and the process of growing diversification and interdependence that would later come to be known as globalization was speeding up. Not just Christians but also all humanists of goodwill faced diverse philosophical challenges from totalitarian ideologies, Marxist and Freudian thought, as well as the hedonism of mass culture. Yet despite all these challenges, hope for lasting world peace and confidence that development efforts could spread prosperity throughout the world were surging.

Doubtless few of the bishops traveling to Rome from around the world initially expected the council to take up such matters, but Pope John sensed the urgency of the modern world's questions and aspirations and longed for the gospel to shine forth through the church more clearly and accessibly.[28] And by the closing days of the council, when the bishops ratified *Gaudium et spes*, the Pastoral Constitution for the Church in the Modern World, they had made John's urgent pastoral concern for all of humanity their own. "The joy and hope, the grief and anguish of the men of our time, especially of those who are poor or afflicted in any way," begins this most original of Vatican II documents, "are the joy and hope, the grief and anguish of the followers of Christ as well." As a human community on journey to God's kingdom, "Christians cherish a feeling of deep solidarity with the human race and its history." Humanity was caught between wonder at its own technological power and troubling, perplexing questions about both contemporary trends and its ultimate destiny.

> And so the Council, as witness and guide to the faith of the whole people of God, gathered together by Christ, can find no more eloquent expression of its solidarity and respectful affection for the whole human family, to which it belongs, than to enter into dialogue with it about all these different problems.

The gospel itself should convince Christians of the dignity of the human person and the value of human society, so deserving of renewal. The church's commitment, therefore, was to accompany humanity in the modern world on its own journey, as a friend who "offers to co-operate unreservedly" and without condemnation. "The Church is not motivated by an earthly ambition but is interested in one thing only—to carry on the work of Christ under the guidance of the Holy Spirit, for he came into the world to bear witness to the truth, to save and not to judge, to serve and not to be served."[29]

Fundamental to the Second Vatican Council, then, was the way in which the Roman Catholic Church came to terms thereby with its own version of the Protestant Principle. If "aggiornamento" was the watchword of the council, in some (though not all) ways it was also a euphemism for reform. To Catholicism of the mid-twentieth century, the very word "reform" remained suspect.[30] It had been hard to pronounce that word without a Protestant accent, after all. For either the word implied an admission that Protestant Reformers had been right all along, or it undermined tenets insisting that the Roman Catholic Church was the unchanging carrier of the divine deposit of faith and truth. The only possible and acceptably Catholic conception of "reform" in pre–Vatican II Catholicism was that re-*formation* whereby Rome might correct any *de*-formations due to decadence or heresy that had come to infect the life of the church; such "reformation" did not really imply change, however, but only the restoration or restitution of a glorious status quo ante.[31] When John XXIII called for aggiornamento, and when the bishops of the council began speaking of the church as a "pilgrim people" on a journey through history, they were putting aside the pious but limited notions of reform in pre–Vatican II Catholicism, as well as their anxious reluctance lest they be seen as making any concessions to Protestantism. They were instead embracing a continuing call to continuing change in the direction of greater faithfulness to Jesus the Christ and Lord of history. John W. O'Malley, SJ, has gone so far as to conclude that "*aggiornamento* was a revolution in the history of the idea of reform" and thus constituted not merely *reform* but also a *reformation* in the full paradigm-shifting sense of the word. If so, this puts Vatican II on par with only two other "great reformations" in Christian history: the Gregorian reformation of the eleventh century and the Lutheran reformation of the sixteenth.[32]

Misunderstanding often arises at precisely this point, however. Vatican II's aggiornamento was not just any kind of reform. But that is *not* because the Catholic Church—the Christian church that everyone, Catholic and non-Catholic alike, thought least likely to change![33]—suddenly lurched forward in a "radically new direction" in order to catch up with the times.[34] When Catholic conservatives bemoan and Catholic progressives celebrate such a lurch, they share the same fundamental misunderstanding. As Alberigo has written, "*Aggiornamento* has been hastily understood by some as a synonym of *reform*, by others as a way to avoid that heated and controverted term, and by still others as an invitation to a pursuit of modernity."[35] In fact, aggiornamento also signaled commitment to stability, which must clearly receive credit for freeing the church to come to terms with the modern world at all.

So yes, aggiornamento was a Catholic way to apply the Protestant Principle at its best. And yes, it signaled the need for the Catholic Church to come to terms with modernity in some way. But the goal, as Alberigo went on to insist, was to place the church in an all-the-better position to "inculturate" the gospel of Jesus Christ that has always, everywhere, spoken to the human condition. Inculturation is the process of translating and embodying the gospel in the language and setting of one culture at a time. Pope John succinctly explained the assumption behind both aggiornamento and inculturation in his opening speech: "The substance of the ancient doctrine of the deposit of faith is one thing, and the way in which it is presented is another."[36] It was long past time to recognize the diversity of cultures that constituted the global life of the church in the modern world, along with a corresponding responsibility to express the gospel accordingly. And it was long past time to do so within the culture of modernity itself.

What hasty commentators too often miss, then, is that aggiornamento bore within itself an immediate commitment to update the church's communication and embodiment of the gospel precisely in continuity with tradition. Not everything was up for grabs all the time. While recognizing with the Protestant Principle that the church must always be open to reform until the day when Christ completes the work of holiness among Christians, the Catholic principle of aggiornamento also signaled the practice of stability and not simply a principle of endless critique.

To be sure, long-standing Catholic approaches to stability might themselves need updating. Indeed, it was the promise and the experience of new patterns of conversation—representing deeper rather than weakened bonds of commitment between bishops from diverse cultures, between theologians and hierarchy, and between the church and the modern world—that did so much to energize council participants in the opening session of the council in 1962. This is not to say that the way forward opened up immediately and unambiguously, as though Pope John XXIII had divided the Red Sea. Alberigo has identified three overarching challenges that quickly emerged in the council: "the conception and structure of the Church, relationships with other Christian traditions, and the role of faith and church within contemporary society."[37]

All these in some way express our problematic. The first challenge includes the question of whether the Catholic Church has the capacity to welcome critique and change in order that it might be more faithful. The second reminds us that other Christian traditions exist and bear the name "Protestant" precisely because some men and women of faith have concluded in their time that the answer to whether the Catholic Church has this capacity was no. The third suggests that if the Catholic Church could find ways to become more faithful and true to itself both by opening itself to the lessons of this history and by engaging the fresh challenges of contemporary society, here would be a way to do what the Protestant Principle calls for, but in a less corrosive way.

Pope John's choice of the word "aggiornamento" was a stroke of genius, then, because the word implied that change would come in firm and accountable continuity with the past. In the game of church politics that Pope John needed to win if his council was to succeed, this was reassuring both to the bishops present and to the entire Catholic world. Few Catholics were prepared for what some say had been a "dirty little secret"[38] and others an "oxymoron"[39]—that their church does change and always has changed. And according to O'Malley, however "psychologically and theologically unprepared" most Catholics may have been to receive the changes that Vatican II wrought, any crisis that it produced was still less dramatic than those of other "great reformations" in Christian history, thanks to the reassuring rhetoric by which the bishops and theologians of the council followed Pope John's lead. The council and its documents were "understated"; they "conciliated and reassured rather than confronted" prophetically.[40]

By invoking change in continuity with tradition, aggiornamento was not just politically savvy, however. Above all and first of all, it

128

was right, deeply right, theologically and pastorally. At its deepest theological level aggiornamento did not really privilege one particular time, the contemporary era. Nor, really, did it privilege one particular space, the church as an institution. Instead, it privileged the work of God's Spirit forming a people of God within history.

Already in convoking the council, Pope John was voicing his hope and his prayer that it would be "a New Pentecost."[41] To associate the council with the dramatic first-century event that marked the church's very founding was surely a way to underscore the theological and historical importance of the council; doing so signaled in yet another way that Vatican II would not just do long-delayed mop-up work that the First Vatican Council had left undone, but would also take the church into a whole new era.[42] It was another way to impress upon the church an awareness of "the exceptional character of [the] historical juncture" that the church faced, and "the extraordinary prospects that it opened up" for a renewed church, which "might be able to show itself to the world and teach humanity the evangelical message with the same power and urgency that marked the original Pentecost."[43]

Above all, however, "the appeal to Pentecost gave first place to the action of the Spirit and not that of the pope or of the Church and its doctrinal universe."[44] Such an orientation helped move the council "beyond a primarily institutional outlook" to "a clearly evangelical conception of the Church."[45] A church as extensive and complex as the Roman Catholic Church cannot live by watchwords and metaphors alone, however inspired they might be. It certainly did need structural and procedural clarity: some of the ambiguities that Vatican II left have contributed to dogged controversies in the postconciliar period. But without a clear and renewing vision of its evangelical purpose and mission, the church's structures had too often taken on a life of their own.[46]

Insofar as aggiornamento offered a significant breakthrough in theological methodology, therefore, that was because it called first the council and then the entire church "to concentrate on what the Church could in fact give the world, namely, the ancient message of the gospel."[47] To make a "leap forward" into engaged service within the world, a church that was committed to reading the signs of the times would need to take its cues from somewhere other than the times alone; it would need "a deeper penetration of the gospel and of the mystery of the Church."[48] Pope John's concern to emerge from the Catholic Church's siege mentality was more rooted, not less rooted, in the very heart of the tradition precisely *because* it was apostolic in the fullest pastoral and missionary sense of the word. As he explained in his opening address to the council,

> Our duty is not only to guard this precious treasure [of sacred doctrine], as if we were concerned only with antiquity, but [also] to dedicate ourselves with an earnest will and without fear to that work which our era demands of us, pursuing thus the path which the Church has followed for twenty centuries.[49]

Elsewhere in the address he held both dimensions of aggiornamento together—ancient fidelity and missionary thrust, each richer for the continuity between them—in this way:

> In order . . . that this doctrine may influence the numerous fields of human activity, with reference to individuals, to families, and to social life, it is necessary first of all that the Church should never depart from the sacred patrimony of truth received from the Fathers. But at the same time she must ever look to the present, to the new conditions and new forms of life introduced into the modern world, which have opened new avenues to the Catholic apostolate.

Aggiornamento, then, really had nothing to do either with "naive optimism" about the world on the one hand, or triumphalism about the church on the other hand, but about hope in Jesus Christ and his Holy Spirit, who had not abandoned the world. Modernity was not without its dangers. The task of inculturating the gospel afresh within the modern world required the church to speak and embody the gospel in the midst of all the ambiguous hopes and aspirations of the modern era, while *also* confronting its degradations and self-deceptions.

Neither Pope John nor the council were blind to the latter. John's opening speech pointed to the "marvelous progress of the discoveries of human genius," but also the need to evaluate them rightly. Central to the church's role was to "admonish [people] so that . . . they may raise their eyes to God, the Source of all wisdom and all beauty." For if moderns attended only to those realities accessible to the senses, "it may happen that the fleeting fascination of visible things should impede true progress." More ominously, Pope John spoke of "fallacious teaching, opinions, and dangerous concepts," which had "produced such lethal fruits that by now it would seem that men of themselves are inclined to condemn them." To be sure, the concurring opinion of these secular commentators allowed John to maintain a stance of accompaniment rather than gloomy judgment. Still, he minced no words as he named "those ways of life which despise God and His law or place excessive confidence in technical progress and a well-being based exclusively on the comforts of life." Likewise, "experience has taught men that violence inflicted on others, the might of arms, and political domination, are of no help at all in finding a happy solution to the grave problems which afflict them." When, in *Gaudium et spes*, the bishops followed John's lead by proclaiming the church's intention to accompany the modern world in solidarity and friendship, the overarching word of hope that some commentators have mistaken for sunnily misplaced optimism did not preclude sustained examination of the dark side of human technological prowess, which was facilitating a chilling array of violations against human dignity.[50]

At least one other biblical image in Pope John's opening address to the council worked in tandem with aggiornamento to unpack the theological insight and guidance that John intended it to carry. If humanity, for all its progress, was nonetheless broken and needy, the church must stand before it not in a Constantinian position of worldly wealth or power but humbly and also needy, with nothing to offer but the treasure of Christ alone. The image here was of the apostle Peter in Acts 3, addressing the lame beggar in the temple of Jerusalem: "To mankind, oppressed by so many difficulties, the Church says, as Peter said to the poor who begged alms from him: 'I have neither gold nor silver, but what I have I give you; in the name of Jesus Christ of Nazareth, rise and walk.'" The church could not offer people in the modern world passing riches or "merely earthly happiness" but did offer them "the goods of divine grace" and a life-giving teaching that originated in Christ, which could help them "to understand well what they really are, what their lofty dignity and their purpose are." As Christians shared this message in "the

131

fullness of Christian charity," nothing would be "more effective in eradicating the seeds of discord, nothing more efficacious in promoting concord, just peace, and the brotherly unity of all."[51]

And nothing would do more to renew the church itself than to rise to this very challenge.[52]

Authority and Dissent in a Richer Theological Context

Conducted under the mantle of aggiornamento, the Second Vatican Council dealt everywhere with the relationship between authority and dissent—yet paradoxically nowhere, at least nowhere in particular. As one might expect, this was both its strength and its weakness, for the ambiguity that such a pattern passed to the church would complicate the reception of Vatican II in the postconciliar period. Eminent theologian and later Cardinal Avery Dulles described that ambiguous legacy:

> No other council in history—not even Vatican I—so exalted the role of the hierarchy. . . . And yet no previous council gave comparable emphasis to religious freedom and the active participation of the laity in the concerns of the Church. Did Vatican II, then, increase or decrease the functions of authority and obedience in the lives of Catholics? No simple answer is possible.[53]

The council, explained Dulles, reaffirmed the teachings of the First Vatican Council concerning papal primacy but simultaneously spoke of the collegial authority of bishops and strengthened the authority of individual bishops theologically. It also acknowledged the rights and dignity of the laity, urging priests and bishops alike to welcome their "prudent advice."[54] To be meaningful, that would have to imply the possibility of dissent, but nowhere did the council directly address or guide the proper functioning of dissent. This, Dulles observed, became a "source of confusion. . . . Vatican II by its reticence unintentionally set the stage for subsequent polarization among Catholics striving to be loyal to the council itself."[55] Still, Dulles insisted, the council did make "a most crucial move" by placing the entire question of authority and obedience into a richer theological context.[56]

The "*everywhere*" of conciliar attention to the question of authority, obedience—and by implication dissent—was manifest in numerous Vatican II documents,[57] but above all in the totality of the conciliar experience itself.[58] Since no churchwide "ecumenical" council had been held for nearly a century, attending bishops were initially unsure of what to expect and had to discover for themselves how to *be* a council in the first place.[59] "A new experience, which caught many bishops off balance, was that of conflict," Alberigo has noted; the Curia had led most to believe that the council would be orderly and quick, but once it began, all bets were off. The council was less calm than they expected, and in contrast to all their formation since seminary days, each bishop had to have a personal opinion.[60] In convoking the council, John XXIII had hoped to open wide the windows of the church, and to his apparent pleasure, the gathered bishops took him up on the proposition. Immediately, in the opening days of the council, they wrested control over the process from the Vatican bureaucracy, rejected the draft documents they had been handed, and reorganized themselves into commissions and consultative regional bodies.[61] As the council proceeded, questions that bishops thought long settled were now "open and debated." What's more, "solutions sometimes diametrically opposed" came into play, and voices or blocs advocating various proposals often lined up in complex and unpredictable ways.[62] Thus, as Cardinal Joseph Bernardin once commented, "recognition and highlighting of dialogue [was] one of the glories of the Second Vatican Council and of the papacies that nurtured and followed it."[63]

That "*everywhere*" by which questions of authority and dissent pervaded the conciliar experience extended far beyond the conclave. The council was not just an institutional phenomenon occurring at the pinnacle of the church. Instead, it involved all of Catholicism and eventually other Christian communities as well; "the conviction . . . spread that the entire community of believers was 'called to council.'"[64] It was not only the bishops and their advisers who felt free to express personal convictions. "While the council was in session, Catholics, not only in the council hall but outside it as well, were living in an uncommon climate of freedom," Alberigo reported. "In that atmosphere it was possible to raise all problems, even if [average Catholics] were limited in dealing with them and solving them."[65] A largely unprecedented number of laypeople did have direct input into the drafting of Vatican II documents, and more had opportunity to comment; some of these were Protestants.[66] The transparency of the entire process contributed to the shock that many Catholics felt as they realized their church could change, particularly as modern media allowed them to view it changing through "behind-the-scenes maneuvering."[67] Whatever the corresponding anxieties, however, the experience also brought what Cardinal Bernardin has called "the privilege of being a conciliar generation," living at what John Courtney Murray termed "the growing edge of tradition," and charged with "the responsibility to appropriate [the council's] meaning, interpret its content and share its significance with succeeding generations."[68]

To be sure, the "*nowhere*" of *explicit* conciliar attention to the relationship between authority and dissent has made it somewhat harder to fulfill that responsibility. The relationship between one authority *and another authority* had been on the agenda for a second Vatican council even before Pope John announced it. The First Vatican Council had closed in 1870 without completing its work; it had underscored the authority of the pope without articulating the corresponding authority of bishops, either within the jurisdiction of their local churches or as a collective body gathered in ecumenical council. Still less did Vatican I imagine a possible role for regional conferences of bishops or articulate the apostolic ministries and vocations of laypeople. The Second Vatican Council did all this, preeminently in *Lumen gentium*, the Dogmatic Constitution on the Church, yet left ambiguity even there. The council did not really explain the relationship between the authority of the pope and the authority of the bishops, after all, but simple affirmed both/and. David Toolan, SJ, Jesuit priest, theologian, and journalist, has suggested that absent a "regularized procedure" detailing the obligations of the pope to consult with local churches by way of the bishops—much less a procedure for calling the pope to account as the apostle Paul once challenged the apostle Peter, according to Galatians 2:11—a "renewal of papal and curial interventionism" in the years following the council "was bound to bring conflict between center and periphery."[69]

And if that was true about the relationship between the twin authorities of pope and bishops, the council was even more "reticent"—

as Dulles put it—to specify when dissent was legitimate on the part of theologians and laypeople. The early draft of one Vatican II document had actually proposed "some helpful, though undeniably cautious, principles regarding dissent," according to Dulles. While warning against giving occasion for scandal, it "stated that subjects, according to their competence, have the right, and sometimes the duty, to declare their views about what affects the good of the Church." Even such cautious language failed to survive the process of redaction and approval, however. "As it turned out, the council's reserve about the question of dissent was a source of confusion during the postconciliar period," Dulles concluded, particularly in the context of the 1967 papal encyclical *Humanae vitae,* on artificial contraception.[70]

In the absence of clear procedures (and on the way to clearer ones), we thus have no choice but to nurture the attitudes and virtues that are ultimately the basis of healthy and sustainable community life anyway. While Vatican II documents may suffer from certain limitations, they still provide many precedents and much guidance for the practices of stability that we need so as to nurture the virtue of fidelity—even or especially when the good of the church requires that stability take the form of loyal dissent. Without claiming to be exhaustive, we may review seven major theological developments at Vatican II that all enrich the theological context within which to negotiate matters of authority and dissent.

The Church as a Pilgrim People

What Dulles considered to be "the most crucial move" of all by the council in regard to authority, obedience, and dissent was "its presentation of the Church as the pilgrim people of God."[71] The theological richness of this concept unfolds throughout the Vatican II documents.[72] A pilgrim people recognizes that its ultimate homeland, purpose, and values transcend every earthly nation and culture, yet finds itself all the freer and more duty bound to help build a better world from within any culture.[73] Realistic about the gap between its present and ultimate locations, it expects trials and sufferings along the way but finds nourishment for its journey by participating in the heavenly liturgy already in its earthly liturgy.[74] Such a concept helps to free the church from Constantinian entanglements but also from the burden of defending all of its own past actions, judgments, and alliances. It is, after all, a people on a journey, still growing and yearning, unfinished, and able to admit that "in the life of the people of God in its pilgrimage through the vicissitudes of human history there has at times appeared a form of behavior which was hardly in keeping with the spirit of the Gospel and was even opposed to it."[75]

Conceiving of the church as the pilgrim people of God has direct implications for the relationship between authority and dissent. Dulles has listed many of these:

- In such a church, authority cannot be a mere matter of handing down official decisions, nor can obedience be mere submission to higher officers.
- The Word of God imparts authority to all who give expression to it, even though they hold no office in the church.
- Obedience—in its original sense of reverent listening—is not the duty of subordinates alone, but of all Christians. All must strive together to hear the Word of God as it is given in the present.
- The gifts of prophecy and interpretation are not bestowed on pastors alone, although pastors have their own distinctive functions in the process of discernment and articulation.
- In a pilgrim church, moreover, the decisions of ecclesiastical authority will be in some respects tentative, as becomes a church whose task, in the memorable phrase of *Lumen gentium*, is "to show forth in the world the mystery of the Lord in a faithful though shadowed way, until at last it will be revealed in total splendour." (*LG* 8)[76]

The pilgrim peoplehood of God, therefore, provides the theological basis for aggiornamento. It elicits a theological methodology that is historically engaged, captive to no one social, cultural, or philosophical order, yet is necessarily open to unanticipated challenges that it encounters along its unfinished journey. Simply put, conceiving of the church as a pilgrim people provides *the* "richer theological context" that orients all our remaining points.

Theological Method

If the deeply Catholic impulse to seek change through continuity was basic to the Second Vatican Council,[77] the name for the theological method that came to fruition at the council was *ressourcement*, a French word used theologically to refer to a "return to the sources." *Ressourcement* differs subtly from the restorationism that is one impulse within Protestantism because it seeks to recover a broader and deeper tradition, not jump back over a tradition that it considers to be deeply flawed or even "fallen." But it also differs from what Tradition (with a capital T) has sometimes become within Catholicism: the notion that authoritative Tradition is simply whatever body of official pronouncements the church's teaching authority or magisterium has now come to make.

Under the banner of *ressourcement*, the council's theological method was to reexpand the range of authorities on which the church's magisterium and theologians base their work. This clarifies that the Tradition is really a centuries-long, authoritatively guided, but still-continuing conversation, not a pure datum that might be reducible to a hefty single catechism. The strength of the Catholic intellectual tradition has long been its commitment to collating Christian theology with the best insights of philosophy and with widely human principles of "natural law," though in pre–Vatican II Catholicism these had sometimes come to eclipse theology or reduce church teaching to highly deductive and supposedly timeless formulations. Vatican II sought to make theology more properly theological again by reorienting it to its biblical sources and to the theological reflections of its earliest centuries (via patristics, studying the thought and practice of the early church fathers).[78] All this requires a far greater historical consciousness, disciplined through modern tools of historical inquiry, even while grounding theology in the biblical and continuing narrative of the pilgrim people of God. Finally, while continuing to insist that "Sacred Tradition and sacred Scripture [together] make up a single deposit of the Word of God, which is entrusted to the Church," the council also made clear that the living teaching authority or magisterium of the church, which bears the responsibility to interpret the Word of God authoritatively, "is not superior to the Word of God, but is its servant."[79]

The import of the council's shift in theological method for the question of authority and dissent is that it reverses some of the historical reasons for the dissent of Reformers. It also loosens some of the theological rigidity that could continue to leave conscientious dissenters feeling that they must choose between the equally destructive options of capitulation and schism.

Liturgical Reform

However technical some of these theological emphases and shifts might seem to be, the wider church began to experience them almost immediately through changes in Catholic practices of worship. Many have made observations similar to this: "Of all the changes in the church's life stemming from the Second Vatican Council, nothing else touched ordinary Catholics so immediately and tangibly as the changes in the liturgy."[80] A core lesson that emerges from *ressourcement* is that as the church prays, so the church believes—*lex orandi, lex credendi*. The very structure of the liturgy is its continual reenacting of the biblical narrative, which ever climaxes eucharistically as it re-presents God's own self-giving through the life, death, and resurrection of Jesus. The most immediate and well-known liturgical change was to conduct the mass in local or vernacular languages rather than Latin, with the obvious intent of allowing the faithful to understand and participate in its meaning more fully. But toward this same end, Vatican II also allowed fuller incorporation of local and regional cultural forms. Meanwhile, many smaller adaptations to the abiding structure of the liturgy aimed to accentuate the drama of the liturgy and its formative impact on the believer, while enlarging the content of biblical readings within the liturgy. The import of liturgical reform for questions of authority and dissent is perhaps indirect. Nonetheless, it remains one of the most tangible expressions of the council's commitment to a greater engagement with culture, based on a clearer expectation that the gospel can and must take shape within every culture. And in the end, week after week, eucharistic celebration is the central place for holding the Christian community's tensions and disagreements together in communion.[81]

Ecumenical Openness

One of the surprises that most enlivened imaginations throughout all of Christendom—and indeed a watching world—was the opening by John XXIII and then the entire council to ecumenical conversation and to a real though "incomplete" communion with other Christian communities. With abrupt nonchalance, non-Catholic Christians suddenly were no longer "heretics" or "schismatics" but "separated brethren." Alberigo has described the impact:

> More than any other aspect, the ecumenical dimension [of the council] elicited surprise, public interest, and some very lively apprehensions. . . . That it should be the Pope who took the first steps toward the unity of the Christian Churches and who presented this process, not in terms of a simple "return," but in terms of a "working together to become a single flock," was so unexpected and almost improbable that it elicited a variety of reactions and called for a rethinking of the entire ecumenical strategy.[82]

Exactly what John's intentions were concerning the relative priority of conciliar work to restore Christian unity remains unclear; so too were his hopes for doing more than simply improve conditions for eventual unity.[83] What is undoubtedly clear is that Vatican II forged an altogether new style of Catholic interchurch relations, and that *Unitatis redintegratio*, the Decree on Ecumenism, represents a commitment to ongoing dialogue that four papacies have now cemented.

True, official Catholic ecumenical openness should not prompt misplaced hopes. Commenting on Vatican II, leading Protestant ecumenist Willem Visser 't Hooft once issued a sober reminder that ecumenical dialogue has often showed that "the most difficult problems to be solved on the way to unity" involve ecclesiology—and the most difficult of these involve the role of the magisterium and the papacy.[84] In other words, what ecumenical dialogue often makes clearest is how *far* the churches still have to go to achieve unity and how many obstacles involve matters related to authority and dissent.

Yet the new era of ecumenical openness that the Second Vatican Council inaugurated has clear import for these questions and represents significant progress nonetheless. Almost by definition, those who have been "separated brethren" vis-à-vis the Catholic Church were dissenters in the first generation and at least by implication remain so even today. For the Roman Church to open itself officially to their perspectives, then, is to open itself to the legitimate challenge of dissent. After all, the church has now pronounced with all the weight of a churchwide council of bishops that in the historic process by which those "separated brethren" "became separated from full communion with the Catholic Church, . . . often enough, men of both sides were to blame."[85] Whenever new obstacles to unity add to old ones, that assessment must in principle remain the case, requiring conscientious and charitable challenge by non-Catholic and Catholic alike.

Principles for Structuring a Pilgrim People

The Catholic Church would hardly be the Catholic Church without a deep conviction, which all but the most radical of its dissidents share at some level: for any theological insight or principle to be sustainable, it must cohere communally, in ways that require those structured relationships we know by the name of institutions.[86] Thus if it was not already clear going into the Second Vatican Council that the conception and structure of the church would be one of its major problematics, this most certainly was clear by the beginning of the second year, according to Alberigo.[87]

As John Courtney Murray, SJ, looked back at the council a year after its close, he observed that Vatican II had taken four traditional themes of ecclesiology and rearranged their emphases by rearranging their presentation. First and foundationally (again) is that before all else, the church is the people of God, and for Murray that meant that through "the common possession of the Spirit," all believers share in a basic equality of dignity, freedom, and "charismatic" ministry. Second, the church is a communion, and as such its interpersonal life as a community is an end in itself. Third, because this communion participates in the divine love of the Trinity, it inevitably reaches out in witness and service toward all humanity. All this reorients but does not alter a fourth point, however: the church remains a visible society and must have a proper authority structure in order to function as such.[88]

That proper functioning of authority, Murray continued, implies responsibilities both on the part of official church authority and the entire people of God, as it exercises its proper freedom *properly*. Matching the "unitive" function of the hierarchy as it builds and strengthens the community through dialogue is the "charismatic" function that God's people exercise as they respond to the hierarchy's invitation to dialogue and to fully deploy their gifts in service within history. Matching the "decisive or directive" function of the hierarchy that is necessary for carrying out its unitive role is the "executive" function of the people of God, which may require obedience and even self-sacrifice, since dialogue is not an end in itself but always "looks toward decisions and directives." Finally, a "corrective" or even "punitive" function of the hierarchy that is necessary to protect community life from "egoisms . . . that would destroy its unity or damage its work" is matched by the "self-corrective" function by which Christians throughout the church avoid abusing their freedom or settling for any freedom other than that which Christ has won for them.[89]

The import for authority and dissent is obvious, even if it is precisely here that more specific details from the council would have been welcome.[90] What is least obvious but most significant is this: following through on the overriding pastoral and missionary orientation of Vatican II will continue to assure that neither the pilgrim people of God nor its guiding authorities will be able to ignore new questions and challenges. Not only that; such an orientation will also help to raise the right questions and invite the proper use of authority. For whatever structures and procedures the church surely needs, what should be clearest is that any proper use of authority must aim to direct God's people toward the larger purposes of the kingdom of God, rather than mere institutional maintenance. But then, as *Commonweal* magazine editor Margaret O'Brien Steinfels has pointed out, the most painful but also most legitimate occasions for dissent arise when those who are trying most to be faithful discover "disjunctures between pastoral experience and existing teaching."[91] Traditional missionaries are her classic example: a missionary church living out the mandate of the Second Vatican Council must expect to experience similar disjunctures as a normal part of its life.

Religious Liberty

To many observers, this was the test. Neither thoughtful Catholics nor hopeful Protestants nor a watching world could quite trust the breakthroughs of Vatican II unless the gathered bishops found a way to move solemnly yet decisively away from Catholicism's long-entrenched willingness to call for, benefit from, and rationalize use of state coercion in religious affairs. Many Vatican II documents recognize the diversity of cultures and political structures within which the church properly lives, worships, and serves; as we have seen, none less than Pope John XXIII hoped that the council would mark the passing of Constantinian entanglements that tied the church to a single outdated model of relations to culture and society. But no embrace of the church's post-Constantinian opportunities would be complete if Catholicism could not live as a pilgrim people within modern democracies, too. The Pastoral Constitution on the Church in the Modern World, *Gaudium et spes*, certainly expanded most broadly on the church's desire to accompany humanity as a friend on its own journey through the modern world, but such friendship meant little if modern men and women could not speak freely along the way. The Dogmatic Constitution on the Church, *Lumen gentium*, and the Decree on the Apostolate of the Laity, *Apostolicam actuositatem*, undoubtedly said the most about the role of the laity in the church and the world, but laypeople could hardly exercise their vocations fully if they seemed to be acting merely as subjects of the clergy. Similarly, the Decree on Ecumenism, *Unitatis redintegratio*, and the Decree on Relationships with Non-Christian Religions, *Nostra aetate*, explicitly committed the Catholic Church to dialogue with other faiths and worldviews; but dialogue partners could hardly trust that the Roman Church would converse in good faith if it still held the possibility of religious coercion in reserve.

The work of the council would have integrity, in other words, only if the gathered bishops found fittingly Catholic language by which to affirm religious freedom, political democracy, separation of church and state, and the dignity of conscience. After protracted deliberation, the council finally did this in its closing weeks. *Dignitatis humanae*, the Declaration on Religious Liberty, states:

> The Vatican Council declares that the human person has a right to religious freedom. Freedom of this kind means that all men should be immune from coercion on the part of individuals, social groups and every human power so that, within due limits, nobody is forced to act against his convictions nor is anyone to be restrained from acting in accordance with his convictions in religious matters in private or in public, alone or in associations with others. The Council further declares that the right to religious freedom is based on the very dignity of the human person as known through the revealed word of God and by reason itself. This right of the human person to religious freedom must be given such recognition in the constitutional order of society as will make it a civil right.[92]

There certainly is more. The declaration required a combination of careful theology and face-saving wording in order to assure many bishops and the faithful that what was patently a *change* in the position of many centuries and recent popes nonetheless amounted to a *development* of doctrine that remained true to the church's long tradition. More than any other Vatican II document, perhaps, the redaction of *Dignitatis humanae* instantiates the council's painful yet fruitful practice of stability.

But the council's altogether crucial and historic Declaration on Religious Freedom still left unfinished business for the postconciliar church. Part of what has long made Constantianism enticing for many Christians has been the promise of help from civil authorities, and from the sword they bear, in exercising church discipline and preserving the quality of their own community life. Some unfinished business presents itself simply as the inevitable task of unlearning old Constantinian habits, as churches speak and Christians work in the public sphere. But further still, learning to do without the help of the state in preserving a Christian culture may, if anything, accentuate conflicts within the Christian community itself.

If, in the midst of "culture wars" and in the face of moral relativism, church leaders must apply any and all disciplinary measures themselves in order to maintain authentically Christian patterns of community life—but must also continue a Vatican-II-style conver-

143

sation with modern culture in order to discern what those patterns and measures really ought to be—then the question of religious freedom and rights of conscience will invariably rear its head within the church itself. And it has. The great continuing debate that *Dignitatis humanae* opened rather than resolved is whether and how the rights of conscience that it named, and the principles it cited, justify free expression of conscience not only in the public sphere but in the ecclesial sphere as well. Scholars such as Daniel Cowdin have argued that because Vatican II grounded freedom of conscience and dissent in moral principles of human dignity and sociability rather than in legal or juridical principles alone, its affirmation of religious liberty must in fact apply within the church too.[93] The *import* for questions of authority and dissent is clear. Yet because the church is a society in which the apostles and their witness to our "Lord" must necessarily exercise some kind of veto power that secular democracies do not know, the *how* of authority and dissent has remained somewhat less clear.

The Coming of a Global Church

Late in his life, looking back at the Second Vatican Council, the twentieth century's preeminent Catholic theologian, Karl Rahner, SJ, identified what he believed to be the single most important implication of the Second Vatican Council. It was the coming of a truly global church. No such epoch-making event had occurred in Christianity since the first century, when Jewish Christianity was transformed into the Christianity of another distinct cultural configuration: Hellenistic and then European Christendom. Even the Protestant Reformation paled in comparison to the Vatican II watershed, Rahner believed. Yet the Roman Catholic Church had only begun to recognize itself as grappling with the coming of global Christianity.[94]

The church will be doing so for a long time, no doubt, for in ways both wonderful and frustrating, the coming of a truly global church complexifies everything I have just said about theological themes running through Vatican II. It especially requires that the exercise of freedom of conscience be mature, self-critical, and accountable to Christian brothers and sisters with quite different cultural assumptions. The coming of a global church makes everything we might say about stability writ large both more difficult and more urgent.

As David Toolan, SJ, has succinctly stated the matter: "The problem, the mystery, is globalization."[95] Yes, the Roman Catholic Church and indeed all Christian churches have needed to come to terms with modernity and thus also with Western commitments to human equality, freedom of conscience, and religious liberty. But modernity is more than these. It is also decolonization, globalization, and the ever-pressing need for just, healthy, and deep-seated patterns of cross-cultural communication. The Second Vatican Council certainly opened up a wider transnational conversation within the church; while a Western agenda may still have dominated there, new faces, hues, voices, and alliances from the global South were gaining prominence.[96] Far from settling specific issues in obvious ways, however, this cultural and geographic widening makes churchwide conversation and deliberation more complex.

Accustomed to thinking of themselves as champions of global justice and multicultural awareness, liberal Catholics in the West often assume that the coming of a truly global church will finally force the church's hierarchy to invest fully in episcopal collegiality at the top, in liturgical and canonical pluralism at the grassroots, and in freedom of conscience and debate throughout. Perhaps. But as Toolan bluntly warned, "If you think we have trouble now, just wait."[97] Yes, as Toolan continued, a "polycentric 'world church'" may well require "a de-Romanized, multilateral church with plural liturgies, plural canon laws, and indeed plural, indigenous proclamations of the gospel message."[98] But not without fierce battles, as he predicted. And not without the weight of global churchwide consensus breaking *against* the habits of individualistic Western Christians on many specific issues.[99] As the religious historian Philip Jenkins has often observed, and as recent crises in the worldwide Anglican communion over homosexuality have underscored, Christians of the global South tend to be more doctrinally orthodox and morally conservative than Western Christians, even when they also advocate more boldly against political and economic injustice.[100] If progressive Christians in the West are going to champion the voiceless of the global South in a truly consistent manner, they had better know how to listen hard and read these signs of the times too.

The reality of a coming global church makes it all the more urgent for Christians, both Catholic and Protestant, to deepen the practice of stability. As the final chapter of this book will argue, therefore, it is not just the Christian community but also a globalizing world that desperately needs models for conducting sustained, painful, but peaceful conversations by which diverse peoples continually learn to hang with one another even as they disagree and struggle. One way that the church must live out its identity as sacrament of the unity of humankind is by offering this model to the world. But one way to avoid the hard work of learning and practicing stability in the global church is instinctively to blame the Vatican whenever churchwide policies do not change quickly enough in one's preferred direction. At least sometimes when Rome seems intransigent, this is not so much because it is being Roman as because it is being global, and in its unitive ministry it must represent the consensus of the global church—not just American and European Catholics who, with a blind spot to a hubris that is no less imperial for being "liberal," are all too sure that they represent the cutting edge of history.

In this light, postconciliar struggles over how to practice and institutionalize authoritative discernment in the church may well be as salutary as they are frustrating. How so? Magisterial and indeed papal authority has set up the very disciplines that Christians need to become more fully a global, cross-cultural, interethnic, international church, capable of gathering the wisdom of the entire people of God. But more on this is coming in chapter 6.

Stability Strained but Holding

The reason to dwell on the Second Vatican Council has been to show that practices of stability are possible on a global, churchwide scale, not to look back longingly on the council as an already-lost golden age. Reflecting on the first decades following Vatican II, some have decried a "promiscuous embrace of novelties" in many sectors of the church, which took the council as warrant for all kinds of experimentation.[101] Meanwhile, others have lamented that this very sort of reaction has stifled "the spirit of the Council," which provides precedent for continuing, thoughtful, discerning change. In some respect, I agree with both laments. Wild experimentation and fearful retrenchment have both been dangers in the postconciliar era. If I look longingly back on the conciliar moment as a continuing model, then, it is precisely because what the Second Vatican Council models is the *commitment to stability and to change through continuity*, which holds both of those tendencies together and thereby *calls to accountability each approach and its respective advocates.*

No doubt the conciliar experience of aggiornamento in 1962 through 1965 and beyond has "summoned up deep feelings about permanence and change, steadfastness and adaptation" for Catholics throughout the world.[102] What the council has provided for the church's continuing pilgrimage through the modern world has been more like a compass than a map. As Alberigo's colleague Peter Hünermann has stated, even *Gaudium et spes*, the Vatican II document that addresses the role of the church in the modern world most directly, did not so much resolve as open "almost all the intra-ecclesial contentious issues of the postconciliar period." It thus stands for the entire council, he explained, in two apparently contradictory ways. On the one hand, Catholic Christendom has tended to use key words from *Gaudium et spes* to summarize the entire conciliar message. On the other hand, almost all the controversies of the postconciliar period emerge from *Gaudium et spes*: contraception, abortion, liberation theology, quarrels over how best to inculturate the gospel in various settings, and clashes over the proper role of the hierarchy.[103]

Still, what Toolan has called "the Catholic taboo against schism," and what I am calling the practice of stability, is (in Toolan's words of 1989) "strained but holding."[104] There should be no doubt whatsoever that Vatican II has provided the Catholic Church and many other Christians with a model of change through continuity, along with much specific guidance that was groundbreaking and historic. In both necessary and less happy ways, the council has also bequeathed tensions, not just despite but because of its process. As we have observed, Vatican II infused ambiguity into the very structure of the church by positing both papal and conciliar authority as preeminent, and it was reticent to offer clear guidance concerning the proper role of dissent in the church's discernment process. Further, a measure of retrenchment began already in the closing phase of the council, as Pope Paul VI sought to guard his conservative flank and reserved a number of key decisions for himself. As we have recognized, it seems no accident that the very issues he reserved—how to establish a worldwide body of bishops, birth control, and clerical celibacy—correspond with the postconciliar controversies that have led many Catholics to feel that the Vatican II promise of consultative churchwide discernment has been betrayed.[105]

Yet as Toolan has most eloquently remarked, "We [Catholics] signed on for these tensions."[106] Hints of tension surface even in Toolan's description of a pre–Vatican II bedrock of Catholic assumptions:

> For better or worse, in sickness and in health, no matter what, one doesn't break with the Patriarch of the West, the Bishop of Rome—so goes the Catholic axiom. Roman Catholics, we liked to congratulate ourselves, stick it out with mother church, digging in our heels if necessary. It almost defined us, or used to, that we have little sympathy for those who were driven—by anathema, by the addition of an "and" to the Nicene creed, by the sack of a city, or by the selling of indulgences—to separate from Rome. . . . We liked to think that in contrast to the purist theatrics of a Protestant "Here I stand, I can do no other," we had chosen a better way: a messier, more human church that had the gumption to take God seriously but also the good-humored sense to take the membership, including the Roman carnival of popes and bishops, less than literally, or even (in Europe) irreverently.[107]

The critical turn of the 1960s may have shaken this axiomatic cultural bedrock, Toolan stated. But it is telling that even when Catholics "began arguing noisily in public about what Vatican II did or did not mean" and "what it ought to mean to be Catholic in a multicentered world," they still preferred to speak of what they were experiencing as a *crisis* and not a looming *schism*.[108] And even the "crisis" could be exaggerated. Surveying the familiar problems of the postconciliar period, Toolan was blunt and sober yet still offered a provisionally hopeful conclusion: "After a period of remarkable transition, . . . the spiritual center arguably holds."[109]

Maybe not the institutional center, though, worried Toolan. The institutional center, he wrote, was suffering (paradoxically) from a resurgent centralization. Even so, if Toolan's analysis of Vatican developments placed him among those who felt some of the promise of the council being betrayed, he continued to exemplify that axiomatic Catholic commitment to both the practice of stability and an authoritative role for the magisterium. For after decrying how the Vatican had been treating a string of contentious but conscientious theologians, Toolan clarified: "This is not to say that there aren't limits, that theological malpractice is not a real possibility, or that we don't need a *respectable* process for identifying it when it occurs." What he and others were denying was not the responsibility of the Vatican, but "that the present Vatican process is at all adequate for the current situation—when so much major rethinking, in so many contexts, is demanded and when Catholic theology around the world is happily so full of spit."[110]

What Toolan was reporting, therefore, he also embodied: "Things are obviously noisier these days than they were fifty or a hundred years ago. . . . Still, for all the recent ventilation of crisis in the Roman Church, the taboo on schism remains relatively intact."[111] Toolan closed with brief reports of discontented religious women and theologians—among them, Brazilian theologian Leonardo Boff, soon to be silenced by Rome for what turned out to be a year. Boff's "summary remark was that 'I prefer to walk with the church rather than to walk alone with my theology.'"[112] Toolan's own summary remark was this: "Give us time, I pray. In the meantime, what can you do? This is my dysfunctional family; these are my people. We Catholics don't believe in divorce."[113]

Oh, and along the way, in Toolan's survey of ways that the center has held, there was this:

> When you consider that in the last quarter century Catholics, at least in the first world, have more or less successfully integrated [the] Protestant principle and the Enlightenment's critical turn with Catholic sacramental substance, what is amazing is not how much upset there's been but, relatively, how little.[114]

5

Stability in Hard Times: Loyal Dissent

We recognize and accept the authority of the Church as we do that of Christ himself. Our Holy Father the Pope is our dear sweet Christ on earth, as St. Catherine called him, even when she was pointing out with the liberty of a saint, how wrong he was at the time, in his conduct of temporal affairs. We accept the authority of the Church but we wonder why it shows itself in such strange ways.

Dorothy Day[1]

STABILITY. PRACTICES THAT engender the virtue of fidelity. The virtue that keeps us together even when we're pissed at each other. Aggiornamento and change through continuity. A "taboo against schism" that is strained but holding.[2] "I prefer to walk with the church rather than to walk alone with my theology."[3]

Despite all the possible ways of naming this Catholic bedrock of assumptions about how to be together as a people, few Catholics think to name the hard-won, always-tenuous virtue that sustains them as a community. Most, I suspect, take it for granted, precisely because it is so basic. As with any virtue, however, it is most visible when forced to rise to a test. In hard times, I have suggested, the practice of stability expresses itself as the tensely paired practice of "loyal dissent." It is then, if well-formed, that we see the practice of stability bearing fruit most evidently in the virtue of fidelity. And this we see through stories.

Obedience and Dissent: Three Archetypal Stories

In 1975, a leader of the Sant'Egidio community in Rome sought a meeting with church authorities. Today, three decades later, the community has more than fifty thousand members in some seventy countries. It has played a direct role in negotiating the end to civil war in Mozambique, worked with the Vatican to organize high-level interreligious gatherings to dialogue and pray for peace, and gained canonical recognition as a "public lay association" within the Catholic Church. All the while, it has integrated prayer and social ministry in ordinary ways through daily gatherings for worship and street-level ministries of friendship with the poor, thus fulfilling the best hopes of the Second Vatican Council.

In 1975, however, Sant'Egidio was scarcely seven years old. The group had begun in 1968 when a small group of high school students started meeting to study the Gospels, pray, and—with all their youthful zeal—try to figure out how to follow Jesus and live in solidarity with the "forgotten ones" at the margins of society. In response, accusations began circulating throughout the archdiocese of Rome.

Although the worldwide Catholic community of 1975 may have been witnessing the blossoming of Vatican II, the culture of the city that had hosted the council a decade earlier could hardly be expected to shed centuries of tradition and habits quickly, if ever. Even otherwise-secular Romans can be quite proud of their historical role as home and protector of the worldwide Catholic Church. Little wonder, then, that in the local Roman Church this Italian version of the Jesus Movement was provoking suspicion. Vatican II had encouraged Catholics to read the Bible for themselves. But to do so with a radical simplicity that went straight from text to life still seemed too "Protestant" for the average Catholic in Rome. Vatican II had also urged Catholic laypeople to take a greater role in

152

the life of the church. But to do so with a vigor that soon required new organizational structures, cutting across parish lines, invited bishops and other prelates to worry that Sant'Egidio was producing parallel lines of authority that might compete with the hierarchy or even result in schism.

In response, Andrea Riccardi of Sant'Egidio met with Cardinal Vicario Poletti. Also present was Fr. Vincenzo Paglia, the first priest to become involved with Sant'Egidio. Years later Paglia would be named bishop of Terni; at the time the young priest was rector of the once-abandoned church where the community had begun to meet, and which lent it the name Sant'Egidio (St. Giles). Riccardi's message was blunt, but not in the way of some renewal movements down through history, when facing off with church authorities: "If we're doing something wrong," Riccardi said, "we'll stop and disband."[4]

What ought we to make of such a posture? On the one hand, the role that Sant'Egido has come to play as a renewal movement favored by none less than Pope John Paul II would be unimaginable without the trust that Sant'Egidio forged by approaching its bishops in friendship and vulnerability. On the other hand, the role that Sant'Egidio eventually came to play as an internationally recognized nongovernmental organization, praised for its effectiveness in work from peacebuilding to HIV treatment among the poor of Africa, would have been lost if church authorities had taken Sant'Egidio up on its winsome but risky offer. Was it worth the risk? To pursue that question would be to indulge in speculation. Behind it, though, another question is likely to nag the modern reader: was Sant'Egidio's offer to disband anything other than cowering, slavish obsequiousness? Far from courageous, were its otherwise groundbreaking leaders not in the lingering grip of that Roman Catholic culture of authoritarianism that moderns have had the good sense to reject in their past and despise in their present? Surely they were wrong to risk not only their movement but also their conscience by placing communion with their church and its bishops over faithfulness to Jesus Christ and his gospel. Or were they?

A single story alone cannot answer these unsettling questions. Nor would I want a single incident from one moment in the life of a single community to serve as the template for every situation in which conscience must find the best available path for attending faithfully to the demands of both authority and dissent, communion and justice. For that very reason, this chapter must necessarily include many stories. Both to sharpen the question and begin to identify an answer—or at least a fruitful pattern of response—let me begin with two other archetypal stories. Deliberately, they come from two of the twentieth century's most formidable and, for many of us, most formative models of principled, conscientious resistance to unjust authority: the Rev. Dr. Martin Luther King Jr. and the Indian architect of modern active nonviolence, Mahatma Gandhi.

Sitting in a Birmingham, Alabama, jail in 1963, Martin Luther King Jr. penned a most eloquent and compelling argument against the sort of patient acquiescence to authority that some *might* see in the Sant'Egidio posture.[5] Imprisoned for leading a campaign of civil disobedience against the brutal and "grossly unjust treatment" of blacks in what he considered "the most thoroughly segregated city in the United States," King had just received an open letter from eight fellow clergymen in Alabama. "White moderates," not segregationists, they sympathized with the cause of civil rights but criticized King's tactics of nonviolent civil disobedience. Counseling him to seek negotiation rather than confrontation, criticizing the campaign as "untimely," and deploring the protesters' willingness to break the law at risk of public order, the clergymen were—as King saw it—telling oppressed and humiliated people to "Wait!" a little longer. King replied that, having already "waited for more than 340 years for our constitutional and God-given rights," blacks could wait no longer. The white power structure of Birmingham had barred every other alternative. Negotiation was actually the goal of the campaign, but oppressors never negotiated willingly, much less relinquished their unjust power voluntarily, without confrontation and a creative heightening of tension. King insisted that he was acting in the best traditions of biblical prophets such as Amos and Jesus when he not only spoke out but also prepared himself and his people "for direct action, whereby we would present our very bodies as a means of laying our case before the conscience of the local and the national community."

An altogether different posture than that of Sant'Egidio—or is it?

If nothing else, the actions of Sant'Egidio and King might be seen as different but related *tactics* that share certain key dynam-

154

ics. Both were taking risks, were prepared to make sacrifices, and were practicing disciplines of vulnerability. Both appealed to the conscience of authorities thereby. Both used psychosocial dynamics that served, intentionally or not, to disarm their opposition or potential opposition.

Similarities between Sant'Egidio and King go deeper than tactics, however. While the desire of the Sant'Egidio folks to work in continuity with their church's tradition is obvious, King's own appeal was all the more powerful because he too was working within tradition. This dimension of his "Letter from the Birmingham Jail" sometimes goes unnoticed. No doubt King's rootedness in the Christian tradition is most obvious in his appeal to its prophetic stream, but there is more. To make his case for civil disobedience against unjust laws, King drew also on the thought of Augustine of Hippo and Thomas Aquinas. Augustine had said that "an unjust law is no law at all," quoted King, and Aquinas had explained that "an unjust law is a human law that is not rooted in eternal law and natural law." Whenever King outlined his own six principles of active nonviolence, one of them restated poetically the very natural law tradition that Augustine and Aquinas represented: "The moral arc of the universe bends toward justice."[6] In his Birmingham letter, King also appealed, as he did throughout his career, to the best traditions of American democracy, citing the Declaration of Independence, the Constitution, and Thomas Jefferson.

The point of all these appeals was that to disobey an unjust law did *not* mean to defy justice, invite anarchy, or undermine public order, but instead constituted a service to the social order and the rule of law. Showing that one was acting to uphold true justice, truly public order, and the rule of law even while breaking unjust laws—that was central to principled and active nonviolence. Only if prophets and protesters were prepared to suffer the consequences of their actions rather than inflict the costs of their campaign on others could this be crystal clear.

Still, in the end a key difference between Sant'Egidio and Martin Luther King Jr. does remain: one was prepared to obey the relevant authorities, and the other was prepared to disobey. To be sure, one case involved church authority and the other civil authority. But even if a Christian ought rightly to bear a greater disposition to

155

obey the former than the latter, we simply face too many examples of ecclesiastical abuse and injustice through the centuries to find a ready rule in that distinction alone.

Instead, a third anecdote may suggest another possibility. Not only do the loyal obedience of the Sant'Egidio folks and the principled disobedience of King each have its own time and place, but it is possible to practice both simultaneously. The example of Mahatma Gandhi demonstrates that each will communicate all the more clearly whenever human creativity discovers ways to combine them both into a strong but flexible alloy.

On March 18, 1922, Gandhi stood trial for "attempting to excite disaffection toward His Majesty's Government," the colonial rule of the British Empire in India.[7] Gandhi had trained as a lawyer in London and had returned to India in 1915 after two decades of legal practice and political activism in South Africa. In South Africa he had developed both his political acumen and the spiritual disciplines he considered essential to the practice of satyagraha—truth-force, or active nonviolence. Though he was already famous in his home-land when he returned from exile, the ensuing years saw Gandhi's growing influence on the independence movement led by the India National Congress party. From 1920 through early 1922, the move-ment launched a series of satyagraha campaigns and boycotts of British goods throughout India. Only when mob violence broke out did Gandhi interrupt it with a hunger fast, to stop the excesses of his own followers. Not until the Congress Party demonstrated its renewed commitment to practicing Gandhi's nonviolent philosophy was he ready to renew his campaign of civil disobedience. But then, after months of hesitation, the government finally arrested him.

The 1982 movie *Gandhi* dramatically summarizes actual court-room accounts with admirable fidelity to the historical record:

ADVOCATE GENERAL [i.e., Prosecutor]: "Non-co-operation has one aim: the overthrow of the Government. Sedition must become our creed. We must give no quarter, nor can we expect any." Do you deny writing it?

GANDHI: Not at all. And I will save the Court's time, M'Lord, by stating under oath that to this day I believe non-co-operation with evil is a duty. And that British rule of India is evil.

ADVOCATE GENERAL: The Prosecution rests, M'Lord.

JUDGE BROOMFIELD: I presume you are conducting your own defense, Mr. Gandhi.

GANDHI: I have no defense, My Lord. I am guilty as charged. And if you truly believe in the system of law you administer in my country, you must inflict on me the severest penalty possible.

JUDGE BROOMFIELD: [*After a long and thoughtful pause.*] It is impossible for me to ignore that you are in a different category from any person I have ever tried, or am likely to try. [*Another pause.*] Nevertheless, it is my duty to sentence you—to six years' imprisonment. [*Commotion in the courtroom. Another pause. The judge briefly lowers his eyes.*] If however His Majesty's Government should—at some later date—see fit to reduce the term, no one will be better pleased than I.[8]

This was not the only time Gandhi insisted on a maximum sentence.[9] As he explained in the 1922 trial, doing so allowed him to communicate how "what in law is a deliberate crime" could also be "the highest duty of a citizen."[10] As he had stated in another trial five years earlier, he did not seek any "extenuation of the penalty to be awarded against me"; instead, he sought to show that he had acted "not for want of respect for lawful authority, but in obedience to the higher law of our being, the voice of conscience."[11]

As a lawyer, a national leader, a citizen in the fullest possible sense, and a disciplined ascetic who described both his political and spiritual development as "experiments with truth," Gandhi was deeply committed to upholding both the rule of law and lawful authority. As far distant as could be from the sort of quasi-adolescent protest that would strike out against any status quo just because it held status—and still quite distant from the postmodern suspiciousness that readily deconstructs without anticipating the need to reconstruct some kind of lawful social order—Gandhi's goal was to bring laws into line with God's just and eternal truth, not tear down the very principle of lawful authority. Truthful dissent will be truly effective only when it does the same.

That intuition holds together the loyal obedience of Sant'Egidio and the principled disobedience of Martin Luther King Jr. And Catholics seem to have internalized that intuition more deeply than have Protestants, who nonetheless need it to keep their Protestant

Dilemma from corroding their Christian communities. The prophetic resistance that Protestants celebrate more readily than Catholics will prove to be prophecy in the Spirit of God only when it discovers creative ways to affirm the principle of proper authority and respect for its human representatives, even while exposing the injustice of specific acts and policies.

The trick is to deal with the challenge that a single person or institution presents when they represent both rightful authority *and* its wrongful use. But that is why the creativity that holds together the creative tension of loyal dissent is so crucial. Discovering the creative gesture that challenges injustice even while situating critique within the continuity of relationship is not so much a technique as an art, and a spiritual discipline.

The Virtue That Catholics Struggle to Name

If there is one way in which Catholic respect for church authority differs from Gandhian respect for legal authority, it is this: the goal and basis for the Catholic practice of stability and the virtue of fidelity is not so much the abstract rule of law (as important as that is) but the deep theological yet organic call to sustain communion. The church needs its own due process, protection of rights, and accountable functioning of rules—sometimes desperately. But the Christian tradition makes clear that the telos, or ultimate purpose of all such guarantees, is the creation, healing, or sustenance of loving relationship among all creatures. Healed relationships of love participate in nothing less than the trinitarian life of God, which Christians know as communion.

We will jump to premature conclusions about a posture such as Sant'Egidio's and be blind to our own cross-cultural misunderstandings if we use only the language of rights, rules, and procedures to read it. Unfortunately, both the Catholic left and the Catholic right run amiss here. The one stresses rights alone while the other stresses rules alone, thus losing touch with the communal framework that gives both rights and rules their raison d'être. Often, when bishops chafe at the counsel of critics on either side, this is what stiffens their backs in reaction. That is all the more so when the preeminence of rights language creates a culture of pressure tactics, media campaigns, and special interest politics within the Christian community itself. The Catholic hierarchy could certainly bear to adjust to the realities of modern mass communications in open societies. But when modern realities carry the assumption that all human relations are at bottom about competition rather than communion—assertion of rights rather than knitting of relationships—they run at cross-purposes with some of the church's deepest theological convictions.

And they miss opportunities for constructive social change. For example, one of the most important breakthroughs of the Second Vatican Council came when Cardinal Alfredo Ottaviani (the ultra-conservative head of the Holy Office, successor to the Inquisition, who had resisted so many other changes at the council) surprised the gathering by rising to speak passionately in favor of a proposed statement on warfare. The draft condemned all use of nuclear weapons, supported conscientious objection, and called for a reevaluation of the classic just-war theory. Ottaviani's speech and the long, thunderous ovation it received helped to ensure the section's passage. Leading to this public climax, however, was a longer and quieter friendship of some fifteen years. It began when the French Catholic peace activist Jean Goss finessed a meeting with Ottaviani in 1950. The cardinal had experienced the horrors of World War II, had harbored his own deep misgivings, and had written that "war is to be altogether forbidden." Still, Ottaviani's theology had kept this as a matter for the church to take up directly with governments, not for the intervention of personal conscience or social movements. It was by seeing past Ottaviani's stern reputation and role as the church's grand inquisitor that first Goss, then his wife, Hildegaard Goss-Mayr, and then a widening circle of Catholic pacifists, including Dorothy Day, all transformed the views of this key prelate through ongoing friendship.[12]

There are two things to notice, then, about a whole series of terms that try to name what I am calling the practice of stability in hard times. First, just as my own term, "loyal dissent,"[13] holds two impulses together in a tight and hopefully creative tension, so too with others. A collection of short biographies about "men and women who loved and changed the Church" bears the title *Faithful Dissenters*.[14] Ex-bishop James Patrick Shannon, who resigned his office

159

in the late 1960s because he could not conscientiously uphold the church's teaching on contraception, described himself as a "reluctant dissenter."[15] More subtly yet still unmistakably, leading scholar of American Catholicism Scott Appleby and his coeditors titled their anthology *Creative Fidelity*.[16] So too, Catholic journalist Paul Wilkes has written of "thoughtful obedience" as an art being practiced by what he calls "good enough Catholics."[17] Janet Somerville, the first Catholic and first woman to head the Canadian Council of Churches, has spoken of "faithful patience."[18]

Second, while each of these terms depends on a tense polarity, the field that they set up is—like a magnetic field—invisible without further instrumentation, even though that very field offers the power and purpose of the pattern. Communion *is* that field, but we need to look for the stories and relationships that disclose what is most important about each of these terms: the sustaining of communion. When we abstract terms like "loyalty" and "dissent" from their stories and relationships, communion will remain invisible. As John Courtney Murray, SJ, once argued, the years immediately following the Second Vatican Council had not produced a crisis of either authority or freedom as much as "a crisis of community." The freedom that expresses itself properly when the Holy Spirit is at work, he wrote, and the authority that is necessary for any structured community—these stand in an "inevitable tension." But Christians must situate "this perennial polarity within the living context of community." Doing so "can serve to make the tension healthy and creative, releasing the energies radiant from both poles for their one common task, which is to build the beloved community."[19]

If we keep the field of communion in view, and not simply the poles of loyalty and dissent, we may notice a subtly distinct yet markedly Catholic approach to social life and the institutions that structure it. Amid all the post–Vatican II conflicts that in other Christian traditions might result in church splits (and that in a civil society dominated by marketplace competition often seem to result in ever-deeper incivility), David Toolan, SJ, has identified not just a taboo against schism but also an enduringly "solid 'we.'"[20] Richard R. Gaillardetz, chair of Catholic studies at the University of Toledo in Ohio, has explored this deeply communal sensibility by comparing Catholic Church membership with lasting marital commitment as exhibited not merely in romantic wedding images, with their "white dresses and black tuxedos, but in mortgages, children, layoffs, illnesses, arguments and reconciliations, boredom and delight."[21]

Communio and the principle of unity consistently keep even the most sharply critical and deeply hurt Catholics in the church, argued journalist David Gibson in *The Coming Catholic Church* in the wake of recent sexual abuse scandals. "Why they will stay" is "the mystery of Catholic identity," which Gibson has explored in a chapter headed by those titles.[22] Actually, the question about why they stay may come naturally to Protestants and Americans generally, but it irritates Catholics all across the theological or ideological spectrum. "The question itself rankles Catholics, because it is posed so often, even in balmier times, and because of the implication that any well-educated, thinking person would leave as a matter of course."[23]

As Gibson sought to answer the question and name the mystery (succeeding as well as anyone), some of his explanations were historical and sociological, but a well-ingrained sensibility toward communion and unity was his deeper answer. What John Chrysostom said in the fourth century still holds, even for twenty-first-century Catholics in an individualistic America: "You cannot pray at home as [well as] at church."[24] Not only has this principle "inculcated an extraordinary social compactness that [goes] beyond obedience to the hierarchy," Gibson observed. Its "glue [has] held throughout the demographic upheavals" that have altered both the cultural and institutional topography of American Catholicism.[25] Rigid parish lines and all-embracing parish culture may have eroded, for example, but a parish mentality survives. Thus the heart of lived Catholicism continues to be local, communal, and stable, whether or not Catholics agree with—or even notice—all that comes down from Rome. It is always in the *very* local, after all, that people experience the sacramental quality of life that is so basic to Catholicism. This is yet another quality that keeps Catholics in the church, its "distinctive aesthetic" or "sacramental vision," which offers a sense of God's presence not only in "icons, statues, ashes, candles, incense, bells, stained-glass, frescoes, holy water, pilgrimages, processions" but also in the richness of ordinary life.[26] What Gibson might have added is that this sacramental vision also populates the entire universe with the communion of saints.

161

No wonder, then, that Catholic thinkers who are quick to defend the place of dissent within their church still seem to be much quicker than their Protestant counterparts to notice what should be logically obvious: *dissent is meaningless outside of communion.* While arguing, for example, that the breakthrough Vatican II document affirming rights of religious liberty in society at large also commits the Catholic Church to rights of conscience and public dissent within the church, Daniel M. Cowdin has recognized that "for the notion of 'dissent' to be intelligible at all," it must take place within "some normative set of beliefs and practices constituting the self-understanding of a given community." More simply: "in order to dissent, one must dissent from something"—something one still largely shares with one's community, thus distinguishing *dissent* from simple *difference* with a community or belief system that is not one's own.[27]

Margaret O'Brien Steinfels, editor of *Commonweal* magazine, has likewise argued that "a true understanding of communion implies dissent, and real dissent demands communion." On the one hand, dissent rarely arises as "an exercise in pure speculation, or the self-aggrandizing acts of disobedience, rebellion, or disloyalty commonly portrayed." Instead, it arises from "painful disjunctures between pastoral experience and existing teaching." However painful *or* disjointed, such disjunctures are possible only through deep participation in the very life of the church. On the other hand, "disagreement can only be meaningful when it takes place within a framework of agreement. . . . One can feel estranged from a family member, but not from a casual vacation acquaintance made twenty years ago." Even as Steinfels wrote in defense of "the dissent that is an inevitable and healthy aspect of communion" and that is done with an attitude of service and affection for the community, therefore, she simultaneously stated: "I take it for granted that somewhere a line must be drawn" between loyal dissent and "the dissent that is no longer compatible with communion." If bishops and the entire papal apparatus in turn ought to exercise their role in drawing that line more judiciously, Steinfels had no interest in doing away with that magisterial role.[28]

Nothing in this thoroughly communal view of human life is entirely unique to Catholicism. Since Catholicism claims that authentic

Christianity fulfills the best of human experience and insists that human nature is inherently social, exclusive claims for Catholic over Protestant community or any healthy community life would actually border on heresy. Still, there is something not just about Catholic teaching but also about Catholic experience that keeps these very convictions in view. Retelling the lives of the saints and others who have gone before us in the faith is integral to that experience. Thus we turn to more stories.

Five Loyal Dissenters

Yves Congar

Loyal dissent has sometimes been vindicated in the Roman Catholic Church in quite dramatic ways. Not always, never easily or predictably, but sometimes spectacularly. Among the *periti*—expert consultants who worked behind the scenes at the Second Vatican Council, lecturing and drafting schemata (outlines) that would eventually become the official pronouncements of Vatican II—were a number of theologians who had been silenced for the very views that later did so much to shape the council. Most prominently, John Courtney Murray, Henri de Lubac, Karl Rahner, Jean Danielou, Dominique Chenu, and Yves Congar had either been barred from teaching, ordered to cease publication, heavily censored, sent into ecclesiastical exile, or seen the Holy Office place their already-published books on its index of prohibited reading for Catholics. In the end, however, Murray guided conciliar thinking toward a breakthrough commitment to the principle of religious liberty. And Congar both articulated a rich theology affirming the role of the laity in the church and formulated key wording on ecumenism. All those I have just listed helped the council to enrich Catholic theology through the fresh appropriation of tradition known as *ressourcement*. When a prominent cardinal addressed the assembled bishops toward the end of the council, everyone present knew he was referring especially to Congar: "There are theologians who once had sanctions against them and were even exiled," he observed, "and who now are the experts to whom we listen." The bishops' response was sustained applause.[29]

Church history has often seen cycles of suppression and then vindication; loyal dissenters can find both lessons and comfort in forerunners who have not only won but also eventually been recognized as saints.[30] Our lesson, however, should not be that if one simply acquiesces long enough, one will inevitably be vindicated. Truly virtuous obedience, according to the practice of stability, may well prepare and even hasten the day of vindication. But reduced to a tactic, mere acquiescence would at best divert one's attention toward crassly winning and away from the true goal of communion that *any* stance within the Christian community should seek. At worst, it would promote an unhealthy psychological pattern of passive aggression. Besides, no formula can tell us how long is long enough to wait, or when, as Martin Luther King Jr. wrote from the Birmingham jail, we can wait no longer. Our question is not how long to wait, therefore, but how to wait long when waiting is necessary.

This is the deeper lesson of French Dominican Yves Congar, deeper than the quite striking one that loyal dissenters often prove right in the long run. This deeper lesson is that those who wait with patience, faith, and love for the church are forging a moral credibility more forceful even than prophetic denunciation. Without these qualities, after all, public actions that claim to be prophetic are simply shrill. Put differently, even when circumstances and the Holy Spirit impel vocal public actions, these cannot really be effective unless they draw on a moral credibility forged through the kind of patient love that Congar and others demonstrated when they accepted their silencing in obedience.

Congar, after all, was hardly a pushover. By his own accounting, he had a temperament not given to compromise or even negotiation.[31] Privately, he had no problem comparing some of the tactics of the Vatican's Holy Office with that of the Gestapo or remarking that many of the French bishops it cowed were "completely boxed in by passivity and servility," with a devotion to Rome that was sincere but "also childish, infantile."[32] By natural disposition, Congar was not even particularly patient: "Those who know me know that I am impatient in little things," he wrote midway through the council. "I can't wait for a bus!" Still, he continued, "I believe I am patient in big things, with a certain active patience" that is "entirely different from just marking time."[33] Trust in God had cultivated this capacity to take a long view:

> It is a certain quality of the spirit or rather of the soul, which has its roots in the profound and existential conviction first, that God is directing the game and is accomplishing a work of grace in us, and secondly, that for every important thing a delay is necessary for maturation. . . . The patient sower, who entrusts his seed to the earth and to the sun, is the very man of hope. If patience is the patience of the sower [in Christ's parable], it is necessarily accompanied by the cross. . . . The Cross is the condition of every holy work, God himself is at work in what is a cross for us.[34]

Those "big things" about which Congar *could* be patient were precisely the lifelong projects that came to fruition at the council. In 1930, as his ordination to the priesthood neared, Congar sensed a special vocation to ecumenical work on behalf of Christian unity. This, however, was a period when the Vatican was altogether suspicious of the fledgling ecumenical movement in Protestant circles. As Congar developed relationships with Eastern Orthodox and with Protestants whom Rome still considered "heretics," he developed a Catholic theology of ecumenical openness toward the work of God in other Christian traditions. This included recognition that the Catholic Church shared responsibility for historical divisions.

Likewise, the church shared responsibility for the unbelief of a searching world as long as its responses were harsh, juridical, and defensive ones that only obscured the gospel. A more adequate proclamation of the gospel required a far richer understanding of the church and the work of the Holy Spirit—ecclesiology and pneumatology. Congar's theology sought to rescue ecclesiology and indeed the hierarchy itself from "hierarchology." Priests and bishops would exercise authentic authority not through privilege but through service—and service not only to ecclesiastical institutions but also the work of all God's people in the world. Amid his most difficult years of exile, Congar thus gave increasing attention to a fuller theology of the laity. A focus on the continuing work of God's Spirit in history must orient the role of both clergy and laity. This orientation should in turn guide the church to express the gospel in new ways for new challenges and cultures. The church's task was not simply to preserve an institutional and doctrinal status quo supposedly handed down from the apostles, especially when that status quo merely represented the single historical moment of recent "Baroque" centuries.

Ressourcement was intrinsic to all these "big things" because it opened access to the much longer and wider tradition, not just to its most recently consolidated—many would say ossified—expression. Congar's circle of French theologians aimed to be more faithful to Catholic tradition, not less, when it invigorated Catholic biblical studies, retrieved insights and interpretations from the church fathers of earlier centuries, and discovered precedents for liturgical reforms that encouraged Catholics to worship more truly as communities rather than simply as the consumers of priestly mediation. One of Congar's biographers, Jean-Pierre Jossua, OP, captured exactly the power of these moves by aptly describing him as a "prophet of tradition."[35]

In theological content, pastoral vision, and strategy of change through continuity, Congar was obviously anticipating the aggiornamento of Vatican II. He models an eminently Catholic way of reform not only in his writings but also in his very person. Congar certainly knew how to identify creative public gestures akin to nonviolent direct action. When the Holy Office prevented him or any Catholic from accepting an invitation to attend the founding assembly of the World Council of Churches in 1948 as observers, he organized a special mass in Paris to commemorate the assembly, manifest sympathy, and pray for its success.[36] Still, what Congar's model most exhibits is not so much a tactic or a formula but also a virtue. If one essential tactic is present here, it is what Jossua has identified as Congar's simple but basic refusal to choose between tradition and reform.[37] Such a refusal sets up the creative tension that marks the practice of stability even in difficult times, forges the virtue of fidelity that is resilient even in dissent, and enables loyal dissenters to discover creatively loving tactics as they proceed.

But not without pain! In hindsight, Congar was obviously doing what Gandhi famously called for when he urged his *satyagrahi* to "be the change you seek in the world." Gandhian practice, however, fully anticipates that change agents will need to suffer the consequences of any clash with injustice, however unjust the consequences may be.[38] Such suffering is precisely the way to deflect cycles of violence, retribution, and the breakdown of relationship that in Christian circles we sometimes call schism. For Congar, this meant enduring, as he described the decade between 1947 and 1957, "an uninterrupted sequence of denunciations, warnings, restrictive or discriminatory measures, suspicious interventions."[39] Near the end of that period, Congar wrote to his mother of his grave discouragement: "Practically speaking, they have destroyed me as far as it was possible for them. Everything I believed and had worked on has been taken away: ecumenism, teaching, conferences, working with priests, [public writing], involvement in conventions, etc." What hurt most was that his very ministry as a Dominican preacher, and his realm of friendships and social activity, was all "at a standstill." The situation had left him "profoundly wounded." Looking back and concluding that indeed "they have for all practical purposes destroyed me," Congar confessed that often "I am overtaken by an immense heartsickness."[40]

What carried Congar through moments—indeed decades—of discouraging obstacles was an abiding love for the church. The church, after all, was finally not the institutions needed to structure its life but a living community that nurtured him despite its foibles. Late in life he insisted that despite his trials, "the Church has been a . . . peaceable place for my faith and my prayer." He was still quite prepared to speak bluntly of its frequent "narrow mindedness and immaturity," of the "many botched works in the Church," and that many spheres of the church remained "unprepared . . . to offer answers to the true questions posed by men." Nonetheless, the burden this had imposed on him and many others was "of no importance when it is balanced against what I can find and actually do find in the Church. The Church has been, and is, the hearth of my soul; the mother of my spiritual being. She offers me the possibility of living with the saints: and when did she ever prevent me from living a Christian life?"[41]

And then there was this final vindication. In 1994, a few months before his death, Pope John Paul II named Congar to the College of Cardinals.

Dorothy Day

One might think that a "radical" Catholic like Dorothy Day would dissent even more vocally and pointedly than someone like Yves Congar. As visionary and persistent as Congar may have been, he still had the traditional formation and obligations of a priest. In contrast, Day was a laywoman and mother whose formation was on the street, first as a socialist in the bohemian culture of 1920s New York, later in launching the Catholic Worker movement as a way to identify with the poor, and always as a sharp-edged journalist. Day advocated for social justice on behalf of even the most unpopular groups. She spoke out against the most popular of American wars long before the Catholic Church officially recognized that pacifism has a legitimate place in the Catholic tradition. Thus at a time when the most urgent task of many United States Catholics was to prove themselves good Americans, Day regularly irritated church officials and upwardly mobile lay Catholics alike. Yet the consistency of her own saintly poverty, works of mercy, and hospitality among the poor would not let them dismiss her, either.[42] Thus as the theologian David Tracy has predicted, "Dorothy Day will probably have a greater impact for American Christian self-reform than any living American theologian."[43]

So yes, Dorothy Day's radicality was a courageous goad within the Catholic Church. Yet that same radicality also prompted her to express her dogged loyalty to the church in the most radical terms possible.

It was early 1967. The United States was bombing North Vietnamese cities and burning South Vietnamese villages. And Day's own archbishop in New York, Francis Cardinal Spellman, was traveling the world not only to bless the troops but also to call for "total victory" in Vietnam. How far from the gospel we *all* live as comfortable Americans, Day wrote in an anguished commentary on the front page of *The Catholic Worker*.[44]

> The works of mercy are the opposite of the works of war, feeding the hungry, sheltering the homeless, nursing the sick, visiting the prisoner. But we are destroying crops, setting fire to entire villages and to the people in them. We are not performing the works of mercy but the works of war. We cannot repeat this enough.

Perhaps it was fear in the face of violence that was leading "princes of the church" to go "against even the Pope" with militaristic words that were "as strong and powerful as bombs, as napalm." Just so, the apostles themselves had "wanted to call down fire from heaven on the inhospitable Samaritans, the 'enemies' of the Jews." Now, however, the government was counting on and paying for words of churchly support in order "to exalt our own way of life, to build up fear of the enemy."

What are we to do in such a time? Day responded: "There is plenty to do, for each one of us, working on our own hearts, changing our own attitudes, in our own neighborhoods." Precisely because all of us stumble and fall daily in thought, word, and deed, we need "the hard words of the Gospel" all the more, calling us to "prayer and fasting, taking up our own cross daily and following Him, doing penance." In all of these confessions of American complacency and sin, Day included herself.

The tough and lingering question that Day's answer undoubtedly left for many readers, though, was whether a follower of Jesus could continue to do and say these things within the church, when too many of its leaders were blunting or even betraying the hard words of the Lord. Her tough but eloquent answer continued to embrace the church in all the poignancy of its exalted yet still-quite-fleshly existence: "As to the Church, where else shall we go, except to the Bride of Christ, one flesh with Christ? Though she is a harlot at times, she is our Mother."

The church as harlot, yet still the one who has given us life and continues to nurture. The church as harlot, yet still the one to whom we might continue to cling with filial loyalty and love. What gave Day the audacity to make such a statement, risking scandal in equal measure for the pious and the disgruntled alike? Nothing short of the character of God: "We should read the book of Hosea, which is a picture of God's steadfast love not only for the Jews, His chosen people, but [also] for His Church, of which we are every one of us members or potential members." For the prophet Hosea, God's command to be faithful to his wandering unfaithful wife had been a revelation of God's unbreakable covenant love. For readers of *The Catholic Worker* (including ourselves), the biblical precedent of Hosea together with the contemporary precedent of Dorothy

Day herself disclose the Catholic practice of loyal dissent in all its excruciatingly creative tension.

This was not the first or last time Day had chafed against the actions or policies of church officials or against Cardinal Spellman in particular. Harvard child psychiatrist Robert Coles worked at a Catholic Worker soup kitchen as a medical student in the 1950s. Decades later he returned to interview his longtime mentor at length. Coles had observed that in her early autobiography, *The Long Loneliness*, Day broke into the narrative of her conversion with a "tough acknowledgment" that she as a convert continued to be a sinner, and that the church she had joined was a thoroughly flawed institution that often deserved "moral outrage." As a new Catholic, she explained, she had remained as mindful as ever of the valid criticism that her secular friends leveled at the church both past and present—for its past wars and persecutions and for continuing to enjoy all the wealth and prestige of a multinational corporation. When Coles asked her, now late in life, about how she had come to pay "intense homage to an institution some of whose practices and policies she strongly disapproved," both the pole of gratitude and that of critique for the church continued to be evident. Day had always been drawn to the church because it gave a home to the poor and workers, however inconsistently, and she now found that it was more committed to them than ever, both in the United States and around the world. Still, Coles reported that he found her "clearly haunted" by a "devastating" quote from theologian Romano Guardini that she cited repeatedly: "The Church is the Cross on which Christ was crucified."[45]

No wonder, then, that Day once identified fidelity and constancy as the virtues she most admired, and another time said that "perseverance is the greatest of all virtues."[46] Without such virtues, she would not have been able to sustain either a life among the poor, in which thoroughgoing identification meant she often had little more to work with than loaves and fishes, or to sustain patience with her church. Not even the greatest of saints would persevere without more joyful sources of sustenance, however. At least four other elements of Catholic faith sustained her practice of stability and upheld her virtue of fidelity.

For one thing, the distressingly eloquent image of the church as both harlot and mother was hardly the only one available to make

170

sense of her struggle. Jesus had compared the church to a net cast into the sea to catch many fish, and that included "some blowfish and quite a few sharks."[47] Saints like John of the Cross and Teresa of Avila were models who "were always getting around their superiors in one way or another in order to do or effect what they considered necessary for the times."[48] Day's reflections on the papacy of John XXIII fused biblical imagery with lessons from a (would-be) saint: if Angelo Roncalli had endured years of priestly obedience, silence, and frustration before becoming pope and convoking the Second Vatican Council, he was like Simeon waiting through years of apparent futility in the temple while God prepared him to present Christ to the world.[49] And as if the long-standing Catholic tradition of calling the church "mother" did not provide a rich-enough vein in itself, Day supplemented it with the image of "that big warm motherly soul in Steinbeck's *Grapes of Wrath*," sitting by her son in a battered pickup truck. The two are "defeated for the moment by the miseries of their lot, but not conquered" and meanwhile, the mother is fulfilling her role keeping the human family together.[50]

Second, but much related, Day simply had an overwhelming sense that the church was her home. "I never go inside a church without thanking God Almighty for giving me a home," Day told Robert Coles in their interviews. "The church is my home, and I don't want to be homeless. I may work with the homeless, but I have had no desire to join their ranks." This, she frankly admitted, made it hard for her to know how to respond when friends called on her "to become a warrior, to take on a cardinal, to take on many cardinals, to wage war with the church." She had not converted "with [her] eyes closed," but neither had she "become a Catholic in order to purify the church. . . . I wasn't trying to reform the church or take sides on all the issues the church was involved with; I was trying to be a loyal servant of the church Jesus had founded." Initially, she recalled, "I felt like a lucky guest for a while, then at home, and then I did decide to try to be as loyal as possible to the example set by the head of the household." Such loyalty was hardly subservience for "if it was achieved," that very loyalty would "be my testimony, my critique."[51]

Third, at the center of this home was the table of the Eucharist. From her earliest days as a Catholic, Day determined to attend mass daily. At first she worried that the ritual might become monotonous, but thirty-five years later she remarked that quite to the contrary, "joy is constantly renewed as I daily receive our Lord at Mass."[52] To be sure, the Eucharist could be the place where the failings of Catholic community were most starkly on display, as when well-dressed Catholics brushed past the poor during the depths of the Great Depression, or when a eucharistic congress was so insensitive as to plan a mass for the military on the anniversary of the dropping of the first atomic bomb on Hiroshima.[53] Yet Day's consistent testimony was that trying times and solidarity with human suffering made the Eucharist all the more necessary—for her an "absolute necessity"—daily, in fact.[54] Throughout her hectic life of activism and hospitality among the poor, her practice was to rise early and walk through the New York streets to morning mass, for "it is our food and drink, our delight, our refreshment, our courage, our light."[55] Whatever church officials might be pronouncing in contradiction to the gospel, insisted Day, "I can go to church and pray to God, and when I pray, I can say anything I want, and He is listening, and no one else."[56]

Speaking her mind with God in solitude hardly precluded speaking her mind in public too, however. A fourth sustenance for her practice of stability was that Day actually experienced great freedom within the church to speak out, act, and experiment. One way she explained her conversion was that obedience to Christ and the church offered freedom from the tyranny of "following the devices and desires of my own heart." Furthermore, church structures set up a domain of freedom. When she and Peter Maurin were first thinking about publishing *The Catholic Worker*, she wondered if they needed permission and asked the editors of other prominent Catholic periodicals. When they told her no permission was needed, she understood that to mean that she and Maurin would be responsible for any mistakes and that "if the work were of God, it would continue." A friend and bishop actually encouraged Maurin: "'Peter, you lead the way, and we [the bishops] will follow.' Peter knew what he meant. He meant that it was up to the laity to be in the vanguard," for they could take risks in the world that priests could not. The laity could "explore the paths of what was possible" and even "make mistakes without too great harm." The incident, said Day, demonstrated "the tremendous freedom there is in the Church, a freedom most cradle Catholics do not seem to know they possess."[57]

Dom Hélder Câmara

Someone, after all, must always begin: call it a vanguard or a pilot project or a creative minority. In any case, far from being a discouragement, the minority status of change agents within any social group—including the church—is not only to be expected but also necessary. Dom Hélder Câmara, archbishop of Recife, Brazil, from 1964 to 1985, knew this well: "I call them 'Abrahamic minorities' in honour of Abraham, the father of all those who over the centuries have continued to hope against hope."[58]

Rightly understood, the most effective model for both social change and ecclesial change shares a common "Abrahamic" dynamic. This does not mean importing the pressure tactics of special interest groups into the church, but living God's own model of social transformation within both church and world. Ever since God offered Abraham and his family the blessing of a distinct identity formed in covenant relationship with God, yet simultaneously called him to make this blessing accessible to all the families of the earth, the pattern has threaded its way through history. Israel, the church, or any family of faith that claims to walk with God is called to demonstrate the viability or "blessing" of the life it offers to the world through loving service to some larger whole. One can think again of Gandhi's aphorism, "Be the change you seek in the world." Such change must always take a distinctive and communal shape. But an Abrahamic community cannot live merely for itself, either in the older form of "sectarian" groups that withdraw from the larger society, or in the newer form of "special interest" groups who compete for a controlling stake within it. The paradoxical identity of an Abrahamic community is that it will lose that identity if it tries to protect the blessing of communal identity by avoiding the risks and tensions inherent in its call to serve and seek the good of the whole.[59]

Perhaps the circumstances of Câmara's flock in the poorest region of Brazil helped him to discover the creative dynamic of Abrahamic minorities. He could not really be a true pastor without being a prophet, or a true prophet without being a pastor. Caring for his church impelled him to travel the world as a fiery orator on behalf of social justice for the peoples of the global South. At the same time, rootedness in the life of his people nurtured an acute suspicion of merely ideological solutions from either right or left. That did not prevent Câmara from drawing the charge that he was a communist, but his famous answer reflected his pastoral orientation: "When I give food to the poor they call me a saint. When I ask why the poor have no food they call me a communist."

As Câmara told an interviewer in 1977, his path moved him "from one error to another" through "a succession of conversions, . . . under the guidance of the Holy Spirit."[60] The 1930s, Câmara's first decade in the priesthood, coincided with the growth of a Brazilian form of fascism, which initially seemed to offer prospects for social development under the influence of the church. But he soon came to see his passing support for the movement as a mistake. In the 1950s and early 1960s, deepening concern for the "sub-human" conditions in which his people lived made him a forerunner of liberation theology and an advocate for the world's poor at the Second Vatican Council. That same concern, however, led him to reject the temptation of violent revolution, which he believed would only perpetuate cycles of violence. The result is that "Dom Hélder is unclassifiable. Capable of dialogue with everyone, he is a challenge to all. In fact, the sovereign liberty in which he practices his faith is something of an embarrassment to all."[61]

Because he was first of all a pastor, Câmara was never so concerned to systematize his thought and theology as to speak out in the name of those "*sem vez e sem voz*," with no hope and no voice.[62] Others had to gather his scattered speeches, homilies, and pastoral letters. Still, animating his words and work was a coherent social strategy, at once thoroughly biblical and sociologically astute. One of those who edited Câmara's writings and speeches thematically, Benedicto Tapia de Renedo, went so far as to contend that "taken as a whole, they constitute a complete treatise on applied psychology and experimental sociology."[63] Câmara did lay out his strategy for social change quite succinctly in three speeches, given on three successive days in November 1972, on the invitation of an Italian Christian movement for third-world development, *Mani Tese*, which means "outstretched hands."[64]

174

Key to Câmara's strategy was the belief that "in the womb of all races, of all religions, in all countries, in all human groups" are change agents whom the Spirit of God is raising up. "They already exist, we do not need to create them." These are the groups he called "Abrahamic minorities," for "like Abraham, they hope against hope and decide to work, even to sacrifice, for a world more just and human."[65]

The way for nonviolent structural change to occur, Câmara said, was for these minorities to form a broad alliance as each works outward from its local problems, local injustices, and local organization toward regional, national, and global concerns. "Each Abrahamic minority can and should preserve its own name, can and should preserve its religious or simply humanist inspiration, can and should continue with its own leaders and its own methods. What is indispensable is not unification or uniformity, but to unite." They need not even unite organizationally, but rather "agree together on certain priority objectives."[66]

The basic posture of the Abrahamic minorities, as Câmara saw it, is to stay within the institutions of the current order, holding them accountable to the values and humanity of the masses who live in poverty and oppression, while working to re-create the structures accordingly. This posture involves permeation, but it is not the diffuse individualistic strategy of some Christians who take Jesus' images of salt, light, and leaven to mean that if only enough well-intended born-again Christians are involved in the system, positive social change will happen automatically. Abrahamic minorities are not simply statistical. They are subgroups working collectively, organized in clusters and networks, yet not acting independently of the larger group or society that they seek to transform. In advocating such a posture, Câmara could chide those who were so *anxious* about change that they habitually counseled patience even as others in the church pressed ahead and demonstrated the viability of change. In nearly the same breath, though, Câmara could also chide those who were so *intent* on change that they thought merely of tearing down. Those on one side were confusing "the prudence of the Holy Spirit and the prudence of the flesh, human prudence." Those on the other side seemed to be motivated by a desire "to overthrow all structures."[67]

The strategic posture of Abrahamic minorities, in contrast, continually negotiates a path between these twin temptations.

When speaking in Italy, Câmara called for Abrahamic permeation at three specific levels:[68]

1. *Abrahamic minorities within the world.* Why, asked Câmara, "don't the hundreds of technicians within the European [economic] community, instead of putting their intelligence and their specialized preparation at the service of increasingly restricted groups, . . . force a change of structures, concretely showing the way to a human economy and sketching sure paths to liberation?" Câmara lamented that while technology may play the role of shock absorber in the modern world, the world was nonetheless becoming increasingly inhuman. As the world became intolerable even to their own children, however, the Abrahamic minority within each profession was questioning its role as shock absorber. "These Abrahamic minorities of technicians—who knows?—at least where conditions are more favorable, . . . [they] could conduct a peaceful rebellion of professionals."[69]

2. *The Abrahamic minorities within the church.* To those with faith, and particularly to Christians, Câmara asked, "Instead of abandoning the faith and rebelling against our church, why don't we root ourselves even deeper in our faith, staying with the church in order to demand coherence, authenticity and the application of those texts that are in our religious literature, with all their beauty and ringing conclusions?" Specifically, he said, let us "demand of each religious group that it not separate love of neighbor from love of God."[70] In other words, why don't we act as an Abrahamic minority, a collective change agent, within the church itself? As Câmara insisted elsewhere, this did not mean acquiescing to the "false prudence" of those within the church who resisted living out the implications of the church's own stated commitments.[71] Instead, it meant a confident trust that the Holy Spirit would raise up Abrahamic minorities within episcopal conferences around the world, and even within the Vatican![72]

3. *That the church may fulfill its Abrahamic calling in the world.* Here Câmara directed his suggestion specifically to his own, Roman Catholic, church, though others can easily make their appropriate analogies. Pope Paul VI had recently created the pontifical commis-

sion Justitia et Pax. Câmara believed it was on its way to becoming "the church's prophetic organ of greatest audacity." It was not lacking in vision or in courage. It enjoyed the mandate of papal encyclicals and Vatican II. Its mandate, according to Câmara, was to be "a sensitive antenna within the church, denouncing the great injustices of our times and stimulating the peoples to promote changes in the structures of slavery, wherever they may exist." Yet the commission lacked support. "Let us help it, lest it only go half-way, . . . [in order that it might] promote concrete measures that free the church of Christ from the entanglements into which our human weakness has taken us." Among those entanglements, Câmara explained elsewhere, was the "anomaly" of the Vatican State itself. Câmara believed that John XXIII and Paul VI shared his own wish that the pope truly be a pastor and not a head of state. "Oh, when will we manage to help the Church of Christ to liberate itself! If we're going to help to liberate the world we must work to liberate the Pope, and the bishops, and all Christians."[73]

The specific program of Abrahamic minorities must necessarily involve many local variants. In the *Mani Tese* speeches, in only three days, Câmara varied his suggestions a little according to each audience. Nonetheless, certain themes came through loud and clear; certain steps are indispensable.

Some of Câmara's points would now be recognizable as the basics of grassroots organizing that "thinks globally and acts locally." Beginning locally, Abrahamic minorities must work outward toward global issues. "We must repeat and underscore this truth," Câmara said. "In order to feel the world's injustices as if they were our own, the best path is to set out from the local injustices."[74] Then work with "the neighbors, the *barrio*, the community, until reaching brothers and sisters of all races, all tongues, and all religions."[75] Don't stop at the local level, however. Here Câmara criticized both philanthropists and protesters alike. Too many activities have been generous and well-intended but have not taken into account the economic, cultural, and political structures that engender local problems.[76]

Throughout his exposition of the Abrahamic social strategy, staying rooted in one's faith tradition was much more than one point among many. The step that makes all others possible, he insisted, is the impulse of grace when we gather in Christ's name. Câmara turned shortly to the obvious question as to where this might leave those who do not profess Christ, but let us first notice his core point: all the talk about "changing structures" could amount to so much rhetorical cackle, never "moving on from theory to practice," never getting beyond "good intentions." Thus he insisted, "As forerunner and sign of the profound changes that must be achieved at the national, continental and global levels, we need something more than the force of an idea: we need a touch of grace, an impulse from on high."[77]

That touch of grace, that divine impulse, he predicted, would happen upon living out the word of Christ, that "where two or three are gathered in my name, there am I in the midst of them" (Matt. 18:20 RSV). "And we are not only two or three, we are thousands upon thousands."[78] The work for justice depends, finally, on more than a program or strategy, whether local or global. It depends on being a people, a people animated by God's grace.

To the many who might not believe themselves religious or to have faith, Câmara did not bring a rebuke or even a direct invitation to faith. Rather, he presented his own inviting faith: "We are and we will be with Christ—even though we may not know it and even though we apparently do not want it—to the degree that our hunger and thirst for justice, truth, and love is sincere."[79]

Even a Christian whose priority is to evangelize those who do not profess Christ might do well to consider Câmara's Abrahamic strategy. The way to demonstrate that one bears a message of truly good news is always to begin where one is, in the locale of one's own life first of all, demonstrating its viability there, through sustainable practices that are life giving, not life draining or life taking. But so too for those who object that they find life in some other name, besides that of Jesus or even Abraham. By name or not, the way to make their best case is still "Abrahamic," for we all do well to argue among one another primarily with our lives. The practical test of arguments both spoken and lived is our personal integrity, yes, and more than that, the sustainability of the communities we are building.

Counterintuitive as it may sound, therefore, the authentic social-change agent will need to value stability as surely as any true conservative. When acting in good faith, the two might even meet, and then wonder how their schism came to seem inevitable.

178

Oscar Romero

In his enthusiasm for a grassroots strategy of social change based on the hopeful initiative of Abrahamic minorities, Câmara might *seem* to be granting only a grudging role to institutional structures. In any case, his message was particularly striking because he delivered it with so much charisma. Still, Câmara *was* an archbishop. His message was all the *more* striking because it *also* came with official church authority. The lesson he exemplifies then can hardly be that top-down authority is without legitimacy. At minimum, there is a complementarity to official authority and charismatic authority, to use a classic distinction many have assumed from sociologist Max Weber. At minimum, the lesson is that each needs the other for its fullest and most effective service, whether to the church or to the world.

In fact, we should scramble standard Weberian assumptions even further, for another lesson emerges from the ministry of Archbishop Oscar Romero, El Salvador's pastor during the darkest days of repression in the 1970s until his assassination in 1980. In Romero's indelible example, charism did not simply coincide with office. Rather, office was itself the bearer of charism.

Actually, the argument here comes from Terrence W. Tilley, and I can do no better than to elaborate. In a 1997 article on "The Institutional Element in Religious Experience,"[80] Tilley's main burden was to counter a long-standing tendency (if not outright anti-institutional bias) that would "identify 'real religion' with personal faith, loving communities, and rich theological traditions, and [would] construe 'institutions' as cold, impersonal, and empty structures" that either have nothing to do with authentic religious experience or stifle and destroy it.[81] Tilley's point was hardly to vindicate all religious institutions or their policies; some of his examples came from people who had converted from one tradition to another or even lost faith. What even the latter demonstrated, however, was that few if any religious experiences are intelligible without accounting for the "institutional element" that is intrinsic to them.[82] Thus Tilley asked us:

> Consider also Oscar Romero's "sudden" acquisition of courage. He acquired charismatic authority, or was empowered to exercise it, only after he had been given institutional authority. He, too, profoundly

affected the faith of many. And he could not have done so had he not had the institutional role of archbishop. In short, institutions and institutional authority do not *necessarily* have, but they *can* have, a profound effect on personal religious faith.[83]

The charisma of office becomes visible in Romero's case because, unlike Câmara, he had not demonstrated a particularly charismatic personality before his early-1977 installation as archbishop of San Salvador. By all accounts, Romero was bookish, shy, ascetic, and scrupulous in the mold of a traditional Catholic spirituality. El Salvador's best-known liberation theologian, Jon Sobrino, SJ, initially found statements by Romero to reflect "a theology straight out of the dark ages."[84] What is certain is that Romero had been critical of liberation theology, suspicious of the progressive political stance that Latin American bishops had taken at Medellín in 1968, and dubious even of Vatican II. To be sure, Romero had grown up in humble circumstances and from his earliest days in parish ministry demonstrated a deep and compassionate engagement with the poor. As repression, torture, and "disappearances" began to increase in the mid-1970s, however, Romero's political theology continued predisposing him to assume the best intentions of government officials. Certain that human rights incidents must have resulted from mistakes and misunderstandings, his practice was to communicate his protests only in private.[85] When John Paul II named Romero to succeed San Salvador's longtime and relatively progressive archbishop, a few popular organizations protested the appointment.[86]

Romero was a won't-rock-the-boat compromise choice. Fellow bishops and observers on all sides expected him to be cautious to a fault. If the conservative prelates who were aligned with El Salvador's wealthy aristocracy and its military protectors worried about anything, it was that Romero would be too weak to crack down on activist priests allegedly tainted by the Marxist ideology of El Salvador's guerrilla movement. Later, when Romero's reputation had changed to the point that he himself became the object of similar allegations, he sought to assure none less than John Paul II of his "'conservative' inclinations and temperament." Only through a "pastoral strength" that came directly from God, Romero told the pope, had he overcome that temperament well enough to fulfill his pastoral duty to "stand in defense of my church . . . at the side of my oppressed and abused people."[87]

The turning point came less than a month after Romero became archbishop. Apparently believing it to be an opportune time for sending a message to activist priests, "security" forces targeted Jesuit Fr. Rutilio Grande, known for his work promoting base communities and defending the rights of peasants against the interests of large landowners. Grande was assassinated, together with an old man and a young boy, as he traveled to an outlying village to conduct mass. Whatever Romero's worries about the political involvement of activist priests, Romero knew Grande well and bore him both affection and trust. Sobrino believes that the experience of traveling to Grande's wake that same evening, viewing both his body and the quiet courage of the peasants present, and conducting mass with them—all prompted a conversion in which scales of fearful caution fell from Romero's eyes.[88] Many factors contributed to this transformation, no doubt: friendship, the power of a martyr's witness, the sense of Christ's presence among the poor of which Romero would now speak often, and a decisively sharpened awareness that what his church was experiencing was not merely the ordinary complications of politics but also outright persecution. All these might change the life of any Christian observer who is even half willing to let solidarity with suffering override whatever privileges one might have to protect. Yet not every Christian has the same duties or channels by which to respond. The shepherd's crook that Romero carried to symbolize the office of bishop curled around to point particular responsibilities in his own direction.

Romero's response to Grande's murder presaged the remaining years of his episcopacy, which an assassin's bullet would also cut short after only three years. In consultation with his priests and other pastoral workers, Romero canceled all masses the following Sunday except for a single memorial mass in San Salvador's cathedral, to which all the faithful of the archdiocese were invited. Most of Romero's fellow bishops in El Salvador objected, as did the papal nuncio. Some argued that their parishioners who could not travel to San Salvador would be deprived of the opportunity to fulfill their "Sunday obligation." But what they really meant was that the rich could not attend mass without worshiping alongside the poor, which was exactly the point. Romero offered a call to reconciliation, not a provocation, unless one refused to identify with the whole persecuted body of Christ in El Salvador and thus found reconciliation itself provocative. For the rest, Romero's suddenly public courage offered hope. In the face of ever-looming death, he now gave himself to the almost hopeless task of stopping the violence. As one biography summarizes:

> Romero, simply by being a pastor, tried to prevent this war that was being waged against the poor. He gave the people hope against all human logic, calling upon their deep reserves of faith in God and defending their right to organize for justice. In his weekly homilies, which were broadcast by radio, he named the massacres and tortures, unmasking the hideousness of a war directed against civilians. He confronted the disinformation apparatus of low-intensity conflict by refusing to allow right-wing sectors in the United States or in El Salvador to characterize either the Salvadoran people or himself as subversives.[89]

Even so, in a profoundly polarized economic and political situation, it was inevitable that Romero would be perceived as a dissident who threatened to subvert the status quo of church, state, and church-state relations. El Salvador's deep division ran through the conference of bishops. The opposition of other bishops in turn prompted persistent scrutiny from the Vatican. One source of Romero's predisposition toward political caution had actually been his commitment to gospel values of nonviolence and service to all people, rich as well as poor. His continuing goal as archbishop was to maintain political neutrality while standing without reservation on behalf of his people. With his people under attack, communicating such a posture became excruciatingly difficult. The charge that Romero was a subversive was deeply unjust. Yet the charge was self-fulfillingly accurate in one way, for what was true of Fr. Grande's memorial mass was true of Romero's entire time as archbishop: nothing could be more threatening than a reconciling posture that was animated by gospel nonviolence and was truthful about the injustices that required repentance for the sake of reconciliation.

One unmistakable sign of Romero's charism of office was the effect he had on others' faith. Tilley's moving example is that of

Jean Donovan, a twenty-seven-year-old lay missioner who would be martyred together with three nuns nine months after Romero's assassination. Donovan had gone to El Salvador out of commitment to the poor but with only a "grudging acceptance" of the institutional church and its patriarchal authority. "I am really at times fed up with the Church and blame God for it," she wrote to a friend. She wondered whether she could "cop out of the institution" and still do her work while maintaining her personal relationship with God through less-formal prayer in small groups of laypeople. Nonetheless, Donovan attended mass at the cathedral whenever she could, drawn to Romero's model of authentic institutional leadership in solidarity with the struggles of ordinary people. She agreed with those who were beginning to speak of him as a saint. "It's done something for me, in that I had become very hard—in believing for example that change comes only through violence. Maybe now I can believe a bit more in prayer." Tilley's comment: Romero "was saying what many said; but it was his position as archbishop that made his voice heard, and led Donovan to nonviolence and prayer."[90]

The compromised bishops who are also part of this story obviously preclude any overstated case that office automatically transforms every officeholder, ex opere operato. From Central America, a yellowing poster depicting Romero hung in my office for many years. It bore the caption *Queremos obispos como Mons. Romero!* That plea, "We want bishops like Msgr. Romero," is sad evidence of a scandal. Too few bishops have responded to injustice with Romero's courage. Yet Tilley's circumspect claim nonetheless stands: "Here was a man of clear institutional authority who also had profound charismatic authority. What is remarkable is that, like Angelo Roncalli [Pope John XXIII], had he not been given the former, he would likely not have had . . . the latter."[91]

Joan Chittister

One moral of the overarching story in this chapter dare not be lost. Bishops and lay champions of top-down authority in the Roman Catholic Church should count their blessings. The loyalty of their loyal dissenters is one of those blessings, and they dare not take it for granted. Few qualities testify more poignantly to the vitality of lived Catholicism than this quite dogged loyalty. Never mind that the terms "dissenter" or "dissident" are often employed hastily and unfairly; even those for whom the terms may be accurate usually demonstrate a deep quality of commitment, love, and patience toward their church. Denominational leaders in Protestant traditions would have reason to envy this quality. Certainly Protestants too can bear a deep and abiding commitment both to Christ and the communities that have formed their Christian lives. Yet as we have seen, Protestant denominationalism itself structures instability into community identity and church life.

Joan Chittister probably has to be classified not just as a so-called dissenter but also as the real thing. Yet she is hardly less loyal to the Catholic Church. Chittister is a Benedictine sister at Mount St. Benedict Monastery in Erie, Pennsylvania, and a prolific writer on everything from Benedictine spirituality to feminism to peace and social justice issues to interreligious dialogue. In one direction, this array of writings includes some of the best expositions available of those very Benedictine practices that sustain stable, committed community through good times and hard. In another direction, though, it includes sharp challenges to the Catholic Church's marginalization of women from much of the life of the church as well as its outright exclusion of women from the priesthood.

In 2001, Chittister's prominence and poignancy on women's ordination drew both an invitation to speak at an international conference on the subject in Dublin and an attempt by the Vatican to silence her. Benedictines vow obedience to the superior who leads their community, so the Vatican congregation that deals with the consecrated life sent a letter to the prioress of Mount St. Benedict, Sr. Christine Vladimiroff. The letter directed her to persuade, or if necessary prohibit, Chittister from addressing the Dublin conference. Believing that ancient Benedictine practices required her as prioress to consult with the community before finalizing any decision, Sr. Vladimiroff initiated a process of community listening. ("Listen" is the first word in the Rule of St. Benedict and the root meaning of "obedience" in Latin.) Vladimiroff also traveled to the Vatican to defend this Benedictine approach to discernment and obedience. The result was a decision *not* to prohibit Chittister from speaking, expressed in a letter to the Vatican that all but one of the 128 members of the

184

community signed. Writing on behalf of her community, the prioress insisted that their actions did not indicate any break in communion with the church but rather fidelity to a monastic tradition that has been intrinsic to Catholicism for over 1,500 years.[92]

The stance of both Chittister and her monastic community, therefore, is clearly less like that of Sant'Egidio and more like that of Martin Luther King Jr. It is a refusal to wait any longer.[93] True to Benedictine traditions of stability, however, Chittister has also called for a "spirituality of endurance" during a time of tension in the church.[94] Likewise, she has rejected individualistic solutions, which propose that each person ought simply to accept one's own truth.[95] At the same time, she has decisively rejected any "spirituality of silence" or quietism.[96] Chittister has recognized that church unity is a "fragile strength," and it might be better to speak on certain topics directly with church officials rather than in public. But since the Vatican has officially refused even to discuss the topic of women's ordination, what women have wanted to say precisely "for the sake of the church" has "had to be said in public because there was nowhere else for a woman to say it."[97]

Unless we are to reduce loyalty to an unquestioning, quasi-military obeying of orders—thus choking out a more organic understanding of loyalty in keeping with deeply Catholic longings for *communio*—then even staunch defenders of authoritative Catholic tradition should be grateful for the sort of dissent that Chittister represents. I suggest at least five reasons.

First, just as the example of Archbishop Romero demonstrates that office can be the bearer of charism, Chittister has remained convinced that *the Catholic Church has been and can continue to be the bearer of the gospel*. In a 1990 essay, Chittister sought to answer the pained and passionate question that a former Catholic had put to her at a feminist conference: "How and why does a woman like you stay in the Catholic Church?"[98] Her answer was "I am a feminist precisely because I am a Catholic—not as a reaction to what is wrong about the Church, but actually as a response to what is right about the Church. . . . [The Church has given me] my Christian feminist commitment to the equality, the dignity and the humanity of all persons." Even if the church had not brought its good news for women into its fullness, she saw "the great, the magnetizing, the empowering, the energizing good that is inherent for women in the Church and promised for women in the Church."[99] At the heart of this good news is Jesus, who was a faithful Jew yet was often most revelatory precisely when he departed from the ancient Middle Eastern conventions of first-century Jewish society by giving women a prominent place in his movement and circle of friendship. So "whatever else it does or does not do, the Church sustains the memory of Jesus with women and always recalls it and has often heeded it, at times in genuinely significant ways."[100]

To be sure, what Chittister has found most "right" about Catholic Christianity usually flows from its prophetic stream, with much less mention of the "kingly" stream of institutional maintenance or the "priestly" stream of sacramental mediation. Still, the second reason Catholic authorities should be grateful for her kind of dissent is that she has evinced an understanding of *the process of change in the church that anticipates the constructive requirements of social life*, thus moving beyond mere critique and "prophetic" deconstruction. Her community's conception of obedience as thorough and attentive listening may not be what some church officials expect, but its authentic practice requires well-knit bonds of social commitment through time. Despite her refusal to wait silently before broaching controversial subjects, she has also respected that change will take time not only because the Catholic Church is a human institution, but also because it is a worldwide "universal institution."[101] Occasionally, in Chittister's more intimate writings (journal entries, meditations in the spirit of Benedictine *lectio divina*), a kind of Gandhian respect for properly exercised authority surfaces too. In a series of pithy meditations on Psalm 112, for example, she dismissed any idealistic notion of interchangeable leadership or the even more idealistic notion that groups can survive without any leadership at all. To be sure, Chittister recognized that authority figures and administrators were not necessarily leaders. Yet she found wisdom in the saying of "some wag" who had written, "Question authority, but raise your hand first." After all, "people who set out to disrupt a system, to attack authority simply for the sake of calling attention to themselves, are not leaders. Leaders always respect authority. It is ideas they question."[102]

Third, *for Catholic conservatives to wish that a gadfly like Chittister would simply leave the church*, if she has so many questions, and find a denomination more to her liking—*this is unwittingly Protestant in the worst sort of way*. One occasionally runs across such an attitude in the freewheeling world of Internet blogs.[103] No doubt there are times when, tragically, the most honest thing for Christians to do is part company. Since church history has left us with multiple traditions, we do well to use them as ways to pursue fruitful debate that clarifies our disagreements through embodied arguments, in pursuit of a renewed and deepened Christian unity.[104] It is another matter, however, to jump to denominational division and church shopping as a quick solution to our disagreements, and that with little sense of tragedy and not a little triumphalism besides. To wish for such "solutions" is thus to acquiesce to the very sort of denominationalism that is at odds with a most Catholic refusal to cease hoping for full Christian communion, and with Catholic practices of stability that accept the hard and uncomfortable work needed to sustain it.

Fourth, the *doggedly loyal dissent* of a Joan Chittister *provides many of the attributes that the church needs for positive service and winsome witness in the world*—too many to be dismissed. I first encountered Chittister not in her feminist critique but in her writings on Benedictine values and practices.[105] Her deep spirituality of "the ordinary" helped me better to comprehend Catholic sacramentality. Her writings on prayer, humility, monastic mindfulness, community life, and yes, obedience, enriched my own life of discipleship and informed my earliest forays into the topic of stability. Encountering her more pointed writings, then, I have had every reason to believe her when she identifies herself with those "who love a system [the Catholic Church] enough to want it to be what it says it is," and who strive to maintain that loving attitude even though "it is so easy to become hardened against any system that has become hardened against you."[106] We should also take seriously her reminder that "suspect" and allegedly "heretical" or "smorgasbord" Christians "are, in many ways, among the most intense Christians of our time."[107] Communities like Chittister's are often on the front lines of service to "the least."[108] If they also press "the woman's issue" within Roman Catholicism, that insistence grows inextricably from a sense of vocation, a willingness to tackle tough issues, and a readiness to take risks for the sake of the gospel. Their "pushing the envelope" is thus in keeping with Jesus' dictum that those who lose themselves for his sake are the ones who actually save their lives. Catholics zealous to "defend the faith" would do well to listen when Chittister warns against a siege mentality, for in the paradox of Christ's dictum, a defensive posture is far more likely to choke the faith than to spread it.[109]

Fifth, and finally, Chittister's *commitment to critiquing church tradition from within that very tradition models the kind of conversation* not only that the church needs but also *that our globalizing world needs*. A Christian community—any Christian community—needs this kind of conversation in order to constitute and extend itself as a *living* tradition through time and in the face of inevitable new challenges. And the Christian churches need this kind of dialogue in order to debate fruitfully among themselves. But still more than that, such a conversation is what the world needs if we are going to live together in a lively peace that does not resort to the false solutions of either violent domination or corrosive relativism. Christians can hardly expect to promote global intercultural practices of stability if they are not training themselves in such practices by holding the imperatives of change and continuity together in their own sustainable communities. My final chapter will elaborate on this claim.

One More Story

Most of the accounts in this chapter have come from prominent figures in the Catholic Church, even heroes. But the practice of stability, the virtue of fidelity, and the quality of church life that we encounter in these leaders would mean little if it did not permeate into apparently ordinary Christian lives. Let us conclude then with another kind of narrative. In the minds of many Catholics, its two leading characters are an antihero, if not a villain, and an apparently ordinary parishioner whose only reason to be in the public eye was one that none of us would celebrate.

Journalist David Gibson has recounted the scene at ground zero of the sexual abuse scandal in the Catholic Church in United States in 2002: the cathedral in Boston where Cardinal Bernard Law presided. Many believed that Law, more than any other church official, bore responsibility for covering up abuses. Protesters had gathered with banners outside of Sunday mass for months. Even those who winced at the harsh language coming from the bullhorns of protesters as they arrived for mass tended to agree that Law was "a disgrace to good Catholics" and should resign. Still, one mother who was a regular at protests made clear that *she* would not be leaving the church that had disappointed her deeply, for she still loved and found the church "a good place to be." Gibson continued:

> Inside the cathedral, the testimony to that stubbornness grew even more compelling. As lines formed for communion, several protesters left their placards outside and walked up the nave, waiting patiently to take the Host from the hands of the man that one of them, victim Arthur Austin, had called "a criminal, a murderer of children, . . . an affront to Jesus Christ." Austin was wearing a "Reject Cardinal Law" button, and he was anticipating a rebuke from the cardinal. But when Law saw Austin, the cardinal recognized him and said, "Pray for me."
>
> Austin later said, "It was a very healing moment because it was not the archbishop or the cardinal who spoke to me. It was my brother, Bernie, who responded to me. I touched him. I touched him literally and I touched him figuratively. And he was able to receive that. That's the radical grace of God in the world."[110]

It is such grace that makes sticking together through hard times worth the pain and struggle.

6

Giving the Gift of Stability to a Globalizing World

What is to be done to prevent increased exchange between cultures (which ought to lead to genuine and fruitful dialogue between groups and nations) from disturbing the life of communities, overthrowing traditional wisdom and endangering the character proper to each people? How is the dynamism and expansion of the new culture to be fostered without losing living fidelity to the heritage of tradition?

Second Vatican Council, *Gaudium et spes*, §56

BUT PERHAPS A reader impatient with the internal workings of Christian communities has been asking what all this has to do with our needy, fractured, yet interdependent world, which can hardly wait for Christians to settle their disputes.

If we may take a hint from Dorothy Day of the Catholic Worker movement, it has everything to do with it. In the previous chapter, I quoted Day's jarring yet somehow reassuring remark that although the church as the "Bride of Christ" "is a harlot at times, she is [still] our Mother."[1] The poignancy of Day's remark and indeed of her faith should not obscure its context, for in that context lies our hint. Day was writing in early 1967, when the United States was napalming Vietnamese villages. Far from breaking with church authorities who vigorously supported the war, however, Day could deny neither her own identification with America nor the moral responsibilities it brought. Day said she must continue to respond to the nation's unjust actions not only in Vietnam but also in South Africa, Nigeria, the Congo, Indonesia, all of Latin America, and the streets of the slums in which Catholic Worker houses of hospitality were located. Despite her "bitterness," then, Day insisted that she had nowhere else to go but the church. She must sustain the practices she had learned as a Catholic Christian in the world with the same trust in God's steadfastness toward all peoples that God demonstrates toward God's wandering church. Her own steadfast commitment to the world was of a piece with her dogged commitment to the church. In her essay she moved seamlessly from one to the other. So too, no doubt, in her heart.

We are not simply adding a postscript about how the practices of stability required for sustaining Christian community are "relevant" to the wider world, therefore, when we widen our attention to that world; the tasks of living together justly and peaceably in a needy, fragmented, yet globally interdependent world require much the same virtue that Christians nurture by hanging in with one another amid their bitterest conflicts. To learn to dissent while respecting authority, to act on personal conscience while recognizing the claims of tradition, to seek change that is not merely a reactive "deconstruction" but a complex aggiornamento or updating—these are capacities that change agents and indeed entire cultures need in order to relate respectfully to other cultures. No global civil society or multicultural polity will be just if its basis is the subtle violence that corrosive individualism inflicts when it trivializes the ancient wisdom embodied in communal traditions. The themes we have explored in this book have as much to do with the world as with the internal Christian debates. If the church is to offer practices of just peacemaking and respectful debate to diverse cultures in our globalized world, it will be able to do so authentically only when Christians first are nurturing the requisite virtues by learning practices that sustain their own community.

A Meditation on Globalization and *Gaudium et spes*

Part of what makes practices of stability worth the painful struggle they sometimes entail is the possibility that self-critical continuity with our own tradition will provide resources for responding wisely and well to the world's challenges.

Even more clearly than when Dorothy Day was writing in 1967, the twenty-first-century shape of our challenges is tradition infused. Our challenge is not just that individuals are competing in dysfunctional ways. Nor is it just that individuals must throw off oppressive yokes of tradition-bound cultures. Rather, traditions themselves are in play, and justice requires us to defend not only individual human rights but also vulnerable traditions. Sometimes traditions are eroding one another, sometimes they are clashing, but always they are at stake, in ways that modernity has not accounted for well.

Modern thought has generally seen tradition as the problem from which it has offered liberation, after all, even as it came to constitute a tradition itself, arrogantly blind to its own hegemonic tendencies. Some theorists of globalization recognize, more fully than others, that the desperation able to spark violence and terrorism in many places around the world is not just (perhaps not even mainly) an economic desperation resulting from inequitable power relations between the haves and have-nots. Rather, it is also (perhaps most deeply) about the dislocation that people experience when the communal practices that had defined their culture for generations, and with it their very sense of identity, are being trivialized and eroded, if not decimated outright.

Benjamin R. Barber is one theorist of globalization who does recognize the cultural dimensions of globalization that can put healthy, life-giving traditions on edge as surely as it does oppressive traditions. Updating his seminal work on globalization from the early 1990s, *Jihad vs. McWorld*,[2] in light of post-9/11 realities, Barber passionately recognized, for example, that it is not at all clear whether "Asian tea, with its religious and family 'tea culture,' [can] survive the onslaught of the global merchandising of cola beverages." Likewise: "Can the family sit-down meal survive fast food, with its focus on individualized consumers, fuel-pit-stop eating habits and nourishment construed as snacking?" Even relatively new cultural traditions like

193

the "national film cultures in Mexico, France or India" face "Hollywood's juggernaut movies geared to universal teen tastes rooted in hard violence and easy sentiment." So then, asks Barber, where is "the space for prayer, for common religious worship or for spiritual and cultural goods in a world in which the 24/7 merchandising of material commodities makes the global economy go round?" Terrorism surely is no answer to the steamroller of trends and pressures that Barber has labeled "McWorld." Yet, Barber pointedly insists, "The truly desperate may settle for terror as a response to our failure even to ask such questions."[3]

We have also failed to attend to those who *have* asked such questions.

The bishops gathered for the Second Vatican Council of 1962–65 were remarkably prescient concerning the challenges, opportunities, and dilemmas that globalization would pose in coming decades; they did ask such questions. For at least two reasons, though, commentators have tended to miss how well Vatican II framed the challenge of globalization. The first and obvious reason is that the terms "globalize" and "globalization" had only recently been coined and were years away from wide circulation. The pivotal Vatican II document *Gaudium et spes* does speak twice of human "interdependence," but readers today must recognize the conceptual link for themselves.[4] A second reason is more complex. In the minds of many, the council stands above all as Catholicism's long-delayed fraternal embrace of the modern world. And that it was. Yet celebration of this breakthrough has often obscured the perceptive warnings that the bishops of the council voiced about the underside of modern life and culture.[5] A general inattention to the council's nuanced reading of modernity, combined with the inevitable fact that the council documents describe the conditions of modernity in the terms of its day, not ours, has thus left its prescient naming of the challenges of globalization largely unnoticed.

Midway through *Gaudium et spes*, the bishops turned in their assessment of especially "urgent problems" to the "proper development of culture."[6] As they did so, the bishops first reiterated the hopeful and befriending embrace of the modern world with which they had famously opened the document. In the process they named in their own words the opportunity that globalization certainly does offer, at its best. The social and culture changes shaping modern life were so profound that one could speak of nothing short of "a new age of human history," offering new opportunities "for the development and diffusion of culture." Those opportunities not only included "tremendous expansion of the natural and human sciences (including social sciences)," and the corresponding "increase of technology" they allow, but also the chief characteristic of what we now call globalization: "advances in developing and organizing media of communication." At that moment in history and this juncture in the document, the bishops offered what we may recognize as the most hopeful vision possible of what globalization *could* mean, at its most just and humane, even as it knits us together through unprecedented economic and cultural ties:

> Customs and patterns of life tend to become more uniform from day to day; industrialization, urbanization, and other factors which promote community living create new mass-cultures which give birth to new patterns of thinking, of acting, and of use of leisure; heightened media of exchange between nations and different branches of society open up the riches of different cultures to each and every individual, with the result that a more universal form of culture is gradually taking shape, and through it the unity of [humankind] is being fostered and expressed in the measure that the particular characteristics of each culture are preserved.[7]

The final caveat here is crucial, however. Any hope-worthy development of a globalized culture must preserve other cultures rather than flatten them out and homogenize them. To "build up a better world in truth and justice," after all, the process of globalization must be participatory rather than imposed:

> In each nation and social group there is a growing number of men and women who are conscious that they themselves are the [artisans] and molders of their community's culture. All over the world the sense of autonomy and responsibility increases with effects of the greatest importance for the spiritual and moral maturity of [humankind].

That growing "sense of autonomy" itself might be constituting "the birth of a new humanism." Yet growing autonomy could be just

195

and mature only if paired with "responsibility to [our] brothers and at the court of history." Otherwise "the unification of the world"—as we may infer from the thrust of the bishops' words—would be no better than the disrespectful hegemony of a single culture, claiming either its own autonomy or that of its individualistic members, without a sense of responsibility or solidarity with others.[8]

So now, in *Gaudium et spes* (§56), comes a remarkable list of unresolved questions, reflecting the underside of modernity, or (we would now add) of globalization. Even in these conditions of apparent scientific, social, and technological development that the bishops had just named hopefully, "it is no wonder that [humanity] feels responsible for the progress of culture and nourishes high hopes for it, but anxiously foresees numerous conflicting elements which it is up to [them] to resolve." Thus the bishops asked:

1. How to Dialogue without Destroying?

The overarching question that the bishops were already foreseeing, in other words, is how to encourage globalization in the *best* sense of the word without contributing to globalization in the *worst* sense of the word.

> What is to be done to prevent increased exchange between cultures (which ought to lead to genuine and fruitful dialogue between groups and nations) from disturbing the life of communities, overthrowing traditional wisdom and endangering the character proper to each people? (§56)

How can we keep "McWorld" from swallowing all other life, culture, and values, in other words? What Benjamin Barber has called "McWorld" is the corporate-driven global culture of consumerism that heeds no borders. It claims it "would like to teach the world to sing in perfect harmony" (Coca-Cola has the catchiest tune!) as it spreads in the name of free trade and respect for choice. By raising doubts, Barber may at first seemed to be questioning Western traditions of democracy, freedom, and individual human rights. Yet he has put his finger on why other societies have resisted those traditions or see them as a decidedly mixed blessing. The freedoms and tolerance that the West offers—whether "free trade" from its right or "free love" from its left—are often blind to the West's own *intolerance* of local communities as it corrodes their cultures. Turning regional cultures into quaint decors and theme parks, McWorld seems to respect but ultimately trivializes other cultures. Thus Barber's deepest worry has been that if anything, McWorld threatens to corrode Western democracy itself, but other cultures are suffering already.[9]

2. How to Change, with Fidelity?

The danger of which *Gaudium et spes* (§56) speaks when it warns that globalization might be "overthrowing traditional wisdom" (or in another translation, "destroying the wisdom received from ancestors") is not just the nostalgia-inducing loss of ancient treasures of the sort that one might store in museums. Rather, it is the potential loss of that very ancient wisdom from classical traditions that could offer fresh perspective on our contemporary realities. Such perspective is what postmodern scholars of various backgrounds and disciplines sometimes seek through what they call "retrieval," the gleaning of insight from ancient sources that offer critical leverage for understanding our own historical situations, precisely because those sources do *not* share our assumptions and worldview.

So the bishops continued:

> How is the dynamism and expansion of the new culture to be fostered without losing living fidelity to the heritage of tradition? This question is of particular relevance in a culture where the enormous progress of science and technology must be harmonized with a system where classical studies according to various traditions have held sway. (§56)

As we saw in chapter 4, the Second Vatican Council, with its strategy of aggiornamento, was an effort to take the church's own sources of ancient wisdom into its encounter with modernity, while rising to the challenge and opportunity that modernity poses for Catholic Christianity. Those sources include Catholicism's experience at appropriating still other sources of human wisdom. Catholic theologians and philosophers have a long record, after all, of enriching the church's thought by engaging and sorting through the best of non-Christian thought, beginning with classical Greek and Roman

197

sources. Hence, no doubt, came the reference in *Gaudium et spes* (§56) to "classical studies."

If Catholics read the bishops as referring narrowly to Western traditions alone, however, the reference could perhaps tie the church so closely to Western culture that it would actually make it harder to become a truly global Christian community. The alternative is to hope that Catholicism's experience of debate and critical appropriation of non-Christian Western traditions has trained the community, or at least its leading thinkers, in the skills that the Christian community needs in order to engage still other cultural and philosophical heritages. Indeed, as we have noticed the preeminent Catholic theologian Karl Rahner arguing, the deepest significance of the Second Vatican Council is precisely that it launched the coming of a truly global Catholic Church.[10] In the documents of Vatican II, aggiornamento vis-à-vis the culture of modernity actually lays the basis for aggiornamento vis-à-vis *any* culture, insofar as the council has committed the church to proclaiming the gospel and translating the liturgy in forms and language that are appropriate to every culture.[11]

Whether the Roman Catholic Church has done enough since the council to realize this vision of a truly global multicultural church would require a larger historical judgment than this book can tender. Indeed, if Rahner was right about the epoch-making scope of Vatican II, it may be generations until *anyone* can tender such a judgment. The final point in this chapter (and this book) will thus need to be more transitional: ever relearning the practices of stability that Christian communities need to participate in the diversity-within-unity that is God's own trinitarian life is *both* what gives the church resources to participate in building a global civil society *and* part of what makes the church itself a gift to our globalizing, culturally interdependent world.

In any case, where *Gaudium et spes* asks how to harmonize ancient heritages with globalizing modernity rather than subsume them, the disquiet the bishops were voicing should sensitize us not only to the eclipse of classical Western sources of wisdom but also to the distress of vulnerable non-Western, non-European ones as well. In the highlands of Guatemala, for example, the Tzutuhil Indians have a reputation for staging some of the Mayan people's most stubborn resistance first to Spanish conquistadores and more recently to the Guatemalan military. Yet an artist and spokesman from the Tzutuhil city of Santiago Atitlán has insisted that television, pop music, designer sneakers, and migration are now doing what neither of those more-obvious oppressors was able to do. Young people "don't want to speak Tzutuhil, only Spanish and English. They are ashamed of their culture. I am afraid that when our elders die, our culture will die with them, unless we do something to stop this trend."[12] (And we wonder, "Why do they hate us?" But I digress.)

3. How to Harmonize the New Sciences with Ancient Wisdom?

The next question on the bishops' list expands on the previous one but moves more particularly to the task of integrating new scientific and post-Enlightenment academic disciplines with older habits of inquiry:

> As specialization in different branches of knowledge continues to increase so rapidly, how can the necessary synthesis of them be worked out, not to mention the need to safeguard [humanity's] powers of contemplation and wonder which lead to wisdom? (§56)

In other words, how can Christians master newly discovered insights and truths of modern scientific and academic disciplines without being mastered by them? Economics and business too, in their own efforts to be scientific and quantitative, have claimed increasing autonomy from moral, religious, philosophical, or even civic considerations. But should they? For if the tools of science, technology, and economics are to serve the global common good, we still need to ask what values and priorities ought to orient their use. How then are we to ensure that new techniques, disciplines, and technologies are the servants and not the masters of humanity?

4. How Can All Partake?

Next we come to the core question of global justice. In many ways the complexity of the modern, industrial, and now perhaps postindustrial world has made the ancient and perennial question of justice all the more complicated:

What can be done to enable everyone to share in the benefits of culture, when the culture of specialists is becoming every day more complex and esoteric? (§56)

Not only do the rich proverbially grow richer while the poor grow poorer; in the information age the well-connected and tech-savvy folks also grow ever more wired while those on the other side of "the digital divide" lack tools to become "competent" in the "more complex and esoteric" technologies required to "share in the benefits of culture."

At least that is the worry. True, the more optimistic commentators of globalization highlight ways that the Internet allows those at the margins of power and wealth to level out various playing fields, or observe how cell phone technology illustrates the possibility that communities in the so-called third world can sometimes leapfrog past the already-wired first world.[13] Still, a term like "the digital divide" would not have emerged if the bishops' worry about some people falling behind and finding it harder and harder to "share in the benefits of culture" were simply out of date. In the years that followed the Second Vatican Council, Catholic social teaching began to name the realities of "structural injustice" because of all the ways that individuals, groups, and entire nations who enjoy economic, social, and cultural advantages can leverage those advantages to create still more self-benefits. Many economists and captains of capitalist industry have argued that economic globalization is already giving billions of people around the world a greater share in resources and opportunities, thus laying the groundwork for greater global equity. As this book goes to press, a new global recession is shaking such confidence. Even if that is true, however, the bishops' prescient probing continues to apply: not only does any moral argument for the global expansion of capitalism require solid evidence that the poor and disadvantaged are benefiting, but we also dare not lose sight of the question of how feverishly "increased exchange" in the globalized economy—taking place not just "between cultures" but also through the hegemony of consumer culture—can promote economic prosperity without "disturbing the life of communities, overthrowing traditional wisdom and endangering the character proper to each people."

5. How to Celebrate Human Dignity without Locking Out the Transcendent?

After all, "prosperity" that is only economic and not also relational, social, cultural, and spiritual is merely quantitative or statistical prosperity, not necessarily the true prosperity of fully human thriving. Hence comes the last explicit question on the bishops' list:

> Finally, how are we to acknowledge as lawful the claims of autonomy, which culture makes for itself, without falling into a humanism which is purely earthbound and even hostile to religion? (§56)

To "prosper" by means of a mechanistic worldview that allows for ever-greater manipulation of the natural world, but that comes to see human beings mechanistically and to treat them manipulatively—that is not really to prosper at all. Though the point should be obvious, that we now tend to associate the words "prosperity" and "wealth" only with their economic, countable, and bankable dimension is actually a sign of human impoverishment. A humanism that truly exalts the dignity of human beings must find a way to celebrate the autonomous culture-building role that human beings play in forging their own histories, while recognizing that our mortal histories may have meaning only if we receive it as a gift from beyond history.

6. And How Can the Church Model Unity in Diversity?

Having laid out the deeply ambiguous set of opportunities and dangers at tension with each other in what we have since come to call globalization, the bishops underscored the fundamental moral requirement that faces all of humanity. Yet in doing so, they implicitly posed one more question for the church itself:

> In spite of these conflicting issues human culture must evolve today in such a way that it will develop the whole person harmoniously and integrally, and will help all [people] to fulfil the tasks to which they are called, especially Christians who are fraternally united at the heart of the human family. (§56)

201

To say "especially Christians" here is not necessarily to privilege one religious tradition, but to press upon Christians their own responsibility, and to name the church's own vocation. In the modern, pluralistic, interdependent, and globalized world, what then is that vocation? A community that crosses borders, embraces many cultures, and calls itself "catholic" *ought* to be distinctly qualified to meet the challenges of globalization. It *ought* to have its own way of being multicultural, diverse, and global—yet thus, paradoxically, to confirm its very identity and convictions thereby rather than sacrificing them to moral or doctrinal relativism. In other words, if it is truly living out its identity as a global and multicultural people in solidarity with one another and hospitable to still others, it will be demonstrating a way to interlace, and not simply to homogenize, long-standing traditions.

Doing so will require practices of stability that nurture virtues of fidelity. But it will also extend them, for any global civil society will require those practices and those virtues too. Exactly what it means to stick together in a community—inevitably conflicting yet doing so peaceably—may well differ tradition to tradition, as distinctive cultural and religious communities draw on their own specific narratives and beliefs, models, and exemplars. But what we all must learn *somewhere*, in some specific community, we all increasingly need *everywhere*, as communities find themselves living in one another's presence. In a globalized world, after all, everyone lives in diaspora now. As communities in diaspora, everyone who still identifies with traditions that have more substance and longevity than mere brands must find ways to preserve their cultural identity while respectfully negotiating their relationships to other communities within an almost incomprehensibly complex larger culture.

A Long-Deferred Objection—Why Now?

How then shall we respond to the bishops' prescient questions at the Second Vatican Council about modernity and globalization? How can we promote the solidarity of the human race amid a globalizing age in a truly respectful way that does not trivialize local cultures or disregard ancient traditions by relying on the false solutions that appear to unify and to avoid conflict only because they assimilate and homogenize? If it is possible for anyone to offer an answer to this globe-sized question, my own attempt will have to be roundabout—by way of attending to an objection that could have arisen at any number of junctures in this book, and that has probably nagged astute readers.

The objection is this: in advocating for practices of stability that nurture the virtues of fidelity, have I not been begging the question of *which* community one ought to hang with or stick with in the first place? Surely stability and fidelity are not absolute principles or exceptionless rules! No form of Christianity can object to the possibility of conversion, after all. If that were the case, Christianity would never have differentiated itself from Judaism, and Abraham should never have departed from Ur of Chaldeans! More realistically and relevant to the topic of whether and how some of us should be "unlearning Protestantism," arguably there were real and legitimate reasons for Reformation Protestants to break with medieval Catholicism, for Anabaptists to separate themselves from the magisterial Reformation, and so on. Eventually we simply must face the issue and argue out that "arguable." We cannot simply brush aside truth-claims concerning faith, works, ethics, the nature of the church, and the demands of Christian discipleship. Surely there are better reasons to stick with some traditions than with others. And that implies that there may be inadequate reasons to stick with some traditions as opposed to others. Which in turn justifies critique and might justify departure, nonstability, or even outright schism. By deferring the question of which tradition to stick with in the first place, have we really gained any leverage over the Protestant Dilemma, or done more than postpone the corrosions of individualism? One way or another, after all, won't we finally have to call on autonomous individual conscience simply to adjudicate the question of where to be stable?

On the way to a reply, the first thing to recognize—and I am hardly being original here[14]—is that there is really no place outside of some tradition from which to judge the adequacy of traditions. The Enlightenment tried, by attempting to construct a value-neutral, commitment-free methodology from which to adjudicate, but in the process the Enlightenment itself came to constitute a tradition.[15]

The Enlightenment's failure to locate a sovereign site of perfectly neutral reasoning becomes apparent when one reviews a whole series of critiques: Marxist, Nietzschean, Freudian. What they all have in common is a relentless exposé of ways that people who claim to derive their positions from disinterested reason have actually been influenced or even determined by interests or other factors in their social environment.[16] Cynicism then tempts many to conclude that rationality is at best a ruse, and rational discourse is a facade for raw power struggles.[17] Perhaps the only way to escape is through a rugged individualism, after all, emboldened by the courage willfully to transgress.

Never mind that rugged individualism has itself become yet another tradition.[18] By now something else should be clear: if this is our only way to adjudicate the claims of rival traditions, then committed Protestants will find little more comfort here than loyal Catholics. Even if I and other commentators have overstated the degree to which a corrosive individualism is the product of Protestant success at shaping the modern world, its acids will delegitimize Protestant communities as surely as both Protestantism and modernity have claimed to delegitimize Catholicism. Protestants have as much of a stake in naming and developing constructive ways to conduct their continuing debate with Catholicism as Catholics have in sustaining their own habits and practices of change-in-continuity-with-tradition.

But that is itself a clue: strengthening patterns of debate *within* one tradition leads to strengthening patterns of debate *between* traditions, and vice versa. If those patterns in turn come to constitute a yet-larger tradition, we are not so much begging yet another question as we are on our way to forging a global civil society of healthy intertraditional debate. Practices of stability, then, are necessary even to answer well the question "Which tradition?" *And* they are relevant to our larger world indeed.

The Rationality of Traditions

This much, at least, should already be clear: if there is a way out of the conundrums that modern culture and Enlightenment philosophy have left us, it will be because it is possible to test traditions from within traditions after all. That is what the philosopher Alasdair MacIntyre has both argued and offered with his notion of "the rationality of traditions."[19] MacIntyre's rationality of traditions not only allows us to chart a response to the question of which tradition one ought to hang with or stick with. It also demonstrates the interdependence between those lively debates we must carry on within a tradition or community in order to sustain and extend it, and the respectful debates we must have between traditions in order to live at peace in a globalizing world. It turns out that we cannot really have either of these without practices of stability. While we cannot expect the virtue of fidelity to one's own tradition to look exactly like the virtues required for civil exchange and debate with rival traditions, they are nonetheless mutually nourishing, or perhaps even mutual prerequisites.

MacIntyre's stress on the role of tradition in human life and moral discourse grows from his Aristotelian conception of the human person. On the one hand, the "self" is inevitably formed and defined through social relationships, so that thriving lives depend on formation and participation within a healthy community or polis.[20] On the other hand, even a single life, if it is to be coherent and meaningful, must be narrative in structure. In other words, others must be able to explain how a life has been well lived by retelling it as a coherent story, while a person in the midst of a still-unfinished life will experience it as a continuing quest and be able to give an account of one's actions by narrating that quest.[21] A quest is itself meaningful, however, only if it aims for some destination, however dimly envisioned and still to be discovered. Furthermore, community life is as much a quest as any individual life. Living a meaningful life as part of a healthy community involves participating in that community's larger project—to discover, debate, test, and embody the community's vision of what it means to thrive as human beings in the first place, its vision of "the good."

With most other modern philosophers, MacIntyre's overarching contention has not been that they have disagreed over what is the good, but that they have given up on even debating it. Instead, they argue that both they and their political communities must call a truce and be agnostic toward any conception of the good, except perhaps that of a neutral arena in which individuals have the right to pursue their own privately defined goods. The fallacy of this philosophically "liberal" approach is that in the name of tolerance, it actually has little tolerance for communal conceptions of the good, having ruled them out of court. Like the philosophers with whom he debates, MacIntyre has not expected or advocated for the hegemonic imposition of a single conception of the good. He has simply insisted that fairness and coherence require that moral, political, and philosophical debates proceed as socially embodied arguments over what is the most adequate vision of good of human beings.

And that is MacIntyre's definition of a tradition: a socially embodied argument over the nature of the good, extended through time, tested and found reliable through encounters with the challenges of new historical situations and worthy rivals.[22] At least that is his definition of a tradition in good working order. Leaders of a community who appeal to the authority of tradition alone may be tradition*ists*, but theirs is probably not a *living* tradition; it has already begun to calcify and die. This distinction between living traditions and mere traditionalism is crucial for avoiding misunderstanding and hearing MacIntyre out. MacIntyre has no doubt espoused some positions that could be labeled conservative, but he has also been pointed in his criticism of conservatism for its own sake.[23] (He is a Scot formed in the British intellectual tradition, where such terms mean something different than they do in the United States; he is formerly Marxist though now Catholic; he has been called a "revolutionary Aristotelian"[24]—these facts should warn us against any easy categorization.) His very effort to demonstrate "the rationality of traditions" has aimed to show what can make it reasonable to assent to a tradition—with a philosopher's emphasis on *reason*. Blind, wooden, and unreasoned obedience to the purported demands of a tradition would only confirm the modern prejudices that MacIntyre has endeavored to undo.

MacIntryre has argued that a viable, living tradition does not have to have anticipated every challenge or newly arising moral dilemma in advance, and some still-unresolved questions are always to be expected. Nor does it have to prove itself right on every last point. What a tradition *does* have to demonstrate is a track record of problem-solving capacity—the coherence that comes from having met past issues and objections in a consistent and trustworthy fashion.[25] To be sure, if too many unanswered questions and unresolved challenges begin to accumulate, a tradition may enter into crisis and face a loss of confidence. But what really demonstrates that it is *un*reasonable to assent to a tradition is when its thinkers and defenders simply refuse to entertain alternative accounts of the tradition that surface from within, or likewise refuse to take on the best objections of rival traditions from without, or generally refuse to stand corrected whether from within or from without.[26]

What this means is that the health that distinguishes a living tradition from moribund traditionalism (to say nothing of outright fundamentalism) depends on the acceptance of challengers, conflict, and dialectic. What the proper destination or telos of our personal and communal quests ought to be will emerge clearly only amid conflict.[27] When a culture is not providing adequate space for people to negotiate the various local and universal claims upon them in order to coordinate the multiple goods that overlapping roles and communities represent, there is a logjam.

> Part of the answer is: by generating just the right kinds of tension or even conflict, creative rather than destructive, on the whole and in the long run, between secular and sacred, local and national, . . . rural and urban. It is in the context of such conflicts that moral education goes on and that the virtues come to be valued and redefined.[28]

If a moral tradition does not take the questions of rival traditions seriously, it may founder, divide, or merge with other traditions. Taking on the questions of rivals, however, rarely means simply defending against their rival claims and going along unchanged. Often a tradition must find ways to reconstitute itself, sometimes in a radically new way. One way or another, if a tradition has the self-awareness to successfully encounter other traditions according to its own internal standards, it provides a rational basis for confidence and adherence.[29]

Conflict *within* a tradition is also to be expected and is not necessarily a sign that a tradition has entered the sort of protracted and irresolvable crisis in which it founders.[30] Contending subtraditions, subcultures, or schools of thought help to keep a living tradition

207

living; it exhibits "continuities of conflict," not the homogenous absence of conflict, that constitute a tradition in good working order.[31] The difference between internal and external debates is that external rivals tend to force reexamination of a community's most basic presuppositions or first principles, while internal debates tend to focus on the implications of a community's shared assumptions and master narratives. Internal debate may not even be so much about "principles" as about the interpretation of sacred texts, the lessons to be drawn from acknowledged heroes and saints, the meaning of communal rituals, and so on.[32] After all, the carriers of a tradition's conception of the good are not so much propositions as narratives, mentors, exemplars, and practices that embody that good. But again, a tradition that suppresses its prophets or dissenters puts itself at risk, for an unpopular Jeremiah or Socrates may offer precisely the account of the master narrative or conception of the good that will enable the community to navigate its current challenge or next crisis.[33] In the face of serious challenges and crises, after all, a tradition may sometimes cease to make progress unless it provides a radically new and conceptually enriched scheme of self-understanding, offers an explanation of what was beginning to render the tradition sterile or incoherent, *and* does both those things in such a way that it *also* exhibits fundamental continuity with the convictions and narratives at the heart of the tradition.[34] In the role of prophets, dissenters, and dialectic within a living tradition, we see the truth of the Protestant Principle—but also the danger of so elevating that principle that we isolate it from the very "*continuities* of conflict" that make protest coherent and purposeful.

Although some moral convictions and the very terms that express them may be fully intelligible only from within the tradition in which they cohere, a tradition that understands itself along the lines of MacIntyre's "rationality of traditions" cannot be sectarian. As with languages, translation between traditions is never perfect. Some terms may simply be untranslatable, yet rough translations remain possible.[35] Thus traditions can overhear one another, and they must do so, for not only do they share certain features and convictions, they also ignore one another only at the cost of excluding reasons that are good reasons, even on their own terms.[36] MacIntyre has even insisted that one does not really understand one's own tradition at all if one has not engaged deeply in empathetic debate with at least one rival tradition, thus testing its claims dialectically.[37]

In MacIntyre's map of the rationality of traditions debating within and among themselves, therefore, we find a vision for globalization and plurality that neither flattens out the differences between traditions, nor guts them through homogenization, nor delegitimizes them, nor expects them to remain unchanged—nor sets them at war. Communities that thrive as traditions have every right to stake their claims on their members and make their cases vis-à-vis rivals. Indeed, such communities have a responsibility to do so, for the vitality of each and the peace of all require honest debate as much as tolerance. "Tolerance" is the wrong word for the character of the interrelationships between communities, for tolerance can as easily be grudging as respectful, with no obligation actually to hear out the claims of one's Other. A person may have been tolerant but has not really been respectful until making oneself vulnerable to the truth-claims of others in precisely the way that MacIntyre's rationality of traditions requires.

Even though a lively debate within traditions and a respectful debate between or among traditions will differ in some respects,[38] they nonetheless require similar skills and virtues, both intellectual and moral. First among these are the patient stability, empathy, and imaginative identification with others that is necessary even to have a fruitful debate. In his exposition of virtue ethics, MacIntyre has observed that institutions alone do not ensure the practices by which a community learns and passes on the virtues that correspond to its conception of the good. Yet the making and sustaining of human community, along with the institutions that structure human life, is one of the most basic of virtue-nourishing practices.[39] Furthermore, for developing the integrity that characterizes any virtuous life, a particularly crucial virtue is what MacIntyre calls "constancy" and I am calling stability or fidelity.[40] But in turn, persons who are engaged in the kind of dialectical conversation between traditions that is necessary for adherence to their own tradition to be rational will require the virtue of empathy. They must develop the capacity to place themselves imaginatively within other traditions despite their continuing disagreements, after all, and must exercise the patience to learn that tradition as a "second first language."[41] Language learning takes time. In other words, it also takes stability.

209

Even if our primary topic had been the building of global civil society rather than the sustaining of Christian community, therefore, an adequate account of that task would have required us to attend to practices of stability within particular communities. For if MacIntyre is right, we can learn virtues only from within a tradition. We must start somewhere. And that is why Christians cannot make their contribution to global civil society unless they first nurture practices of stability and the virtue of fidelity from within their own community.

So even though MacIntyre has not told us which tradition to adhere to, he has showed us how to proceed with deciding: put one's roots down even farther within the tradition in which one finds oneself, but do so by testing its claims through sustained dialogue and imaginative debate with at least one other tradition.

As I hope that readers will have discovered by now, this book is among other things an exercise in doing precisely that. I have not argued that Protestants must become Catholic. What I have done, I hope, is bring these two traditions of Christianity into deep conversation, thus bringing to light certain oft-unnoticed presuppositions that Catholics and Protestants sometimes share, sometimes dispute, but often act on unreflectively. It is possible that some Protestant readers will come away from this book deciding that Catholicism—despite certain problems that Catholics dispute among themselves—coheres better than Protestantism and thus invites assent. But it is also possible that other Protestant readers will find themselves enriched in a way that makes them better Christians who are more faithful to their Protestant communities. It is likewise possible that some Catholic readers will have understood their tradition better precisely because they have seen why they must incorporate what is right about the Protestant Principle of dissent while sustaining continuity with their own tradition. MacIntyre's rationality of traditions anticipates all these possibilities. He has also described how traditions may reach such a point of crisis that schism results, how they sometimes recover, and how occasionally they even merge. Except for further schism, I welcome all these possibilities. For my purposes, all of them—even perhaps the divisions that some historical situations make tragically inevitable—will proceed in healthier ways if Christians in all of their communities have learned to practice stability. And whenever greater church unity does become possible, our having disputed in the healthy ways that result from hanging in there with one another even amid deep disagreements will have done much to make it so.

My point then stands: if we need stability and fidelity even toward our rivals, and if we need first to learn such practices and virtues by sustaining our own communities, then we need them in every case, in any case.

Notes

Introduction

1. Or in less polite company: "even when they're pissed off at one another."

2. For more information on Bridgefolk, visit Bridgefolk.net or see the following: Gerald W. Schlabach, "The Bridgefolk Movement in Ecumenical Context," *Ecumenical Trends* 32, no. 3 (March 2003): 14–15; Schlabach, "Catholic and Mennonite: A Journey of Healing," *One in Christ* 42, no. 2 (Winter 2008): 318–40; Ivan Kauffman, "On Being a Mennonite Catholic," *Mennonite Quarterly Review* 76, no. 2 (April 2003): 235–55, www.goshen.edu/mqr/pastissues/apr03kauffman.html.

3. For a somewhat more complete accounting of what I have called non-Roman reasons for having become Roman Catholic, see Gerald W. Schlabach, "You Converted to What? One Mennonite's Journey," *Commonweal*, June 1, 2007, 14–17—but please note that the title was not of my choosing. As someone who was already a Christian and whose trinitarian baptism the Catholic Church accepts, I regard the term "convert" as misleading. Rather, as I have already had occasion to do in this introduction, I call myself "a Mennonite who has entered into full communion with the Catholic Church."

4. I invite my fellow theologians to recognize here and in the surrounding paragraphs something of a Barthian act of *Aufhebung*. Due to poor initial translation, readers in English received the impression that Karl Barth understood the work of Christ as "abolishing" all religions because they amounted only to misguided human efforts to find God. Yet the word *Aufhebung*, which Barth used to describe what God in Christ does to religion means—yes—to fundamentally change or even to put aside, but also to preserve in the process. *Aufhebung* thus is like pickling, which changes the cucumber forever but also preserves it. By analogy, my vision for our current Christian identities—whether Catholic or Mennonite or a multitude of other denominational qualifiers—is to simultaneously preserve and change them by moving beyond current patterns.

5. Robin W. Lovin, "Niebuhr at 100: Realism for New Realities," *Christian Century*, June 17, 1992, 605.

6. Cardinal Joseph Ratzinger, *Church, Ecumenism, and Politics: New Essays in Ecclesiology* (New York: Crossroad, 1988), 87; Walter Cardinal Kasper, "Current Problems in Ecumenical Theology," *Reflections* 6 (Spring 2003): 64–65.

213

Chapter 1 The Protestant Dilemma

1. Stanley Hauerwas, "The Importance of Being Catholic: Unsolicited Advice from a Protestant Bystander," in *In Good Company: The Church as Polis* (Notre Dame, IN: University of Notre Dame Press, 1995), 98.

2. More information on the Ekklesia Project is available at www.ekklesiaproject.org.

3. Such themes run throughout Robert N. Bellah et al., *Habits of the Heart: Individualism and Commitment in American Life* (New York: Harper & Row, 1985), but see esp. vii, 21, 47, 65, 139, 142–44, 167–68, 177–78.

4. Years after the publication of *Habits of the Heart*, Bellah made this connection explicit in "Religion and the Shape of National Culture: Flaws in the Protestant Cultural Code," *America*, July 31–August 7, 1999, 9–14. Also note the claim by Paul Tillich that traces of the Protestant spirit run through all creators of modern autonomous culture, in *The Protestant Era*, trans. James Luther Adams (Chicago: University of Chicago Press, 1948), 195. Though Tillich no doubt celebrated the role of Protestantism in shaping modern culture, Stanley Hauerwas has observed the same phenomenon but lamented what it has done to the church; see "The Importance of Being Catholic: Unsolicited Advice from a Protestant Bystander," in *In Good Company: The Church as Polis* (Notre Dame, IN: University of Notre Dame Press, 1995), 98, where Hauerwas concludes: "In short, Protestantism helped to create, but even more, to legitimate, a form of social life that undermined its ability to maintain the kind of disciplined communities necessary to sustain the church's social witness."

5. Tillich, *The Protestant Era*, xi, xxii, 163, 195–96, 202–5.

6. Tillich, *The Protestant Era*, xi.

7. Tillich, *The Protestant Era*, 163.

8. Tillich, *The Protestant Era*, xi, xxii, 163, 203; quotation from xxii.

9. Tillich, *The Protestant Era*, 205.

10. Tillich, *The Protestant Era*, 205.

11. Tillich, *The Protestant Era*, xi.

12. The Shepherd of Hermas, *Visions* 2.2.6 and 3.9.17. The Shepherd of Hermas is not canonical yet nearly made it into the New Testament canon; for centuries, church fathers recommended it for devotional reading.

13. See Augustine, *Letter* 82, in reply to nos. 72, 75, and 81.

14. Martin Luther, "The Freedom of a Christian," 1520, trans. W. A. Lambert, rev. Harold J. Grimm, in *Luther's Works*, vol. 31, ed. Harold J. Grimm, gen. ed. Helmut T. Lehmann (Philadelphia: Fortress, 1957), 336.

15. Catholic historian of the Reformation Joseph Lortz defended his own bleak portrayal of the state of the church as the Protestant Reformation began: "If some feel that the picture could not be as black as I have painted it, I would point to the weighty judgment pronounced by the most religious-minded pope of the period, Adrian VI of Utrecht, the last German pope. What he said comes down to this: So widespread are the sins of the Curia, that those who run it are no longer aware of the foul stench." Joseph Lortz, *The Reformation: A Problem for Today*, trans. John C. Dwyer (Westminster, MD: Newman, 1964), 79–80.

16. John Calvin, *The Necessity of Reforming the Church*, in *Tracts and Treatises*, trans. Henry Beveridge, with a short life of Calvin by Theodore Beza, intro. Thomas F. Torrance (Grand Rapids: Eerdmans, 1958), 125.

17. Calvin, *Necessity of Reforming the Church*, 183.

18. Calvin, *Necessity of Reforming the Church*, 184.

19. Actually, there would now be versions of what I name here that also divide Protestants from Protestants.

20. Jacques de Senarclens, *Heirs of the Reformation* (Philadelphia: Westminster, 1964), 85–87.

21. All quotations in this paragraph are from de Senarclens, *Heirs of the Reformation*, 11.

22. All quotations in this paragraph are from de Senarclens, *Heirs of the Reformation*, 12.

23. This paragraph summarizes arguments in de Senarclens, *Heirs of the Reformation*, 85–87, 108; quotation from 108. The source for de Senarclens is Calvin's first *French Catechism* of 1537.

24. At least in part, these issues are at stake in de Senarclens's claim that Protestant faith and theology "differ sharply from all movements operating on the basis of a prior union between God and man in terms either of the analogy of being or of man's likeness to God in feeling, duty or historical development." See de Senarclens, *Heirs of the Reformation*, 108.

25. De Senarclens, *Heirs of the Reformation*, 108.

26. De Senarclens, *Heirs of the Reformation*, 146.

27. Lortz, *The Reformation: A Problem for Today*, 27–28, 92–93. While it is probably no coincidence that this book was translated and published during the Second Vatican Council, the original German edition was a decade and a half earlier: *Die Reformation als religiöses Anliegen heute: Vier Vorträge im Dienste der Una Sancta* (Trier, [W. Germany]: Paulinus Verlag, 1948).

28. Lortz, *The Reformation: A Problem for Today*, 75, 78.

29. Lortz, *The Reformation: A Problem for Today*, 78–79.

30. Lortz, *The Reformation: A Problem for Today*, 31–32.

31. Lortz, *The Reformation: A Problem for Today*, 42–43, 51.

32. Lortz, *The Reformation: A Problem for Today*, 37.

33. Joseph Lortz, "The Basic Elements of Luther's Intellectual Style," in *Catholic Scholars Dialogue with Luther*, ed. Jared Wicks, SJ (Chicago: Loyola University Press, 1970), 7. Other essays in this volume fill in Lortz's picture with additional detail; see esp. Harry J. McSorley, CSP, "Erasmus Versus Luther: Compounding the Reformation Tragedy," 106–17. For a contrasting view of Luther in a decidedly pre–Vatican II mode, see Hartmann Grisar, *Martin Luther, His Life and Work*, adapted from the 2nd German ed., 1930 (Westminster, MD: Newman, 1950); Grisar's view that Luther's rash and stubborn willingness to divide the church owed to mental illness finds summary expression on 574.

34. Second Vatican Council, *Unitatis redintegratio*, Decree on Ecumenism (1965), §6. All quotations of council documents are from Second Vatican Council, *Vatican Council II: The Conciliar and Post-Conciliar Documents*, new rev. ed., general ed. Austin Flannery, Vatican Collection 1 (Newport, NY: Costello; Dublin, Ireland: Dominican Publications, 1996).

35. Cultural historian Eugene McCarraher does trace numerous lines of influence, particularly on that sector of radicals or that dimension of the New Left "whose critical discourse relied heavily on psychology and existentialism." See McCaharar's *Christian Critics: Religion and the Impasse in Modern American Social Thought* (Ithaca, NY: Cornell University Press, 2000), 121, 136–43; quotation from 136. McCarraher also notes on 141 that "existential theology, often introduced to students through Tillich's work, saturated the intellectual atmosphere of numerous campus fellowships and student groups that became key nuclei of the New Left."

36. McCarraher put it this way: "Tillich inhabited the footloose and bureaucratic world of a mostly white, educated, and mobile religious intelligentsia. Among them, [Tillich's] personalism [i.e., the existential theology of personal fulfillment] inspired an equally political

[as compared with radical student and other leftist movements surveyed in previous pages] but also more purely therapeutic gospel of personality that gradually weakened the symbolic and institutional structures of mainline Protestantism." McCarraher, *Christian Critics*, 143. Behind McCarraher's summary of Tillich's class location are his fuller recounting of Tillich's narrative on 121–36.

37. In *The Protestant Era*, Tillich identified three broad human phenomena that Protestantism, as an impulse more universal than Protestant Christianity alone, addresses: (1) It insists on "the radical experience of the human boundary-situation" in which ultimate threat confronts human existence. Protestantism protests all attempts by human beings to evade their vulnerability, whether through political ideologies, philosophical systems, scientific method, pedagogies of social transformation, therapeutic psychology, active engagement with the world, or "religious expedients." (2) It pronounces the "'Yes'" that comes to human beings once they face their boundary-situation in all its "ultimate seriousness." (3) It witnesses to the "'New Being'" that is "manifest in Jesus as the Christ" and that is efficacious in individual personalities, community life, and nature itself. The Protestant Principle, having broken down all boundaries in the face of universal judgment, can be open to everything, secular and religious, individual and social, within which the New Being finds cultural expression. Tillich, *The Protestant Era*, 203–5.

38. Cf. McCarraher, *Christian Critics*, 126–28, 132–33, 135–36, 143.

39. McCarraher's judgment is that "Tillich pushed the liberal Protestant idiom of religion and personality to its farthest limits of discursive abstraction and psychological form." *Christian Critics*, 143. Also note the judgment of Hannah Tillich herself, as McCaharer reports it on 146.

40. At a number of different points, McCarraher confirms the tendency of Tillich's theology and "'the Protestant principle' of prophetic iconoclasm" (132) to corrode committed participation in any actual church or denomination. See *Christian Critics*, 132–33, 136, 143. On 136 he writes: "Religious intellectuals in particular found in Tillich's harvest abundant justification for dismissing churches as potential political sites, thereby crippling rather than strengthening religion as a vehicle of moral imagination."

41. See James M. Kittelson, *Wolfgang Capito: From Humanist to Reformer*, Studies in Medieval and Reformation Thought, vol. 17 (Leiden: Brill, 1975), 5, 182, 186–87, 201.

42. Quoted in Lortz, *The Reformation: A Problem for Today*, 149.

43. Lortz, *The Reformation: A Problem for Today*, 21.

44. The classic source for tracing such cycles is Ernst Troeltsch, *The Social Teaching of the Christian Churches*, trans. Olive Wyon, intro. H. Richard Niebuhr (New York: Macmillan, 1931; repr., Chicago: University of Chicago Press, 1981). Though Troetsch did not schematize his findings under the name of a "sect cycle," sociologists of religion inspired by his work recognized a recurring pattern and gave it that name: First, broad social discontent issues in broad social movements against the status quo and those established churches associated with the status quo. Then when adherents of a social movement fail to achieve their more utopian goals, some of them retreat into smaller "sectarian" religious groups where they can retain greater hope that life according to an ideal of fraternal love and justice is possible. By the second or third generation, however, these groups find that they must accommodate the realities of "the world" or wider society; thus they begin to look more like the established churches against which they once protested. Eventually some of their adherents conclude that their church has become too compromised, and so the cycle begins again.

45. Oliver Read Whitley, *Trumpet Call of Reformation*. (St. Louis: Bethany, 1959), 44.

46. All quotations to this point in the paragraph are from Whitley, *Trumpet Call of Reformation*, 49.

47. Whitley, *Trumpet Call of Reformation*, 137.

48. This is akin to an argument I first made in a critique of the better-known and influential Lutheran thinker Anders Nygren. See Gerald W. Schlabach, *For the Joy Set before Us: Augustine and Self-Denying Love* (Notre Dame, IN: University of Notre Dame Press, 2001), 151, which in turn owes a debt to Oliver O'Donovan, *The Problem of Self-Love in St. Augustine* (New Haven: Yale University Press, 1980), 155–59. One could also develop a similar argument vis-à-vis H. Richard Niebuhr. Eugene McCarraher indicated how this argument would run when he supplemented his critique of Paul Tillich by showing that Niebuhr's notion of "radical monotheism" finally succumbs to some of the same problems as Tillich's Protestant Principle. Niebuhr was quicker than Tillich to recognize that the biblical prophets were always intimately bound up with "the concrete life of the people," yet his radical monotheism still tended (in McCarraher's word) to "evade and erode" that life by allowing no special place, time, community, or person to represent the One God in any particularly intense and theologically significant way. See McCarraher, *Christian Critics*, 144–45. I have chosen to engage the lesser-known de Senarclens here only because he has more directly engaged the question of what makes Protestants Protestant.

49. All quotations in this paragraph are from de Senarclens, *Heirs of the Reformation*, 125–26.

50. De Senarclens, *Heirs of the Reformation*, 108.

51. Charles Marsh, *God's Long Summer: Stories of Faith and Civil Rights* (Princeton, NJ: Princeton University Press, 1997), 45–46, 147–49.

52. Marsh, *God's Long Summer*, 82–115, and esp. 106–12.

53. Marsh, *God's Long Summer*, 109.

54. Marsh, *God's Long Summer*, 98–100, 107–10.

55. Marsh, *God's Long Summer*, 127–41.

56. The overtly segregationist "Christianity" of KKK Grand Wizard Samuel Bowers in the previous chapter of *God's Long Summer* (49–81) is still more extreme.

57. Cf. William Cavanaugh, "Stan the Man: A Thoroughly Biased Account of a Completely Unobjective Person," in *The Hauerwas Reader*, ed. John Berkman and Michael G. Cartwright (Durham, NC: Duke University Press, 2001), 17.

58. Sometimes, in Hauerwas's telling, "high-church Mennonite" is what it should still mean to be a Methodist, though this hardly exhausts the puzzles or the possibilities that Hauerwas's term evokes: "For we Methodists are a people with Catholic practices of ministry and eucharist [sic], but at the same time we have a free church ecclesiology. We began as a lay attempt to reform an established church. We have never wanted to let the state establish us. We are established by God, thank you. As free church Catholics we think we stand in a peculiar position to bind up the wounds of the Reformation." Stanley Hauerwas, "Why *Resident Aliens* Struck a Chord," with William Willimon, in *In Good Company*, 62. For more on Hauerwas's ecclesial stance, see *In Good Company*, 10–11, 27, 66–67, as well as Cavanaugh, "Stan the Man," 24. Finally, together with Samuel Wells, Hauerwas explained why he believes arguments intending to identify marks of "the true Church" are unhelpful in Hauerwas and Wells, "The Gift of the Church and the Gifts God Gives It," chap. 2 in *The Blackwell Companion to Christian Ethics*, Blackwell Companions to Religion (Malden, MA: Blackwell, 2004), 22–24.

59. Hauerwas, "The Importance of Being Catholic," 99. See also Hauerwas, "Why *Resident Aliens* Struck a Chord," 62–63, where he wrote that

one of the oddities of mainstream liberal Protestant social theory [is] that because we have an intrinsic social nature, the church must be about social action. But the social theory that informs that social action would create liberal democratic societies that intrinsically privatize religious convictions. Indeed, such a strategy cannot help but reduce Christian practice to religious belief. Thus the widespread assumption that you can be a Christian without going to church. . . . Put differently, liberal societies make religion more important than the church.

60. Cf. Stanley Hauerwas, *Character and the Christian Life: A Study in Theological Ethics*, based on the author's thesis, Yale University, Trinity University Monograph Series in Religion 3 (San Antonio: Trinity University Press, 1975), 5–8, 29; Stanley Hauerwas, "Situation Ethics, Moral Notions, and Moral Theology," in *Vision and Virtue: Essays in Christian Ethical Reflection* (Notre Dame, IN: Fides, 1974; repr., Notre Dame, IN: University of Notre Dame Press, 1981), 11–29.

61. Stanley Hauerwas, "Must a Patient Be a Person to Be a Patient? Or, My Uncle Charlie Is Not Much of a Person but He Is Still My Uncle Charlie," in *Truthfulness and Tragedy: Further Investigations in Christian Ethics* (Notre Dame, IN: University of Notre Dame Press, 1977), 131.

62. Stanley Hauerwas, "Whose Church? Which Future? Wither the Anabaptist Vision?" in *In Good Company*, 73.

63. Cavanaugh, "Stan the Man," 24. For an expression of Hauerwas's respect for Roman Catholicism, see Hauerwas, *In Good Company*, 14. Yet note Hauerwas's critique of Roman Catholic patterns of hierarchical authority when it silences weaker members of the community, in Stanley Hauerwas, "Christianity: It's Not a Religion, It's an Adventure" (1991), in Berkman and Cartwright, *Hauerwas Reader*, 527–28: "Listening to the weakest member is the kind of church government that is at the very heart of the Gospel. One of the deep problems in Catholicism is when the weakest member is shut up. The weakest brother or sister is always there to speak as a Christian and to be a witness to Jesus Christ. Giving power to those weakest members is necessary; otherwise, the entire community is always dependent on the good nature of the leadership."

64. Stanley Hauerwas and Samuel Wells, "How the Church Managed before There Was Ethics," chap. 4 in *Blackwell Companion to Christian Ethics*, 48.

65. Hauerwas and Wells, "How the Church Managed before There Was Ethics," 48.

66. Hauerwas, "Whose Church? Which Future?" 73. Cf. Hauerwas and Wells, "How the Church Managed before There Was Ethics," 48–49; and Hauerwas, *In Good Company*, 4.

67. See Stanley Hauerwas, "A Retrospective Assessment of an 'Ethics of Character': The Development of Hauerwas's Theological Project" (1985), repr. in Berkman and Cartwright, *Hauerwas Reader*, 75–89. Note esp. 79, where Hauerwas described his first book as "a door that, once opened, forced [him] to see things [he] had no idea existed when [he] first began the work."

68. Hauerwas has called this "occasionalism." Protestant theologians and ethicists may rarely if ever have stated their position so baldly, so part of the task of Hauerwas's first book, *Character and the Christian Life*, was to demonstrate that this was its underlying logic; he thus begins his closing summary (229–30) this way:

The basic concern of this book has been the inability of contemporary Christian ethics to develop an adequate way to articulate the nature of the Christian moral life. This inadequacy has become more apparent with the gradual loss of the vitality of central Christian symbols. The decay of our language has revealed some of the systematic inadequacies that have been endemic to the Protestant understanding of the Christian life. In particular the concentration on justification tended to impede the development of an ethic concerned with the nature and moral formation of the self. Moreover, the dominance of the metaphor and language of command in Protestant thought encouraged an occasionalistic ethic concerned with decision and judgment about specific acts. Situation ethics is a natural development of a theological tradition that provided no means to develop an ethic of character.

69. Hauerwas, *Character and the Christian Life*, 2–5, 8–10, 229–33. Cf. Hauerwas, "A Retrospective Assessment," 87.

70. See Stanley Hauerwas, "On Keeping Theological Ethics Theological" (1983), repr. in Berkman and Cartwright, *Hauerwas Reader*, 72–73; Hauerwas, "A Retrospective Assessment," 88–89; Hauerwas, "Reforming Christian Social Ethics: Ten Theses" (1981), repr. in Berkman and Cartwright, *Hauerwas Reader*, 111–15.

71. Stanley Hauerwas, "Character, Narrative, and Growth in the Christian Life," in *A Community of Character: Toward a Constructive Christian Social Ethic*, Readings in Moral Theology 4 (Notre Dame, IN: University of Notre Dame Press, 1981), 130. Although this essay takes on the developmental theories of Piaget, Kohlberg, and Fowler most explicitly, it also provides an excellent introduction to Hauerwas's arguments against Kantian autonomy, assumptions of which stand behind those theories.

72. Stanley Hauerwas, "Abortion, Theologically Understood" (1991), in Berkman and Cartwright, *Hauerwas Reader*, 612.

73. I am not sure whether Hauerwas has ever said all this in one place, but it seems to me to be implied by his simultaneous emphasis on virtue and hospitality, on truthfulness and nonviolence. I also believe it accords with his portrayal of the task of theological ethics, communally based biblical interpretation, and community discernment (or casuistry) in chaps. 4, 5, and 7 of his book *The Peaceable Kingdom: A Primer in Christian Ethics* (Notre Dame, IN: University of Notre Dame Press, 1983), respectively, along with his comments on hospitality and vulnerability to the presence of the other (e.g., on 44–49 of *Peaceable Kingdom*). To "begin in the middle" of church life (as Hauerwas stated matters in chap. 4 and implicitly continued to develop in chap. 5) means that not everything is open to theological reformulation or biblical reinterpretation, but must be obeyed to be understood. Likewise, casuistry requires a working conception of the good if it is to proceed coherently. And yet in all of these modes of discourse within the Christian community, the community and its leadership must be vulnerable to challenge and revision if the church's discernment is to be reasoned rather than merely authoritarian. (Such a view of authoritative yet vulnerable discernment, by the way, owes an important debt to Alasdair MacIntyre's portrayal of "the rationality of traditions" in the closing chapters (18–20) of *Whose Justice? Which Rationality?* (Notre Dame, IN: University of Notre Dame Press, 1988), which I will discuss at length in my final chapter. This debt is especially evident in chap. 7 of Hauerwas, *Peaceable Kingdom*.

74. Here I quote myself, in a formulation of Hauerwas's position that he has endorsed for "say[ing] what I have been trying to say better than how I have said it." See Stanley Hauerwas, "The Christian Difference: Or, Surviving Postmodernism," in *A Better Hope: Resources for a Church Confronting Capitalism, Democracy, and Postmodernity* (Grand Rapids: Brazos, 2000), 43–44; as well as Stanley Hauerwas, *After Christendom?* 2nd ed., with a new preface by the author (Nashville: Abingdon, 1999), 7–8.

Chapter 2 The Matter of Continuity

1. John Howard Yoder, "Methodological Miscellany #2: Have You Ever Seen a True Church?" Historical mss. 1–48, box 187, section: ethics, 1938–1997, John H. Yoder Collection, Mennonite Church USA Archives, Goshen, IN (1988), 4.

2. See Hauerwas, *Peaceable Kingdom*, xxiv; Cavanaugh, "Stan the Man," 21–22.

3. John Howard Yoder, "The Anabaptist Dissent: The Logic of the Place of the Disciple in Society," *Concern: A Pamphlet Series* 1 (June 1954): 45–68. See also John H[oward] Yoder, "The Prophetic Dissent of the Anabaptists," in *The Recovery of the Anabaptist Vision: A Sixtieth Anniversary Tribute to Harold S. Bender*, ed. Guy F. Hershberger (Scottdale, PA: Herald, 1957), 93–104.

4. See the title of one of Hauerwas's early collections of articles, *A Community of Character*.

5. Hauerwas, *Peaceable Kingdom*, xxiv.

6. Stanley Hauerwas, "Why Truthfulness Requires Forgiveness: A Commencement Address for Graduates of a College of the Church of the Second Chance" (1992), repr. in Berkman and Cartwright, *Hauerwas Reader*, 311–12; Stanley Hauerwas, "Reconciling the Practice of Reason: Casuistry in a Christian Context," in *Christian Existence Today: Essays on Church, World, and Living in Between* (Durham, NC: Labyrinth, 1988), 67–87.

7. Hauerwas, "Whose Church? Which Future?" 67.

8. This is one way to summarize a major theme running through the whole of Hauerwas's *Peaceable Kingdom*, but see esp. chaps. 4 through 6. Also see Hauerwas, "Whose Church? Which Future?" 67, where he wrote: "I am often accused of romanticizing both Catholicism and Anabaptist, and no doubt that is a danger. But the reason I am so attracted to those traditions is that they have managed to keep some practices in place that provide resources for resistance against the loss of Christian presence in modernity. For that is the heart of the matter—namely practices."

9. While recognizing that it is an affront to the gospel whenever a church reproduces ethnic divisions ("Whose Church? Which Future?" 71), Hauerwas also chided Mennonites in the same essay for being too embarrassed about their ethnic identity: "[Today's] Anabaptists are embarrassed about their ethnicity, but it may be that 'ethnicity' is one way God provided and continues to provide for your survival as a people capable of remembering the martyrs that have made you what you are. [Harold S.] Bender rightly understood that historiography is a theological enterprise, but discipleship, the voluntary nature of church membership, and nonresistance must be embedded in a thicker history if they are to continue to provide us with the skills of Christian faithfulness" (73).

10. Hauerwas and Wells, "How the Church Managed before There Was Ethics," 48. John Courtney Murray, SJ, a thinker with a quite different view of the role of the church in American society, concurred in a way with Hauerwas's characterization of modernity when he wrote: "My generalization will be that the political experiment of modernity has essentially consisted in an effort to find and install in the world a secular substitute for all that the Christian tradition has meant by the pregnant phrase, the 'freedom of the Church'" (*We Hold These Truths: Catholic Reflections on the American Proposition* [New York: Sheed & Ward, 1960], 201). The difference is that Hauerwas has been more concerned about sustaining specifically Christian ecclesial practices, while Murray was more concerned about sustaining a Christian foundation for American civilization, which Hauerwas counts as a dubious proposition.

11. Occasionally one finds a scholar objecting that "modernity" is a concept *so* vast that it lacks all precision and defines almost nothing. Yet just because water covers three-fourths of the earth's surface, and a vessel without map or rudder might float on it for months or decades without seeing anything else, that hardly means that there is no difference between floating at sea and standing on land—or even canoeing a river.

12. Dennis D. Martin, "Nothing New under the Sun? Mennonites and History," *Conrad Grebel Review* 5, no. 1 (Winter 1987): 2. Also see Russell R. Reno, *In the Ruins of the Church: Sustaining Faith in an Age of Diminished Christianity* (Grand Rapids: Brazos,

2002), 15–26, where Reno found surprising commonality in the Enlightenment philosopher René Descartes and the Anglican-priest-turned-dispensationalist John Nelson Darby; their shared "strategy of separation" in search of conceptual or ecclesial purity in the face of the corruptions of the age "typifies the modern project" (17).

13. Troeltsch, *Social Teaching*, 1010–12.

14. Robert N. Bellah, *The Broken Covenant: American Civil Religion in a Time of Trial*, The Weil Lectures 1971 (New York: Seabury, 1975), 143. For critiques (which I share) of Bellah's ongoing attempt to find a remedy for this situation in American civil religion, see Hauerwas, "Why *Resident Aliens* Struck a Chord," 55–56; Stanley Hauerwas, "A Christian Critique of Christian America" (1986), repr. in Berkman and Cartwright, *Hauerwas Reader*, 459–80.

15. Still other dimensions of modernity that philosophers and theologians see behind the *sociology* of modernity are a certain kind of trust in reason, and the assumed universality of that reason. See, for example, Murray, *We Hold These Truths*, 200; Alasdair MacIntyre, *After Virtue: A Study in Moral Theory*, 2nd ed. (Notre Dame, IN: University of Notre Dame Press, 1984), 327; MacIntyre, *Whose Justice? Which Rationality?* 385–87.

16. Both among emerging Mennonite academics and among the sophisticated folk sociologists in the leadership of Anabaptist-Mennonite groups that have shunned higher education, anxieties and analyses of modernity could be found in almost any group and decade of at least the last century. Suffice then to note the subtitle of a major historical study of Mennonites in twentieth-century America by Paul Toews: *Mennonites in American Society, 1930–1970: Modernity and the Persistence of Religious Community*, vol. 4 of *The Mennonite Experience in America* (Scottdale, PA: Herald, 1996).

17. Findings have been compiled and interpreted in J. Howard Kauffman and Leland Harder, *Anabaptists Four Centuries Later: A Profile of Five Mennonite and Brethren in Christ Denominations* (Scottdale, PA: Herald, 1975); J. Howard Kauffman and Leo Driedger, *The Mennonite Mosaic: Identity and Modernization*, foreword by Donald B. Kraybill (Scottdale, PA: Herald, 1991). I have made greatest use of the latter, but it sometimes makes comparisons with the former.

In 2006 a similar survey was conducted, with results published the following year in Conrad L. Kanagy, *Road Signs for the Journey: A Profile of Mennonite Church USA* (Scottdale, PA: Herald, 2007). The 2007 book does not readily or consistently allow for longitudinal comparison, however. One legitimate reason may be that denominational restructuring prevents comparison with exactly the same demographic population as in the previous studies. A more difficult reason is that Kanagy has presented survey findings with a greater overlay of theological editorializing. Observe, however, that neither the 2006 survey data nor the lessons that Kanagy has drawn from that data suggest a more optimistic reading of trends than those I have drawn from the 1972 and 1989 data. Kanagy (25) framed his interpretations, after all, with an early comparison of the North American church with the Laodicean church that is the object of the biblical seer's warning in Rev. 3, and with a running comparison with the prophetic warnings of Jeremiah.

18. Kauffman and Driedger, *Mennonite Mosaic*, 82; cf. 71.

19. Kauffman and Driedger, *Mennonite Mosaic*, 99.

20. Kauffman and Driedger, *Mennonite Mosaic*, 83.

21. Kauffman and Driedger, *Mennonite Mosaic*, 182, 241.

22. Kauffman and Driedger, *Mennonite Mosaic*, 83–84.

23. Kauffman and Driedger, *Mennonite Mosaic*, 83, 182, 241.

24. Kauffman and Driedger, *Mennonite Mosaic*, 46, 84, 254–56.

25. Kauffman and Driedger, *Mennonite Mosaic*, 208–9.

26. Kauffman and Driedger, *Mennonite Mosaic*, 209, 253–56. Cf. Robert Wuthnow, *The Restructuring of American Religion: Society and Faith since World War II* (Princeton, NJ: Princeton University Press, 1988).

27. Kauffman and Driedger, *Mennonite Mosaic*, 124.

28. Kauffman and Driedger, *Mennonite Mosaic*, 99.

29. So warned another leading Mennonite sociologist, Donald Kraybill, at a preliminary conference on the 1989 survey (Leo Driedger and Leland Harder, *Anabaptist-Mennonite Identities in Ferment* [Elkhart, IN: Institute of Mennonite Studies, 1990], 113). Kauffman and Driedger acknowledged that the transformation of Mennonites' sense of peoplehood was "still very much in the testing stages" (*Mennonite Mosaic*, 163).

30. One indicator of things to come might have been that even though Mennonite youth were no more individualistic, materialistic, or secular than their elders, their sense of ethnic identity and their commitment to traditional moral codes was less than their grandparents. See Kauffman and Driedger, *Mennonite Mosaic*, 269–70.

31. Commenting on an early draft of this chapter, Mark Thiessen Nation of Eastern Mennonite Seminary wrote:

> It is my impression that the "acids of modernity/postmodernity" have been eating away quickly at the fabric of Mennonite life since those surveys [of 1972 and 1989] were conducted. I see huge evidence of that among the Mennos I encounter. . . . My impressions: many of the less educated and sophisticated Mennos are rather unreflective Evangelical Christians totally but unknowingly sucked in by the peculiar forms of modernity within that subculture; many of the urbane, educated Mennos are quickly becoming unreflective, unrepentant liberal Protestant Christians. These are gross generalizations. There are traditions still somewhat alive that challenge some of this—on both fronts. But such generalizations seem to have too much truth. (Personal correspondence, January 1, 2005)

32. Kauffman and Driedger, *Mennonite Mosaic*, 95–96.

33. Kauffman and Driedger, *Mennonite Mosaic*, 100–101. Taken alone, an inverse relationship between secularization and religious commitment is probably a truism.

34. Kauffman and Driedger, *Mennonite Mosaic*, 162, 183–84. Kauffman and Driedger refer to this as "in-group identity," "in-group identification and solidarity," a "sense of peoplehood," and "communalism."

35. Kauffman and Driedger, *Mennonite Mosaic*, 271. Driedger has also argued more recently that some forms of individualism may express themselves in the kind of creativity and initiative that leads people to take responsibility for their community and engage in community-building activities. See Leo Driedger, *Mennonites in the Global Village* (Toronto and Buffalo: University of Toronto Press, 2000), 68.

36. Kauffman and Driedger, *Mennonite Mosaic*, 100.

37. Here I am reminded of the warnings of ecological disaster from pesticide use in the groundbreaking book by Rachel Carson, *Silent Spring* (Boston: Houghton Mifflin, 1962). Critics of the environmental movement have sometimes used the fact that its most dire predictions did not come to pass as evidence that we need not be so apparently alarmist about current dangers, such as global warming. But Carson's worst predictions were actually allayed precisely because publics and governments took her warnings seriously and began to outlaw at least the most dangerous pesticides, such as DDT.

38. This is my own interpretation, as an alumnus of Goshen College and the son of a faculty member. But also see Susan Fisher Miller, *Culture for Service: A History of Goshen College, 1894–1994* (Goshen, IN: Goshen College, 1994), 1–3, 44–45.

39. Harold S. Bender, "The Anabaptist Vision," *Church History* 13 (March 1944): 3–24; "The Anabaptist Vision," *Mennonite Quarterly Review* 18 (April 1944): 67–88. In later footnotes, however, I will be citing the article's pagination as it appeared in Bender's Festschrift: Hershberger, *Recovery of the Anabaptist Vision*, 29–54.

40. John Howard Yoder once characterized Bender's vision this way: "For Bender's generation the retrieval of his particular vision of the Swiss Brethren origins was not disinterested historiography; it was a weapon in the struggle for Mennonite identity in the face of the mid-century challenges of urbanization, acculturation, and global war." John Howard Yoder, "Historiography as a Ministry to Renewal," *Brethren Life and Thought* 42 (Summer–Fall 1997): 218.

41. Complementing my own account of the Mennonite intellectual debate that centered in Goshen at midcentury are the following: Paul Toews, "The Concern Movement: Its Origins and Early History," *Conrad Grebel Review* 8, no. 2 (Spring 1990): 109–26; Steven M. Nolt, "Anabaptist Visions of Church and Society," *Mennonite Quarterly Review* 69 (July 1995): 283–94.

42. The Amish will come to mind for most readers, along with the Hutterites for a few more. But I mean this strategy to be broad enough to include other "Old Order" groups who are Mennonite rather than Amish, as well as the kinds of communities in Western Canada and elsewhere that had literally transplanted entire Mennonite villages from Ukraine and Russia in the 1870s and afterward. On the former, see Theron F. Schlabach, "Keeping the Old Order," chap. 8 in *Peace, Faith, Nation: Mennonites and Amish in Nineteenth-Century America*, vol. 2 of *The Mennonite Experience in America* (Scottdale, PA: Herald, 1988), 201–28. On the latter, note that Leo Driedger dedicated chap. 4 to what he called "the Sacred Village" in order to provide a kind of sociological baseline for his contemporary (2000) study of *Mennonites in the Global Village*.

43. Again, I mean this category to be broad enough to include efforts to find a niche among both early twentieth-century fundamentalists and modernists, and later among both evangelical and liberal Protestants. All the defining differences here are important, yet they share the same basic strategy and differ mainly around which conception of the mainstream seemed most important to catch up with and join.

44. I am grateful to Alan Kreider, longtime Mennonite mission worker in Great Britain, now teaching at the Associated Mennonite Biblical Seminary (AMBS) in Elkhart, Indiana, who reminded me of this possible fifth strategy after reading an earlier version of this chapter. Kreider pointed out that mission, both as missionary and as service activity, was "vitally important in Goshen in the 1950s, and animated some of its most gifted people. . . . I suspect that in the Goshen dorms in the 1950s there was intellectual buzz about mission, [which] . . . didn't last forever but left a genuinely important legacy."

The leading exemplar and advocate for the strategy of mission was J. D. Graber, who had served with his wife, Minnie Swartzendruber Graber, in India and later headed his denomination's mission agency. The strategy attracted people like David Shank, one of the original Concern Group members; as well as brothers Ralph and Albert Buckwalter, who served in Japan and Argentina, respectively; John Driver, who has greatly influenced Anabaptist thought throughout the Spanish-speaking world; and Wilbert Shenk, who later became the leading Mennonite missiologist. Throughout the 1960s the strategy would continue to inspire future leaders such as Marlin E. Miller, theologian and president of AMBS; his brother Larry Miller, executive secretary of Mennonite World Conference; and Alan Kreider, together with his wife, Eleanor Graber Kreider.

To be sure, the mission strategy drew insight from the other strategies: indeed, not only did David Shank of the Concern Group play a role in both movements, but so did John

Howard Yoder. Yoder was employed for a time by the Mennonite Board of Missions as an adviser to J. D. Graber, was involved in discussions leading to Mennonite involvement in providing Bible teaching for African Initiated Churches (AICs), and is now being studied by missiologists as a missiological thinker of significance.

Nonetheless, the mission strategy had its own understanding and its own sense that the church is renewed not by going back but by reaching out according to the slogan "Every church a mission outpost," whether into Japan or Belgium or Nigeria or across town. The formative articulation of its vision was J. D. Graber's *The Church Apostolic: A Discussion of Modern Missions* (Scottdale, PA: Herald, 1960). Its effect was to help move the Mennonite world away from Harold S. Bender's North Atlantic axis to a genuinely worldwide church.

45. Theron F. Schlabach, "To Focus a Mennonite Vision," in *Kingdom, Cross, and Community: Essays on Mennonite Themes in Honor of Guy F. Hershberger*, ed. John Richard Burkholder and Calvin Redekop (Scottdale, PA: Herald, 1976), 23–24.

46. See esp. Reinhold Niebuhr, "Why the Christian Church Is Not Pacifist," in *Christianity and Power Politics* (New York: Charles Scribner's Sons, 1940), 1–32.

47. For a new biography of Hershberger, see Theron F. Schlabach, *War, Peace, and Social Conscience: Guy F. Hershberger and Mennonite Ethics* (Scottdale, PA: Herald, 2009). For a chapter-length biography, see T. Schlabach, "To Focus a Mennonite Vision," 15–50.

48. Mennonites of the first half of the twentieth century objected to participation in labor unions for at least two reasons. The most often stated reason was that labor action relied on coercive tactics at best and violent ones in extreme cases; Mennonites intuited and thinkers such as Hershberger explicated that even nonviolent coercion fell short of nonresistant Christlike love. In addition, labor unions could easily constitute a social group that would compete with the local congregation for a member's primary loyalty; for this reason they also objected to fraternal organizations such as Moose Lodge, Elks Club, or Rotary Club.

49. T. Schlabach, "To Focus a Mennonite Vision," 29–30, 32–33.

50. Guy F. Hershberger, *War, Peace, and Nonresistance*, 3d ed., Christian Peace Shelf Selection (Scottdale, Pa.: Herald, 1969). Until John Howard Yoder's work began to become prominent, mainstream Protestant ethicists who wished to cite a representative of the Mennonite peace position would site this book by Hershberger; see Reinhold Niebuhr, "Why the Christian Church Is Not Pacifist," 4–5, 30–31; John C. Bennett, *Christian Ethics and Social Policy*, The Richard Lectures in the University of Virginia (New York: Charles Scribner's Sons, 1946), 41–46.

51. Nolt ("Anabaptist Visions," 286) summarized the movement's "fundamentally distinctive" approach to social ethics this way:

> The movement's method began with the affirmation that social ethics grow out of particular social settings and community patterns and that those particular settings must be the starting point for active Christian witness. Normative standards of scripture cannot be applied or understood theoretically apart from concrete human situations. Specific Mennonite communities, therefore, possessed ethical resources which were not only theological but also social and relational. As such, they offered not so much havens of withdrawal from the world but viable, valuable contexts in which to think ethically and to apply social justice principles in order to gain experience for subsequent engagement with surrounding society.

52. Nolt ("Anabaptist Visions," 293) asked: "In light of some present Mennonite misgivings about the ahistorical and perfectionist irrelevance of the Anabaptist vision, and amid stirring among some Mennonites for a new communitarian approach to social ethics, might the Mennonite Community movement [sic] deserve a second look—not because the Community vision offered the right answers (often its answers were far too rurally oriented),

but because it was beginning to ask the right questions and to employ helpful historical and contextual methods?"

53. Albert N. Keim, *Harold S. Bender, 1897–1962* (Scottdale, PA: Herald, 1998), 13.

54. Against a range of other views of the Anabaptists, Bender ("Anabaptist Vision," 37; cf. 41) wrote: "There is another line of interpretation which is being increasingly accepted and which is probably destined to dominate the field. It is the one which holds that Anabaptism is the culmination of the Reformation, the fulfillment of the original vision of Luther and Zwingli, and thus makes it a consistent evangelical Protestantism seeking to re-create without compromise the original New Testament church, the vision of Christ and the Apostles." Note the historiographic claim, but also the way that such a portrayal might serve to buttress Mennonite self-respect.

55. H. Richard Niebuhr expressed something of this approach in the opening pages of his book *Christ and Culture*, Harper Torchbooks/Cloister Library (New York: Harper & Row, 1956): "The belief which lies back of this effort . . . is the conviction that Christ as living Lord is answering the question in the totality of history and life in a fashion which transcends the wisdom of all his interpreters yet employs their partial insights and their necessary conflicts." This was with reference to the various "types" of Christian involvement in the world that Niebuhr was to lay out. With regard to denominations per se, see H. Richard Niebuhr, *The Purpose of the Church and Its Ministry: Reflections on the Aims of Theological Education*, in collaboration with Daniel Day Williams and James M. Gustafson (New York: Harper & Row, 1956), 16–17. John Howard Yoder ("Anabaptist Dissent," 57) recognized this developing understanding of denominationalism by implicitly protesting it near the very start of his career, in the early 1950s: "The Anabaptist-Mennonite tradition, theologically understood, is seen to represent not simply a branch of Protestantism with a particular 'talent,' but [also] a historical incarnation of an entirely different view of the Christian life, of the work and nature of the church, and fundamentally also of the meaning of redemption."

56. While clearly uncomfortable with crassly nationalistic answers to Protestant uncertainty about the whole of which denominations are a part, H. Richard Niebuhr gave unmistakable evidence of that uncertainty in *The Purpose of the Church and Its Ministry*, 5–17, in a subsection titled "Denomination, Nation or Church?"

57. Keim, *Harold S. Bender*, 354–55.

58. Bender, "Anabaptist Vision," 42. Later, for his transition from his elaboration of point 1 to point 2, Bender wrote: "As a second major element in the Anabaptist vision, a new concept of the church was created *by the central principle* of newness of life and applied Christianity," aka discipleship (47).

59. Bender, "Anabaptist Vision," 30–31.

60. Bender, "Anabaptist Vision," 31.

61. Gerald Mast also noted a tendency toward abstraction in Bender's "Anabaptist Vision," held in tension with an attempt to name essences that were actually concrete practices rather than purely formal categories. See Gerald Biesecker-Mast, *Separation and the Sword in Anabaptist Persuasion: Radical Confessional Rhetoric from Schleitheim to Dordrecht*, The C. Henry Smith Series 6 (Telford, PA: Cascadia; Scottdale, PA: Herald, 2006), 48–50.

62. Bender, "Anabaptist Vision," 43, but also see 44–46.

63. Bender, "Anabaptist Vision," 42.

64. The "practice of true brotherhood and love among members of the church" was a "principle" that should not express itself merely as "pious sentiments, but in the actual practice of sharing possessions to meet the needs of others." Bender, "Anabaptist Vision," 49.

65. Keim, *Harold S. Bender*, 310, 314.

66. In that sense, Bender was preparing the way for the Concern Movement of younger Mennonites influenced by Bender, who sought to break even more radically with ethnic and institutional ways of sustaining Mennonite community, as we will shortly see. One may also recognize a telling use of the language of "essence," for example, in Paul Peachey, "What Is Concern?" *Concern: A Pamphlet Series* 4 (June 1957): 18 (calling for an "inner recovery of essence"); and Peachey, "Spirit and Form in the Church," *Concern: A Pamphlet Series* 2 (1955): 16, contrasting the New Testament's realization of the "spiritual essence of the people of God" with Jewish traditionalism, but no doubt using the latter as a foil for ethnic Mennonite traditionalism. Steven Nolt also saw an increasing tendency to abstraction as one moves from Hershberger to Bender to the Concern Group; see Nolt, "Anabaptist Visions," 289–93.

67. Irvin B. Horst, John W. Miller, Paul Peachey, Calvin Redekop, David A. Shank, A. Orley Swartzentruber, and John Howard Yoder.

68. The terms here come from the title of an essay that John Howard Yoder wrote a decade and a half later: "Anabaptist Vision and Mennonite Reality," in *Consultation on Anabaptist-Mennonite Theology: Papers Read at the 1969 Aspen Conference*, ed. A. J. Klassen (Fresno, CA: Council of Mennonite Seminaries, 1970). From the beginning, however, the Concern Movement had been all about the strategy of critically examining Mennonite reality in the harsh light of the "Anabaptist Vision." The 1969 essay actually seems to have a strong genealogical link to an acerbic memo that Yoder first drafted near the end of the Amsterdam meeting of 1952, sent to Bender with devastating effect, and circulated in various drafts among the Mennonite Church intelligentsia in the following years: "Reflections on the Irrelevance of Certain Slogans to the Historical Movements They Represent. Or, the Cooking of the Anabaptist Goose[.] Or, Ye Garnish the Sepulchres of the Righteous," Historical mss. 1–48, box 6, file 1, John H. Yoder Collection, Mennonite Church USA Archives, Goshen, IN (1952).

69. Nomenclature is not standard, but when I refer to the Concern *Group*, I mean the original seven men who met in Amsterdam in 1952 (see n. 67, above). When I refer to the Concern *Movement*, I mean the larger group of friends, peers, and correspondents who contributed to *Concern* pamphlets in the following years.

70. P[aul] P[eachey], "Preface," *Concern: A Pamphlet Series* 2 (1955): 3, with original emphasis.

71. See Peachey, "What Is Concern?" 14. "What led to the 'Concern' conversations," wrote Peachey, was a certain disillusionment with the attempt to revive ethnic Mennonitism by means of a strong denominational and academic program." This not only failed to halt Mennonite acculturation but also confirmed it. The Concern Group, therefore, was not simply criticizing the gap in performance that is inevitable when measured against ideals, but was also criticizing the way that an "ethnic plus denominational . . . Mennonitism" had actually widened that gap.

72. Here they were certainly in continuity with Bender. But with a radicalized form of his vision, they were also seeing more radical precedents in the sixteenth and first centuries.

73. Proposed answers varied: *Yes* in the technical sense, by which they believed that authentic Christian communities must always stand over against the violence-rooted ways of a fallen world (Yoder, "Anabaptist Dissent"). *Probably*, insofar as this posture also forced the Anabaptists to break with established churches ("Epistolary: An Exchange by Letter," *Concern: A Pamphlet Series* 4 [June 1957]: 9, 12–13). *No*, in that they did not want to provoke a fresh schism in their own church (Peachey, "What Is Concern?" 14). And *no*, in their desire to release themselves from parochial home communities and take their faith into robust engagement with the challenges of their age (Toews, *Mennonites in American*

Society, 235, with hints of what Toews calls their rejection of "sociological sectarianism" in "Epistolary," 7, 10).

74. Paul Peachey, "Toward an Understanding of the Decline of the West," *Concern: A Pamphlet Series* 1 (June 1954): 8–44.

75. Toews, *Mennonites in American Society*, 232.

76. Yoder, "Anabaptist Dissent," 48.

77. Toews, "The Concern Movement," 123. Whether out of embarrassment, convenience, lack of information, or common sense, Mennonite intellectuals of later decades, under the influence of the Concern Movement, have generally ignored this part of the Concern program. The critique of Mennonite parochial schools appeared more often in the Concern Group's personal correspondence than in their published writings. I am thus indebted to the unpublished senior seminar paper of one of my peers at Goshen College in the 1970s; see Ronald S. Kraybill, "The 'Concern' Group: An Attempt at Anabaptist Renewal," History Seminar paper, Mennonite Historical Library, Goshen College (Goshen, IN, 1976), 20–21. Nothing hints more clearly, however, that attitudes toward parochial schools mark a fundamental divide than this: Guy F. Hershberger apparently picked up on the significance of the point immediately. The decision-making process that had led to Mennonite church schools in recent decades, in keeping with the Mennonite Community Movement, was something he immediately sought to clarify and defend. See "Epistolary," 10–11.

78. John W. Miller, "Organization and Church," *Concern: A Pamphlet Series* 4 (June 1957): 35.

79. C. Norman Kraus and John W. Miller, "Intimations of Another Way—a Progress Report," *Concern: A Pamphlet Series* 3 (1956): 7–11.

80. Kraus and J. Miller, "Intimations of Another Way," 12–17, quoting from 17. Toews has summarized Concern Movement advocacy of house churches and small groups within established congregations, which appeared especially in the 1956 issue of *Concern*: These would be "a place to recapture something of the fellowship, intimacy, empowerment, visibility, and purity of the New Testament ideal." Toews, "The Concern Movement," 120.

81. "Epistolary," 9. Though this remark by J. Miller is drawn from personal but published correspondence, when Miller elaborated on his ecclesiology in a paper that pointedly contrasted "church" with "organization," he closed by pressing the same perspective in a less offhanded way:

> The point must never be lost that the decision to stake one's lot with the people of God in the assembly of the "two and three" is still the most important thing that anyone can do. Here is the place where the real cause of Christ is represented and the work of God done. Here is the place where the concept of "full-time commitment to the work of the Church" should find its truest expression. Where this sense of the importance of the congregational gathering becomes alive the various organizational programs of the Church will probably of themselves assume their true significance. (J. Miller, "Organization and Church," 41)

In this article J. Miller had marked the Mennonite drive toward denominational organization off to assimilation into the culture of an American or Western culture that did more and more of its work through the "organizational revolution" of proliferating voluntary associations. What is ironic is that J. Miller betrayed an assimilationist tendency of another kind, into another wing of mainstream culture—a bohemian romanticism that found its way through a troubled century by seeking solace in an existentialist drive for authenticity.

82. "Introduction," *Concern: A Pamphlet Series* 1 (June 1954): 5–6. There were other oppositions in the series here. Standing over against "our own compromised life and at-

home-ness in the world" was "the more complete discipleship of the early Christians coupled with a fervent expectancy of the *parousia*" (Christ's soon appearing). Over against "world conformity within church life conterminous [*sic*] with society" was "the validity of the Anabaptist dissent and 'exodus.'" Though this dichotomous formulation and the entire pamphlet introduction bears the marks of Peachey's authorship, the piece is unattributed and must be assumed to speak for all seven participants in the original Concern Group. Yoder made exactly this dichotomy between denominational "machinery" and the "pneumatic" character of the church proper in "Epistolary," 7.

83. I had the privilege of presenting an early draft of this chapter in a seminar at Eastern Mennonite University (Harrisonburg, VA) in April 2006. Present were two members of the original Concern Group, Peachey and Calvin Redekop. With Peachey nodding graciously, Redekop commented that these issues were continual matters for lively debate among the Amsterdam seven, and that Peachey represented an anti-institutional view that was on the far end of their continuum of positions. Yoder, Redekop said, stood somewhere in the middle.

84. See John Howard Yoder, "What Are Our Concerns?" *Concern: A Pamphlet Series* 4 (June 1957): 23–24, 29.

85. "Epistolary," 7.

86. Though the following paragraphs trace the nuances of Yoder's later thought on tradition, dissent, and "continuity," the reader who knows Yoder's mature arguments about nonviolence, the "politics of Jesus," Constantinianism, counter-Niebuhrian notions of social responsibility, eschatology, and so on—this reader will recognize the contours of his mature thought and career already taking marked shape in this essay. Mark Thiessen Nation, a leading interpreter of Yoder's thought, concurred in finding an "amazing consistency" in Yoder from beginning to end of his theological career. See Mark Thiessen Nation, *John Howard Yoder: Mennonite Patience, Evangelical Witness, Catholic Convictions* (Grand Rapids: Eerdmans, 2006), 75, as well as 77–78, 189, 197.

87. John H[oward] Yoder, "The Hermeneutics of Peoplehood: A Protestant Perspective on Practical Moral Reasoning," *Journal of Religious Ethics* 10–11 (1982–83): 52–53, with emphasis added. Also note the allusion to this same text in John Howard Yoder, "To Serve Our God and to Rule the World," in *The Royal Priesthood: Essays Ecclesiological and Ecumenical*, ed. and intro. Michael G. Cartwright, foreword by Richard J. Mouw (Grand Rapids: Eerdmans, 1994), 139–40.

88. John Howard Yoder, "Is There Historical Development of Theological Thought?" in *The Witness of the Holy Spirit: Proceedings of the Eighth Mennonite World Confer-ence, Amsterdam, The Netherlands, July 23–30, 1967*, ed. Cornelius J. Dyck (Elkhart, IN: Mennonite World Conference, 1967), 379–88; Yoder, "The Authority of Tradition," in *The Priestly Kingdom: Social Ethics as Gospel* (Notre Dame, IN: University of Notre Dame Press, 1984), 70; Yoder, "The Kingdom as Social Ethic," in *The Priestly Kingdom*, 86; Yoder, *Body Politics: Five Practices of the Christian Community before the Watching World* (Nashville: Discipleship Resources, 1992), 10, 59.

89. Yoder, "Is There Historical Development?" 384–85; also Yoder, "A People in the World," in *The Royal Priesthood*, 68–73.

90. John Howard Yoder, "That Household We Are," keynote address, conference on "Is There a Believers' Church Christology?" (Bluffton College, Bluffton, OH, 1980), 1.

91. John H. Yoder, "The Free Church Syndrome," in *Within the Perfection of Christ: Essays on Peace and the Nature of the Church; In Honor of Martin H. Schrag*, ed. Terry L. Brensinger and E. Morris Sider (Nappanee, IN: Evangel; Grantham, PA: Brethren in Christ Historical Society, 1990), 174, with original emphasis.

92. Yoder, "The Free Church Syndrome," 175.

93. Yoder, "Is There Historical Development?" 388–89. After a series of nine concluding theses, which all revolved around the congregation, Yoder concluded the essay with the following paragraph:

> Thus the promise of the Spirit to lead the Church "into all truth" has led us to examine not faith or order, doctrine or organization, in their own right, but rather to seek their rootage and their legitimation in the reality of the believing, forgiving congregation. It is because that Spirit is a permanent Presence in the church that bishops and synods, creeds and councils may be used of God; it is because the congregation is the locus of that presence that no creed or council, synod or bishop may stand in judgment over the congregation as in each age and in each place men gather around the Bible and confess that Jesus Christ is Lord.

94. Yoder, *Body Politics*. For skepticism of tradition as succession or priesthood, see 51, 55, 60. For skepticism of classical understandings of sacrament, see 1, 15, 21, 44, 72. In some of these instances, Yoder was reporting the view of free-church Protestants who associate the term "sacrament" with superstitious, mechanical, or magical workings of grace—and in other instances (3, 33, 71) he criticized Protestant theologies that would disallow any mediation of grace through the Christian community—but never did Yoder distance himself at all from Protestant assumptions that classical sacramentalism is quasi-magical and thus unworthy of consideration. The sacramentality that Yoder affirmed, wherein God is fully present in the distinctive yet public practices of the Christian community, certainly contributed important insights toward ecumenical understandings of the sacraments. And as an exercise in demonstrating how, as the subtitle puts it, "five practices of the Christian community" prove to be accessible public models "for a watching world," the book is quite successful. Still, any effort to translate Christian convictions into empirically verifiable and religiously neutral language must risk reductionism, and it is not always clear that Yoder avoided a merely functionalist view of the Christian sacraments. Mark Thiessen Nation, though generally a vigorous advocate for Yoder's thought, has agreed that Yoder is at least vulnerable to this critique; see Nation, *John Howard Yoder*, 197.

95. Yoder, "The Authority of Tradition," 69.

96. Yoder, "The Authority of Tradition," 69–70. Cf. Vigen Guroian, "Tradition and Ethics: Prospects in a Liberal Society," *Modern Theology* 7, no. 3 (April 1991): 217–18.

97. As Yoder ("The Authority of Tradition," 69–70) explained:

> This renewed appeal to origins is not primitivism, nor an effort to recapture some pristine purity. It is rather a "looping back," a glance over the shoulder to enable a midcourse correction, a rediscovery of something from the past whose pertinence was not seen before, because only a new question or challenge enables us to see it speaking to us. To stay with the vinedresser's image, the effect of pruning is not to harm the vine, but to provoke new growth out of the old wood nearer to the ground, to decrease the loss of food and time along the sap's path from roots to fruit, and to make the grapes easier to pick. *Ecclesia reformata semper reformanda* is not really a statement about the church. It is a statement about the earlier tradition's permanent accessibility, as witnessed to and normed by Scripture at its nucleus, but always including more dimensions than the Bible itself contains, functioning as an instance of appeal as we call for renewed faithfulness and denounce renewed apostasy.

98. Yoder began his important essay "The Hermeneutics of Peoplehood" (40–41) by making an explicit cross-reference to Tillich's Protestant Principle. Cf. *The Priestly Kingdom*, 15.

229

99. John Howard Yoder, "The Burden and the Discipline of Evangelical Revisionism," in *Nonviolent America: History through the Eyes of Peace*, ed. Louise Hawkley and James C. Juhnke, Cornelius H. Wedel Historical Series 5 (North Newton, KS: Bethel College, 1993), 22.

100. Yoder, "The Authority of Tradition," 79. I have already cited Yoder's faithful-tradition-as-vine metaphor from 69–70 of this essay; another much improved version of the Protestant Principle appears on 67. Still another example is John Howard Yoder, "Discerning the Kingdom of God in the Struggles of the World," in *For the Nations: Essays Public and Evangelical* (Grand Rapids: Eerdmans, 1997), 237–45; the essay contrasts sharply with any kind of romantic Tillichian bias toward social movements outside the church.

101. Yoder, *The Priestly Kingdom*, 3.

102. John Howard Yoder, "Methodological Miscellany #2: Have You Ever Seen a True Church?" Historical mss. 1–48, box 187, section: ethics, 1938–1997, John H. Yoder Collection, Mennonite Church USA Archives, Goshen, IN (1988). I am most grateful to Mark Thiessen Nation of Eastern Mennonite Seminary for pointing out this document to me.

103. Yoder, "Methodological Miscellany #2: Have You Ever Seen a True Church?" 4. Yoder's main point was that later disappointment does not refute a founding or renewing vision. Still, there is more circumspection in the following paragraph:

If the renewal vision is confirmed as real because renewal happens, but then it is lost in the second or the fourth [*sic*] generation, does that not prove it false after all? It may prove that the vision which triggers initial steps of renewal is not sufficient to face other questions of renewal. This I should insist on strongly. Yet to measure the second generation and third . . . by the idealism of the first generation is not a fair test either of the community or of the ideal, precisely because the situation of later generations poses new questions which are not automatically either answered or set aside by appealing to the truth of the earlier right answers.

Though these remarks are part of a larger argument, they seem to cast a retrospective judgment (probably unintentional) on the ways the early Concern Group had measured a later generation of Mennonites against first-generation Anabaptists. The younger Yoder had been little short of snide when he circulated the conclusions of the first Concern Group meeting in Amsterdam 1952 in his unpublished memo, "The Cooking of the Anabaptist Goose." Some of that same tone remained in the 1969 essay "Anabaptist Vision and Mennonite Reality."

104. Yoder, "Methodological Miscellany #2: Have You Ever Seen a True Church?" 3.

105. Yoder, "Historiography as a Ministry to Renewal," 219. Interestingly, here and elsewhere Yoder's purpose was to counter a certain free-church or believers-church impulse to trace an alternative underground line of unbroken apostolic succession of faithful dissenters who have remained faithful to the gospel. Believers churches, by the very nature of their ecclesiological case, need not compete to authenticate themselves in this way, he argued. Also see John Howard Yoder, "Anabaptism and History," in *The Priestly Kingdom*, 133–34.

106. Paul Peachey, "The Modern Recovery of the Anabaptist Vision," in Hershberger, *Recovery of the Anabaptist Vision*, 332.

107. Toews, "The Concern Movement," 119–21; Nolt, "Anabaptist Visions," 287.

108. "Epistolary," 11; John Howard Yoder, "The Recovery of the Anabaptist Vision," in *Radical Reformation Reader*, issued as *Concern: A Pamphlet Series* 18 (Scottdale, PA: [n.p.], 1971), 22.

109. "Epistolary," 9–12. At various points on these pages, participants in the Concern conversation returned to the concept of historical Pietists, that of *ecclesiola in ecclesiam*,

or small church cells within an established church. They apparently recognized affinities to what they were doing and proposing but were not satisfied with Pietist ecclesiology.

110. For both points, see Peachey, "What Is Concern?" 14.

111. Keim, *Harold S. Bender*, 469; John W. Miller, "Concern Reflections," *Conrad Grebel Review* 8, no. 2 (Spring 1990): 141, 144–45, 148.

112. Two expressions of this work are readily accessible: Yoder, "The Hermeneutics of Peoplehood"; and John Howard Yoder, "Binding and Loosing," in Cartwright, *The Royal Priesthood*, 323–58.

113. It also is worth remembering what we noted in chap. 1, in the section on "The Puzzle of Protestant Identity": congregationalism can just as easily support racial segregationism as the liberation of a long-oppressed minority.

114. Table 3-3 in Kauffman and Driedger, *Mennonite Mosaic*, 71, lists the following survey items as indicative of Anabaptist convictions: "Baptism is unnecessary for infants and children." "Should follow the lordship of Christ even if persecuted." "Church discipline is necessary for the unfaithful." "Christians should take no part in war." "Christians cannot perform in some government offices." "It is against God's will to swear civil oaths." "Must follow Jesus in evangelism and deeds of mercy." "Should not take a person to court even if justified."

115. Kauffman and Driedger, *Mennonite Mosaic*, 257.

116. Kauffman and Driedger, *Mennonite Mosaic*, 85.

117. Kauffman and Driedger, *Mennonite Mosaic*, 77.

118. Kauffman and Driedger, *Mennonite Mosaic*, 257.

119. All quotations to this point in the paragraph are from Kauffman and Driedger, *Mennonite Mosaic*, 271.

120. Kauffman and Driedger, *Mennonite Mosaic*, 263.

121. Yoder, "What Are Our Concerns?" 23–24, 21, 29.

122. John Howard Yoder, *The Fullness of Christ: Paul's Revolutionary Vision of Universal Ministry* (Elgin, IL: Brethren Press, 1987), 9–17, 46–47, 66.

123. Yoder, "What Are Our Concerns?" 23.

124. Yoder, "The Hermeneutics of Peoplehood," 48. This article also appears in *The Priestly Kingdom*, 15–45.

125. Yoder, "The Hermeneutics of Peoplehood," 48.

126. During the last two decades I have enjoyed close-enough friendships with at least a half dozen Mennonite pastors that they have all confided their frustrations at some point. None are power-hungry authoritarian personalities; all are deeply committed to congregational, consensus-building discernment processes. One pastor's frustration reached its peak when a church member objected not to *his* decision, but rather tried to veto a decision the congregation had reached after months of processing. This kind of pastoral experience surfaces at various places in John A. Esau, ed., *Understanding Ministerial Leadership*, foreword by Ross T. Bender, Text Reader Series 6 (Elkhart, IN: Institute of Mennonite Studies, 1995). Within this volume, see especially Esau, "Recovering, Rethinking, and Re-Imagining: Issues in a Mennonite Theology for Christian Ministry," 5, 12; Erick Sawatsky, "Helping Dreams Come True: Toward Wholeness—Articulating the Vision," 35; Marlin E. Miller, "Some Reflections on Pastoral Ministry and Pastoral Education," 58–59; George R. Brunk III, "The Credibility of Leadership," 117–19. Crucial for reassessing the claim that the notion of "the priesthood of all believers" as Mennonites were using it in the latter half of the twentieth century could claim New Testament or sixteenth-century precedents was Marlin E. Miller, "Priesthood of All Believers," in *Mennonite Encyclopedia*, vol. 5 (Scottdale, PA: Herald, 1990), 721.

127. Esau, "Recovering, Rethinking, and Re-Imagining," 5.

128. Marlin E. Miller, "The Recasting of Authority: A Biblical Model for Community Leadership," in *Theology for the Church*, ed. Richard A. Kauffman and Gayle Gerber Koontz (Elkhart, IN: Institute of Mennonite Studies, 1997), 109–10; Sawatsky, "Helping Dreams Come True," 32–35; Brunk, "The Credibility of Leadership," 117.

129. Sawatsky, "Helping Dreams Come True," 32, 35.

130. Esau, "Recovering, Rethinking, and Re-Imagining," 11.

131. De Senarclens, *Heirs of the Reformation*, 125; see chap. 1 (above), in the section "The Permanent Principle of Reform."

132. Peachy, "The Modern Recovery of the Anabaptist Vision," was part of a Festschrift for Harold S. Bender and thus more "polished" and scholarly than any of the *Concern* pamphlets. Heightening its importance is its placement as the climactic chapter of the volume. The whole book may well be the single most serious scholarly project that Concern Movement leaders ever took up (cf. Keim, *Harold S. Bender*, 450–51, 469–70), though they did so in collaboration with Guy F. Hershberger, the named editor. As an effort to honor and perhaps mend fences with Bender, Concern Group collaborators were surely paying attention to how they would communicate. Peachey's essay seems to be the place where, after more historical and less programmatic essays, Hershberger allowed or they allowed themselves the luxury of coming back into the present—"The Modern Recovery of the Anabaptist Vision"—cashing in on the capital they had built up through all the previous chapters, and offering an apologia for Concern agenda. Though the essay certainly bears the stamp of Peachey's own theological tendencies, his role as spokesman can hardly have been accidental, much less self-appointed.

133. Peachey, "The Modern Recovery of the Anabaptist Vision," 339. On the next and final page, Peachy summarized: "I would therefore propose that the genius of the Anabaptist vision lies not merely in the heroic act of men who dared to abandon the apostate *Volkskirche* culture inherited and developed by medieval Christendom, but above all in the reassertion that *the church is always truly the church in the living existential community*" (340; emphasis added). More work needs to be done on the influence of philosophical existentialism on the Concern Group and Movement. Existentialism was in its ascendancy after World War II, and young Mennonites in Europe were experiencing the climate that favored it most. One of the group's other teachers of Anabaptist history was Robert Friedmann, who would later argue explicitly that Anabaptist theology was existentialist; see Robert Friedmann, *The Theology of Anabaptism: An Interpretation*, Studies in Anabaptist and Mennonite History 15 (Scottdale, PA: Herald, 1973), and note his enthusiastic support for the Concern Movement in "Epistolary," 9–10. And yet explicit references to existentialism are rare, and so are hints that the Concern Group was reading existentialist writers.

134. Peachey, "What Is Concern?" 16–17.

135. Note: Peachey ("What Is Concern?" 16) did not even say here that Christ's presence is realized in the local church, but in the *fellowship* of the local church.

136. Peachey, "Spirit and Form in the Church," 15.

137. Peachey, "Spirit and Form in the Church," 21.

138. Peachey, "Spirit and Form in the Church," 23–24.

139. After all, the prospect that the church's visible expression is not its reality seemed to imply that the church's reality is invisible after all. See Peachey, "Spirit and Form in the Church," 24–25.

232

140. Cf. Peachey, "Spirit and Form in the Church," 19, 24. One correspondent, Paul Verghese, who described himself as "a Catholic (not a Roman one) by conviction," noticed the issue right away; see "Epistolary," 11.

141. Peachey, "Spirit and Form in the Church," 24. The "confusion" here is one that Peachey associated with centuries of "Catholic dogma."

142. Peachey, "The Modern Recovery of the Anabaptist Vision," 339. For an account of internal debates and frustration within the Concern Movement over how to realize their ideals, see Toews, "The Concern Movement," 121–22. Also note the chapter on the Concern Group in Keim's biography of Harold S. Bender; in relation to Concern Group idealism, see the chapter's final paragraphs (*Harold S. Bender*, 450–71), which end with these sentences: "In the 1950s Harold Bender and John Howard Yoder embodied the dilemma, but left it unresolved. The dilemma lay in the limits of Christian perfection."

143. Wrote Yoder: "The Anabaptists of the sixteenth century, like others before and after them, believed that Christendom, in ceasing to be the primitive church and becoming medieval Europe, had taken the wrong path. They called for a return to the Christianity of the New Testament, and to a very great degree succeeded in reproducing in their day what the church of AD 50 or 80 had been. They believed not only that their church should take this form, but [also] that every true church should do likewise, and that their own church should keep this form. They condemned the 'Sect cycle' itself." See John Howard Yoder, "Christian Education: Doctrinal Orientation," prepared as the beginning of conversation about Mennonite Church-administered high schools, Historical mss. 1–48, section 1, box 02, unpublished writings 1947–1997, John H. Yoder Collection, Mennonite Church USA Archives, Goshen, IN (1958), 2.

144. Yoder, "Christian Education: Doctrinal Orientation," 4.

145. Yoder, "Christian Education: Doctrinal Orientation," 5.

146. Douglas K. Harink, "For or against the Nations: Yoder and Hauerwas, What's the Difference?" *Toronto Journal of Theology* 17, no. 1 (Spring 2001): 167–85; Joseph J. Kotva Jr., "For or against the Nations? John Howard Yoder vs. Stanley Hauerwas on the Nature of Christian Politics," conference presentation, Society of Christian Ethics (Chicago, 2001); Craig A. Carter, *The Politics of the Cross: The Theology and Social Ethics of John Howard Yoder* (Grand Rapids: Brazos, 2001), 227–28 et passim; Paul Doerksen, "Share the House: Yoder and Hauerwas among the Nations," in *A Mind Patient and Untamed: Assessing John Howard Yoder's Contributions to Theology, Ethics, and Peacemaking*, ed. Ben C. Ollenburger and Gayle Gerber Koontz (Telford, PA: Cascadia, 2004), 187–204; Craig R. Hovey, "The Public Ethics of John Howard Yoder and Stanley Hauerwas: Difference or Disagreement," in Ollenburger and Koontz, *A Mind Patient and Untamed*, 205–20.

147. Yoder, *For the Nations: Essays Public and Evangelical*; Stanley Hauerwas, *Against the Nations: War and Survival in a Liberal Society* (Minneapolis: Winston, 1985).

148. On this latter point, cf. Yoder, "What Are Our Concerns?" 23–24, 29.

149. John H. Yoder, "The Ambivalence of the Appeal to the Fathers," in *Practiced in the Presence: Essays in Honor of T. Canby Jones*, ed. Neil Snarr and Daniel Smith-Christopher (Richmond, IN: Friends United Press, 1994), 248.

150. Perhaps this is what has drawn an accusation by Patrick Madigan (who identifies himself as a pacifist) that Yoder's thought verges on gnosticism. See Patrick Madigan, review of John Howard Yoder, *The Jewish-Christian Schism Revisited*, *Heythrop Journal* 47, no. 2 (April 2006): 301–2. Though I find Madigan's critique overwrought, he does identify a vulnerability to which Yoder's students should attend.

151. Hauerwas, *A Community of Character*, 2; Hauerwas, "Character, Narrative, and Growth in the Christian Life," in *A Community of Character*, 150. Cf. Hauerwas, "The Moral Value of the Family," in *A Community of Character*, 155–66; Hauerwas, "The Family: Theology and Ethical Reflections," in *A Community of Character*, 167–74; Hauerwas, "Abortion: Why the Arguments Fail," in *A Community of Character*, 212–29.

152. Stanley Hauerwas, "Response," in *On Baptism: Mennonite-Catholic Theological Colloquium, 2001–2002*, ed. Gerald W. Schlabach, The Bridgefolk Series (Kitchener, ON: Pandora, 2004), 101–3.

153. Stanley Hauerwas, "The Liturgical Shape of the Christian Life: Teaching Christian Ethics as Worship," in *In Good Company*, 153–68; Stanley Hauerwas and Samuel Wells, "Christian Ethics as Informed Prayer," in *Blackwell Companion to Christian Ethics*, 3–12.

154. Hauerwas has not made this critique of Weber in print, though he has done so in personal conversation. His rejection of a divorce between charismatic and official authority is evident in "Clerical Character," in *Christian Existence Today*, 133–48; and "The Pastor as Prophet: Ethical Reflections on an Improbable Mission," in *Christian Existence Today*, 149–67. "Clerical Character" also makes clear his assent to sacramental and priestly understandings of ministerial office, wherein office is understood precisely as a carrier of charism or grace.

155. Hauerwas, "Whose Church? Which Future?" 73. Cf. "What Could It Mean for the Church to Be Christ's Body?: A Question without a Clear Answer," in *In Good Company*, 19–31.

156. Hauerwas, "The Importance of Being Catholic," 94. For Hauerwas on authority more generally, see "The Moral Authority of Scripture: The Politics and Ethics of Remembering," in *A Community of Character*, 60–63. For his juxtaposition of John Paul II and John Howard Yoder, see *With the Grain of the Universe: The Church's Witness and Natural Theology*, Gifford Lectures delivered at the University of St. Andrews in 2001 (Grand Rapids: Brazos, 2001), 216–31.

157. Emblematic of this is Hauerwas's juxtaposition of John Howard Yoder's account of practical reasoning or casuistry with that of Mennonite farmer Olin Teague in "Reconciling the Practice of Reason," 72–82.

Chapter 3 The Practice of Stability

1. Thomas Merton, *The Sign of Jonas* (New York: Harcourt, 1953), 9–10.

2. Carole King, "So Far Away," *Tapestry*, Ode Records, 1971.

3. For historical background, see Derek G. Smith, "Oblates in Western Monasticism," *Monastic Studies* 13 (Autumn 1982): 47–72.

4. Like many people in recent years, I first learned about Benedictine oblates from Kathleen Norris's best-selling book *The Cloister Walk* (New York: Riverhead Books, 1987), but all I needed to decide to explore this option was the raw fact that non-Roman Catholics could become oblates, which appears in her first paragraph.

5. Cf. Hanna-Renata Laurien, "The Benedictine Monastery—a Challenge for Society?" in *As We Seek God: International Reflections on Contemporary Benedictine Monasticism*, ed. Stephanie Campbell, OSB, Cistercian Studies Series 70 (Kalamazoo, MI: Cistercian Publications, 1983), 62–76 (including responses).

6. Sherman Kauffman, executive secretary of the Indiana-Michigan Conference of the Mennonite Church, and a former pastor.

7. Cf. Hobbes's and Locke's accounts of men in the "state of nature," in *Leviathan* (book 1) and the *Second Treatise on Civil Government* (chap. 2), respectively.

8. This is because a radically perspectivist epistemology has nowhere to stop positing the construction of world and realities except in the ultimately unique perspective of each individual.

9. For a plea that cross-cultural understanding should extend to premodern communities, see Dennis D. Martin, "Journey to a Far Country: Premodern History as Crosscultural Education," *Conrad Grebel Review* 11, no. 3 (Fall 1993): 249–63. Also see the opening and closing essays in Robert L. Wilken, *Remembering the Christian Past* (Grand Rapids: Eerdmans, 1995), 1–23, 165–80.

10. Wendell Berry, "The Work of Local Culture," in *What Are People For?* (San Francisco: North Point, 1990), 153–69. For a discussion of "fidelity" that parallels somewhat the practice of "stability," see Wendell Berry, "The Body and the Earth," in *The Unsettling of America: Culture and Agriculture* (New York: Avon, 1977), 120–23.

11. Scott Russell Sanders, "Settling Down," in *Staying Put: Making a Home in a Restless World* (Boston: Beacon, 1994), 102. Sanders noted that he was quarreling with Rushdie "because he articulates as eloquently as anyone the orthodoxy that I wish to counter: the belief that movement is inherently good, staying put is bad; that uprooting brings tolerance, while rootedness breeds intolerance; that imaginary homelands are preferable to geographical ones; that to be modern, enlightened, fully of our time is to be displaced" (103).

12. Sanders, "Settling Down," 105, 103.

13. Sanders, "Settling Down," 106.

14. Sanders, "Settling Down," 114. Sanders has also cited Benedictine stability as a model in the chapter on "Fidelity," in Scott Russell Sanders, *Hunting for Hope: A Father's Journey* (Boston: Beacon, 1998), 88.

15. All quotations from the Rule (abbreviated as RB) are taken from St. Benedict, *RB 1980: The Rule of St. Benedict in English*, ed. Timothy Fry, OSB (Collegeville, MN: Liturgical Press, 1982). I am also consulting Terrence G. Kardong, *Benedict's Rule: A Translation and Commentary* (Collegeville, MN: Liturgical Press, 1996), abbreviated as BR, using p. or pp. when page numbers are cited. Finally, for various clarifications concerning the Rule, I am indebted to Fr. Michael Brunovsky, OSB, the oblate director at St. Andrew Svorad Abbey in Cleveland, who is well trained in patristic and monastic history.

16. RB 1 has provided terrain for a long and continuing debate over the conceptual relationship between anchorism and cenobitism. RB 1.3–5 seems to present anchorites as graduates of cenobitic communities who are now strong enough to go out to wrestle with the devil and their own vices in one-on-one combat. Yet that would seem to make monastic community life into something merely instrumental; besides, 1.13 calls the cenobites the strong or (as Kardong translates) "most vigorous" of monks. See BR, pp. 31, 43, 599–600.

17. Cf. RB 1.2, where cenobites are described as "those who belong to a monastery, where they serve under a rule and an abbot."

18. Cf. RB 2.7, in which the abbot-shepherd is reminded that he is not actually the owner of the sheepfold, since the owner is rather the Lord God.

19. Political chieftains in the Latin/Germanic West had abandoned the last pretense of continuity with the Roman Empire in 476, yet the Eastern emperor Justinian tried to regain control after 526. Whatever one thinks of that combination of political stability and militarism that the Roman Empire had once represented, its disintegration no more brought freedom from oppression and violence than the demise of the Soviet Union has brought freedom and prosperity to all of its regions. Whatever local improvements came from the fall of these respective empires, the improvements did not come without new dangers.

20. So at least suggests Fr. Brunovsky, OSB, of St. Andrew Svorad Abbey in Cleveland, Ohio.

21. MacIntyre, *After Virtue: A Study in Moral Theory*, 263. For a short monograph that applies MacIntyre's thought to the challenge of Christian mission in modern culture, and frames its proposals as "a new monasticism," see Jonathan R. Wilson, *Living Faithfully in a Fragmented World: Lessons for the Church from MacIntyre's "After Virtue,"* Christian Mission and Modern Culture (Harrisburg, PA: Trinity Press International, 1997).

22. Hauerwas, *In Good Company*, 26, 73.

23. Jeffrey Stout has been an especially cogent critic of MacIntyre's dire diagnosis. See Jeffrey Stout, "Liberal Society and the Languages of Morals," in *Community in America: The Challenge of Habits of the Heart*, ed. Charles H. Reynolds and Ralph V. Norman (Berkeley: University of California Press, 1988), 127–46; Stout, *Ethics after Babel: The Languages of Morals and Their Discontents* (Boston: Beacon Press, 1988); Stout, *Democracy and Tradition*, New Forum Books (Princeton, NJ: Princeton University Press, 2004).

24. "Habits and practices [of] community life" approximates the initial meaning of *conversatio morum* (RB Prol. 49; 58.17) rather than "conversion of life," which became one of the three traditional Benedictine vows. But the point of conformity to the former was growth in the latter. See Kardong's discussion of RB 58.17 in BR, pp. 473–74 and 483.

25. The Benedictine commentator Kardong suggested that as Benedict added to his Rule over time, he began to recognize the dangers in this formula; hence, he inserted a new chapter calling for abbots to exercise their authority with gentle discretion (RB 64, in contrast to RB 2; see BR, p. 541), along with a key chapter inviting monks to object to impossibly burdensome commands in a way that would elicit truly pastoral guidance from their superior (RB 68; see BR, p. 572). Even so, Kardong recognized that in another chapter (RB 71) Benedict abjectly failed to "take account of community life in any realistic sense," for although he began the chapter with a call for *mutual* obedience (but also see RB 72), he ended by insisting on the "capitulation and self-accusation" of junior monks to seniors, and no such system "can be said to be healthy" (BR, p. 586). Still, Kardong's harsh criticism of the saintly founder of his own religious order attests to possibilities of critique and accountability within the order that outsider observers may not always discern. See also Terrence Kardong, OSB, "RB 71.6–9 in the Light of Gandhi's Non-Violence," *Tjurunga* 27 (1984): 3–16.

26. See BR 2.1, p. 49.

27. In any case, Kardong has observed that Benedict, in redacting a more succinct and workable "rule" out of longer and harsher sources such as the anonymous "Rule of the Master," drastically reduced the number of references to the abbot as a "master" or "father," and to the monk as "son," thus reducing paternalistic overtones as well. See BR, pp. 5, 66.

28. Cf. BR, pp. 67–68.

29. Commenting on the first draft of this chapter, Kardong commented that this reluctance to accept the position of abbot tends to be the case today, though not necessarily for reasons Benedict would have expected: "There is no question that Benedict makes his abbot a huge factor in the life of the monk and the monastery. So much so, that I think it scares the daylights out of modern monks. Hence monasteries have a tough time finding anyone who is willing to be abbot! In reality, most abbots today are anything but authoritarian. American abbots tend to be rather shy and retiring; some do not do much teaching in the monastery. At any rate, the problem is the same all over society: where to find people with vision?"

30. See note 25, above.

31. Kardong has observed that Benedict never reversed the order of the repeated pair "under a rule and an abbot," thus implying the clear priority of the Rule over the abbot (BR, p. 36; see RB 1.1, 6–8; 3.7–9; 23.1).

32. See RB (chaps.) 4 and 7 for what are only the most marked examples of this distillation. Cf. BR, pp. 36, 117.

33. T. Schlabach, *Peace, Faith, Nation*, 201–3.

34. Since Vatican II, many Benedictine congregations have been electing their abbots until age sixty-five, rather than for life, with longer terms possible only through reelection. Another obvious example is that, according to Kardong (BR, p. 251), "there may not be a single monastery in the world today that carries out literally [Benedict's] prescriptions for punishing monks," particularly through corporal punishment.

35. Merton, *The Sign of Jonas*, 9–10. For a more thorough exploration of the role of stability in monastic life and sanctification, see Michael Casey, OCSO, "The Value of Stability," *Cistercian Studies Quarterly* 31, no. 3 (1996): 287–301. Casey suggested: "Solemn profession of stability means that the whole cosmic drama of salvation is transferred to the microcosm of the monastery—at least as far as the individual is concerned. . . . It is precisely the containment of ultimate events within the human scale that enables the monk to live more intensely. . . . Monastic life is not a means of escape from anything. On the contrary, it has the effect of bringing monastics into sustained confrontation with realities they might otherwise avoid, disguise, or deny" (291). Likewise, Casey (292–93) contrasted the lessons of stability with the lures of what I have called hypermodernism:

> The first effect of stability is that it brings lofty dreams of spiritual growth down to earth. Present opportunities are to be taken seriously since nothing much is going to change. . . . Once the idea sinks in, there is no excuse for postponing effort under the pretext that opportunities are lacking or that the time is not ripe. In our supermarket culture it is possible to spend a lifetime toying with alternatives, convinced that one is a genuine spiritual seeker, but never committing oneself to anything beyond the first flush of enthusiasm. Stability puts an end to this sort of searching. The monk accepts to live in a microcosm, where the spiritual combat remains firmly on a human scale.

36. Cf. RB 2.7, where God is decisively made the paterfamilias or owner of the sheepfold, and the abbot is a shepherd who must give account. Those who would reject this image of God will have to excise those parables by which Jesus himself spoke of God as a landowner or vineyard owner.

37. See Kardong, BR, pp. 5, 8, 22, 32, 62, 75, 254–55, 403, 431–32.

38. See BR, pp. 5, 66–67, on RB Prol.1. Although the filial language of the Rule's opening words is prominent, it is also unique, for as Kardong has pointed out, the only other place where the RB refers to the monk as "son" (RB 2.29) is a biblical quotation.

39. Cf. John Howard Yoder, "The Christian Case for Democracy," in *The Priestly Kingdom*, 151–71.

40. Casey's observations ("The Value of Stability," 298) may help us understand why:

> There is an obscurity inherent in any human commitment. When we oblige ourselves to do something, we can never know in advance whether the circumstances in which we are to render our debt will have changed. Before binding ourselves we make an assessment on the basis of both objective and subjective information, but no practical judgment can be infallible. What we decide comes into being only *after* our decision; we can never know what would have been if we had decided otherwise. Every commitment we make involves an element of risk-taking. On the other hand, once we have taken the step, we are honor-bound to a certain obstinacy not only in keeping our promises but [also] in actively pursuing the purposes for which the promises were made.

41. I do not have the time or expertise in sixteenth-century sources to prove my suspicion that the contentious students of Harold S. Bender's "Anabaptist Vision" have been far too quick to read their own late-twentieth-century antiauthoritarianism back into formative Anabaptism. One example, from a scholar who actually tries hard to avoid such things, may however illustrate the grounds for suspicion. In his biography of Michael Sattler, Arnold Snyder rightly sought to show points of both continuity and discontinuity between Sattler's Benedictine and Anabaptist thought. Comparing Benedictine and Anabaptist processes of discernment, he argued that in the latter, the community rather than its leaders decide, and the Holy Spirit witnesses through their unity and unanimity. Snyder concluded that "the monastic community is obedient to Christ *via* its obedience to the Rule and its abbot" while "the Anabaptist community is to be obedient *directly* to Christ, his Word and his Spirit" (C. Arnold Snyder, *The Life and Thought of Michael Sattler*, Studies in Anabaptist and Mennonite History 26 [Scottdale, PA: Herald, 1984], 191–92). A footnote on this page, however, leads the reader to a letter of Sattler's admonishing the church of Horb to assemble constantly for prayer and breaking of bread. "In such meeting together you will make manifest the heart of the false brothers, and will be freed of them more rapidly" (in John H[oward] Yoder, ed., *The Legacy of Michael Sattler*, Classics of the Radical Reformation 1 [Scottdale, PA: Herald, 1973], 62). How? The letter does not say. But since no actual community can beg the question of who the "false brothers" are in the way in which the letter *seems* to do, a more sensible reading is that some one or some party within the group has only achieved "unanimity" by deciding which voices count. The criticism here is not necessarily of Sattler, for elsewhere he in turn provided ways to make the community's shepherd accountable (see art. 5 of the Schleitheim Confession, in Yoder, *The Legacy of Michael Sattler*, 38–39). The criticism is of recent historiography that tends to romanticize sixteenth-century Anabaptist communities as radically egalitarian, in order to legitimize antiauthoritarian assumptions that may actually derive from late modernity. If I am right that Snyder erred at this point, his mistake was not so much egregious as symptomatic.

42. In troubled and tragic marriages among fundamentalist Christians, for example, rigid theologies of obedience and submission to male "headship" as unto Christ have exacerbated domestic abuse. Such situations require all the best efforts of moral and pastoral theology to adjudicate.

43. Kathleen Norris, *Amazing Grace: A Vocabulary of Faith* (New York: Riverhead Books, 1998), 93, 135, 192, 203–4, 238, 258–61, 268–76, 309–10.

44. Gary Gunderson, *Deeply Woven Roots: Improving the Quality of Life in Your Community* (Minneapolis: Fortress, 1997), 86–90.

45. Sanders, "Settling Down," 119–20, with original emphasis.

46. Michael Goldberg, "Corporate Culture and Corporate Cult," in *Against the Grain: New Approaches to Professional Ethics*, ed. Michael Goldberg (Valley Forge, PA: Trinity Press International, 1993), 13–36.

47. Joanne B. Ciulla, "Leadership and the Problem of Bogus Empowerment," in *Ethics, the Heart of Leadership*, ed. Joanne B. Ciulla (Westport, CT: Quorum Books, 1998), 63–86.

48. Luther, "The Freedom of a Christian," 364–71; Martin Luther, "Treatise on Good Works" (1520), trans. W. A. Lambert, rev. James Atkinson, in *The Christian in Society I*, vol. 44 of *Luther's Works*, ed. James Atkinson, gen. ed. Helmut T. Lehmann (Philadelphia: Fortress, 1966), 23–26.

49. Cf. Martin Luther, "The Babylonian Captivity of the Church," trans. Charles M. Jacobs, rev. James Atkinson, in *Three Treatises*, 2nd ed. (Philadelphia: Fortress, 1970), 198–203.

50. Kasper, "Current Problems in Ecumenical Theology," 64–65. Note similar remarks by Joseph Cardinal Ratzinger in *Church, Ecumenism, and Politics: New Essays in Ecclesiology*, 87.

51. MacIntyre, *After Virtue: A Study in Moral Theory*, 263.

52. Translation here is from *The Psalms: An Inclusive Language Version Based on the Grail Translation from the Hebrew* (Chicago: G.I.A. Publications, 1993), as used in Maxwell E. Johnson and the monks of Saint John's Abbey, comps. and eds., *Benedictine Daily Prayer: A Short Breviary* (Collegeville, MN: Liturgical Press, 2005), 130.

Chapter 4 Stability Writ Large

1. Pope Benedict XVI, "Address of His Holiness Benedict XVI to the Roman Curia Offering Them His Christmas Greetings" (December 22, 2005).

2. Terence L. Nichols voiced this judgment in *That All May Be One: Hierarchy and Participation in the Church* (Collegeville, MN: Liturgical Press, 1997), 135–36. However, he also recognized Benedictine practices of community consultation (134–35) and implied that they provide precedents for the polity of the worldwide Roman Catholic Church (307, 318).

3. Cf. Ann Elizabeth O'Hara Graff, "Transforming Today's Church," *Chicago Studies* 32, no. 2 (August 1993): 140–41.

4. This sentence could stand as a summary of Nichols's entire book, *That All May Be One*, and of a shorter article based on it, "Participatory Hierarchy," in *Common Calling: The Laity and Governance of the Catholic Church*, ed. Stephen J. Pope (Washington, DC: Georgetown University Press, 2004), 111–27. But see esp. 5–20 and 316–35 in the former, and 111–13 and 125 in the latter.

5. Nichols, *That All May Be One*, 14–17; Nichols, "Participatory Hierarchy," 113–14.

6. Nichols noted that Jesus allowed himself to be called rabbi and teacher, while referring to his followers not as "equals" but as "disciples" or learners. With the kingdom of God at the core of Jesus' message, with a selection of twelve apostles who are one day to sit on thrones of judgment, there is an undeniably hierarchical element in the Jesus movement. And yet this "is not dominance or command hierarchy." Jesus defies social convention; he teaches and practices an authority exercised through service. When he sends out his disciples, he is in command and yet "His aim seems to be to bring the disciples into the kind of loving relationship with the God that he himself experiences. He thus exercises the kind of hierarchy characteristic of teachers, parents, and religious masters." The same is later true of the apostle Paul, who insists on his own apostolic authority precisely in order to "to open the way to participation" by more and more active and gifted members of the body of Christ. Nichols, "Participatory Hierarchy," 116–17.

7. Nichols, "Participatory Hierarchy," 114.

8. John W. O'Malley, "Developments, Reforms, and Two Great Reformations: Towards a Historical Assessment of Vatican II," *Theological Studies* 44, no. 3 (1983): 399.

9. Joseph A. Komonchak, "Ordinary Papal Magisterium and Religious Assent," in *The Magisterium and Morality*, ed. Charles E. Curran and Richard A. McCormick, Readings in Moral Theology 3 (New York: Paulist Press, 1982), 67–90.

10. Cardinal Joseph L. Bernardin, "Address on the Common Ground Project," *Origins*, November 14, 1996, 353.

11. Nichols, *That All May Be One*, 241. For Nichols's observations concerning the two matters that Paul VI reserved for papal decisions, see Nichols, "Participatory Hierarchy," 122. Cf. Giuseppe Alberigo, ed., *History of Vatican II*, 5 vols., English version edited by Joseph Komonchak (Maryknoll, NY: Orbis Books; Leuven, Belgium: Peeters, 1996), 5:541–43.

12. Nichols, *That All May Be One*, 239–41. Corroborating Nichols's assessment of Vatican II, as well as those of O'Malley and Bernardin (cited above), are those of still others: Giuseppe Alberigo, editor of the monumental *History of Vatican II*, stressed that the council was not simply a set of texts but was an *event* in which bishops who had never experienced an ecumenical council for themselves learned amid growing excitement to take counsel together, found to their surprise that the world was paying close attention, and discovered the fruitfulness of a wide-ranging conversation within the church and indeed beyond (*History of Vatican II*, 2:583). The bishops could speak confidently of the role of the church accompanying modern humanity on its journey because they had experienced exactly that; cf. Second Vatican Council, *Gaudium et spes*, Pastoral Constitution on the Church in the Modern World (1965), §§1, 45.

13. All quotations from the Second Vatican Council are from Second Vatican Council, *Vatican Council II*.

14. Nichols, "Participatory Hierarchy," 123.

15. The liberal narrative sees the Holy Spirit working through Pope John XXIII and the council he called in order to end the war that the church had been waging for two centuries against modernity, and to restore the church's self-identity to that of a true community on a journey through history in service to humankind. The moderately conservative narrative agrees that the council was the work of the Holy Spirit and recognizes its contributions to church reform and renewal, but believes that "politicized media, liberal theologians, and restless clergy" badly misrepresented the council and encouraged changes that both defied established church teachings and departed from the council. The other two narratives obviously lie at either extreme of these. The radical narrative sees the council as having broken insufficiently with patterns of patriarchy, dogma, and Roman imperialism that have misshaped Catholicism for centuries. The ultraconservative story line sees the council as "an unfortunate mistake, rooted in mischievous theological enthusiasms and perpetrated by naive bishops." See Peter Steinfels, *A People Adrift: The Crisis of the Roman Catholic Church in America* (New York: Simon & Schuster, 2003), 32–36.

16. Alberigo, *History of Vatican II*, 1:xii, 42; 2:583; 5:628, 643.

17. John Courtney Murray, "Freedom, Authority, Community," *America*, December 3, 1966, 734.

18. Readers wishing to pursue such details might wish to consult Richard R. Gaillardetz, *By What Authority? A Primer on Scripture, the Magisterium, and the Sense of the Faithful* (Collegeville, MN: Liturgical Press, 2003).

19. Graff, "Transforming Today's Church," 128.

20. Peter Steinfels (*A People Adrift*, 356) seems to have been calling for something like this shift from proceduralism to virtue when he warned against overtheologizing post–Vatican II debates among American Catholics: "Too many debates about American Catholicism are 'over-theologized,' at least if theology is identified with reasoning about relatively abstract propositions rather than reflection grounded in the actual practices of a believing and worshiping community, both in the present and through time." Likewise, Margaret O'Brien Steinfels has argued that while bishops and theologians must resolve their debate over the proper line between responsible and irresponsible dissent, "in the practical everyday life of the church, the question . . . is less than we often suppose a matter of intellectual propositions, and more often a matter of conduct, of attitude, of affection, and of heart." Margaret O'Brien Steinfels, "Dissent and Communion: You Can't Have One without the Other," *Commonweal*, November 18, 1994, 11.

21. In an otherwise well-balanced article on issues in Catholic higher education, for example, M. Cathleen Kaveny observed the way that, for some people, "aggiornamento"

has become a "catchword" simply meaning "openness to modernity." M. Cathleen Kaveny, "The Perfect Storm: 'The Vagina Monologues' and Catholic Higher Education," *America*, May 8, 2006, 16–17.

22. Peter Steinfels (*A People Adrift*, 36–37) has concurred: Yes, one may legitimately argue in the name of "the spirit of the Council" for ongoing reforms that continue the trajectory of the council beyond the positions of the council itself. But part of that "spirit of the Council" is "an appreciation and receptivity toward tradition at least equal to any hermeneutic of suspicion. Vatican II cannot be invoked to justify sweeping dismissals of whole periods and major themes in the church's history or all the council fathers' caveats and compromises."

23. Alberigo, *History of Vatican II*, 1:505.

24. Pope John XXIII, *Gaudet mater ecclesia*, Mother Church Rejoices, opening speech to the Second Vatican Council (1962), §4.2.

25. The most often cited instance is *Gaudium et spes* 4. But also see *Dignitatis humanae*, Declaration on Religious Liberty, or, On the Right of the Person and Communities to Social and Civil Liberty in Religious Matters (1965), §15; *Unitatis redintegratio* 4; *Apostolicam actuositatem*, Decree on the Apostolate of the Laity (1965), §14; *Presbyterorum ordinis*, Decree on the Ministry of Priests (1965), §9.

26. *Gaudet mater ecclesia* 4.5. Cf. Alberigo, *History of Vatican II*, 2:16: "The 'princes'— and this was something new—remained outside the realm of the Council's decisions. The church of Vatican II had no privileged connections with politics or with any model of a state."

27. Alberigo, *History of Vatican II*, 1:42. Also see 5:540–641.

28. According to Alberigo:

Very few bishops consciously related the now opening council to the changed conditions of a planet that had shortly before emerged from a destructive conflict and was still divided by opposing ideologies and living under the threatening shadow of a nuclear war. Humanity wanted peace but was incapable of attaining it; it was caught up in an exciting period of scientific, economic, and technological development, but troubled by formidable social imbalances. Councils had traditionally had for their purpose to pass judgment [sic] on preceding situations of Church-conflict, that is, they were motivated essentially by problems that had arisen in the past and for which no solution had been found. But the context of Vatican II was of a quite different kind. (Alberigo, *History of Vatican II*, 2:565; also see 1:14, 34, 56–59).

29. All quotations in this paragraph are from Vatican Council, *Gaudium et spes* 1, 3.

30. Alberigo, *History of Vatican II*, 1:72.

31. See Alberigo, *History of Vatican II*, 5:633; cf. 2:15–16.

32. O'Malley, "Developments, Reforms, and Two Great Reformations," 373, 376–78, 392–93.

33. Peter Steinfels (*A People Adrift*, 6) articulated this expectation well: "For Catholic and non-Catholic alike, the [Roman] church had come to symbolize unyielding permanence, whether interpreted as an anachronistic obstacle to modern progress or as a solid rock in a convulsive landscape."

34. I borrow the phrase "radically new direction" from one of the places where Alberigo similarly lamented "a hasty and superficial reading" of Vatican II reforms that fails to account for the deep continuities on which the council drew even as it made those reforms. See Alberigo, *History of Vatican II*, 5:593, 578.

35. Alberigo, *History of Vatican II*, 5:578.

36. John XXIII, *Gaudet mater ecclesia* 6.5.

37. Alberigo, *History of Vatican II*, 3:493.

38. Garry Wills, *Bare Ruined Choirs: Doubt, Prophecy, and Radical Religion* (Garden City, NY: Doubleday, 1972), 21; as quoted in P. Steinfels, *A People Adrift*, 247.

39. Jay P. Dolan, *In Search of an American Catholicism: A History of Religion and Culture in Tension* (Oxford and New York: Oxford University Press, 2002), 253; also see 193–95.

40. O'Malley, "Developments, Reforms, and Two Great Reformations," 398, 396.

41. Pope John XXIII, Apostolic Constitution *Humanae salutis*, Of Human Salvation, convoking the Second Vatican Council (1961), §23.

42. Alberigo, *History of Vatican II*, 1:42, 50.

43. Alberigo, *History of Vatican II*, 5:605.

44. Alberigo, *History of Vatican II*, 5:605.

45. Alberigo, *History of Vatican II*, 3:512.

46. Alberigo, *History of Vatican II*, 3:498.

47. Alberigo, *History of Vatican II*, 2:17.

48. Alberigo, *History of Vatican II*, 2:17, commenting on John XXIII, *Gaudet mater ecclesia*.

49. John XXIII, *Gaudet mater ecclesia*.

50. All quotations in this paragraph are from John XXIII, *Gaudet mater ecclesia* 5.6; 7.2. The most oft-cited list of human injustices and violations of dignity in *Gaudium et spes* appears in §27, but a critique of human hubris runs through much of the document.

51. John XXIII, *Gaudet mater ecclesia* 7.3.

52. Cf. Alberigo, *History of Vatican II*, 1:168–70.

53. Avery Robert Dulles, "The Vatican II Revolution: Authority and Obedience," *Tablet*, December 18, 1982, 1264.

54. Second Vatican Council, *Lumen gentium*, Dogmatic Constitution on the Church (1964), §37.

55. Dulles, "Authority and Obedience," 1264–65.

56. Dulles, "Authority and Obedience," 1265.

57. Dulles's summary:

In its Constitution on Revelation, Vatican II insisted on the living authority of God's word in Scripture, adding that the magisterium of the Church is under the word of God, not over it. The Decree on Ecumenism spoke of the Church's need to undergo continual reform and to rectify deficiencies in its own doctrinal formulations. In the Declaration on Religious Freedom, and in the Pastoral Constitution on the Church in the Modern World, the council taught that the present age calls for an assent of faith that is free, personal, and reflective, rather than coerced, mechanical, or uncritical. In the Constitution on the Liturgy, the council called for the lively participation of the faithful in the Church's worship. In the second chapter of the Constitution on the Church, the common priesthood of the faithful was recognized, though this priesthood was described as differing in essence from the ministerial priesthood of the ordained. In its Decree on the Pastoral Office of Bishops, the council called for the reorganization of the Roman Curia; it also recommended pastoral councils in which representatives of the clergy, religious, and laity might have a voice. (Dulles, "Authority and Obedience," 1265)

58. Alberigo (*History of Vatican II*, 5:643) has insisted that "the most important novelty of Vatican II cannot consist in its new formulations but rather in the very fact that it was convoked and held. From this point of view the council represents a point of no return; the conciliar age has begun again and has found a very important place in the consciousness of the Church."

242

59. For evidence that the bishops were not completely aware of what they were doing in the first session of the council, nor of its significance, and thus had to discover the method of the council as they proceeded, see Alberigo, *History of Vatican II*, 2:566, 568, 575–76.

·60. Alberigo, *History of Vatican II*, 5:618–19.

61. Alberigo, *History of Vatican II*, 2:26–36.

62. Alberigo, *History of Vatican II*, 5:618–19. Joseph Komonchak has emphasized the latter point in Joseph A. Komonchak, "What Road to Joy? How Vatican II Changed the Church, Pt. 8," *Tablet*, November 30, 2002, 11–12; though it is common to portray the council as a struggle between a large bloc of progressives and a small but influential cadre of conservative holdouts, leading voices in the "majority" sometimes differed sharply, and some debates moved forward dramatically when well-known conservatives took unexpected stands, as, for example, when Cardinal Ottaviani spoke passionately in opposition to atomic weapons.

63. Bernardin, "Address on the Common Ground Project."

64. Alberigo, *History of Vatican II*, 2:580.

65. Alberigo, *History of Vatican II*, 5:602.

66. Alberigo, *History of Vatican II*, 5:123–24.

67. P. Steinfels, *A People Adrift*, 20.

68. Cardinal Joseph L. Bernardin, "The Impact of Vatican II: Church in the Modern World," *Origins*, October 17, 1985, 307.

69. David Toolan, SJ, "The Catholic Taboo against Schism: Strained but Holding," *Religion and Intellectual Life* 7, no. 1 (Fall 1989): 46.

70. Dulles, "Authority and Obedience," 1264.

71. Dulles, "Authority and Obedience," 1265.

72. *Sacrosanctum concilium*, Constitution on the Sacred Liturgy (1963), §8; *Lumen gentium* 7, 21, 48, 50; *Unitatis redintegratio* 2, 3; *Dei Verbum*, Dogmatic Constitution on Divine Revelation (1965), §7; *Apostolicam actuositatem* 4; *Ad gentes*, Decree on the Church's Missionary Activity (1965), §2; *Dignitatis humanae* 12; *Gaudium et spes* 45, 57.

73. Vatican Council, *Gaudium et spes* 57–58.

74. Vatican Council, *Lumen gentium* 7, 48; *Sacrosanctum concilium* 8.

75. Vatican Council, *Dignitatis humanae* 12.

76. Dulles, "Authority and Obedience," 1265. I have broken Dulles's prose into bullet points for emphasis.

77. "The Catholic style admits of change—indeed requires change, but it is change rooted in continuity. Anyone familiar with Catholic history knows that Vatican II was a surprise but not an aberration from [this] law of development." Bernardin, "The Impact of Vatican II," 307.

78. Cf. *Optatam totius*, Decree on Priestly Training (1965), §§15–16.

79. Vatican Council, *Dei Verbum* 9–10.

80. P. Steinfels, *A People Adrift*, 167.

81. Cf. M. Steinfels, "Dissent and Communion," 15. On the tensions that Christians hold together through participation in the Eucharist or Lord's Supper, see Gerald W. Schlabach, "Breaking Bread: Peace and War," in Hauerwas and Wells, *Blackwell Companion to Christian Ethics*, 366–73.

82. Alberigo, *History of Vatican II*, 5:585.

83. Alberigo, *History of Vatican II*, 1:501. On p. 5:486, Alberigo identified yet another ambiguity concerning the precedent that the Vatican II ecumenical breakthrough set: was it a "milestone" on the way to yet more changes, or a "boundary marker" identifying the outer limits of change?

84. Willem A. Visser 't Hooft, "Teachers and the Teaching Authority: The Magistri and the Magisterium," *Ecumenical Review* 38, no. 2 (April 1986): 186.

85. Vatican Council, *Unitatis redintegratio* 3.

86. Margaret O'Brien Steinfels may not have been quite as certain about a wide sharing of this conviction, but reflected it nonetheless when she opened one article this way: "My premise is that the state of the church, its institutional vitality, makes a difference. I say that because it is not a premise everyone accepts." See Margaret O'Brien Steinfels, "The Unholy Alliance between the Right and the Left in the Catholic Church," *America*, May 2, 1992, 376.

87. Komonchak, "Ordinary Papal Magisterium and Religious Assent," 3:492–93.

88. Murray, "Freedom, Authority, Community," 736–37.

89. Murray, "Freedom, Authority, Community," 737–41.

90. A postconciliar revision of the Code of Canon Law did some of this by specifying new roles for the laity in the life of parishes and dioceses—some of them mandatory—that had formerly been reserved for priests. As John O'Malley, SJ, noted however, the code nonetheless reaffirms "traditional Roman-law theories" of institutional structure, while admitting "a pastoral practice and theology that in certain ways runs counter to an older structure." O'Malley, "Developments, Reforms, and Two Great Reformations," 402

91. M. Steinfels, "Dissent and Communion," 10.

92. Vatican Council, *Dignitatis humanae* 2.

93. Daniel M. Cowdin, "Religious Liberty, Religious Dissent and the Catholic Tradition," *Heythrop Journal* 32, no. 1 (January 1991): 26–61.

94. Karl Rahner, "Towards a Fundamental Theological Interpretation of Vatican II," *Theological Studies* 40, no. 4 (December 1979): 716–27.

95. Toolan, "The Catholic Taboo against Schism," 37.

96. For general commentary in this regard see Alberigo, *History of Vatican II*, 3:499, 5:624. For ways that these dynamics influenced specific deliberations over religious liberty, the nature of priestly ministry, and the role of bishops—not just global poverty, injustice, or missionary activity—see Alberigo, *History of Vatican II*, 5:74–79, 5:135–36, 5:239–41, 5:622–23, 5:638–40.

97. Toolan, "The Catholic Taboo against Schism," 47.

98. Toolan, "The Catholic Taboo against Schism," 47–48. Toolan was here paraphrasing the Rahner article cited above, in note 94.

99. Even such a champion of progressive American Catholicism as *Commonweal* editor Margaret O'Brien Steinfels ("Dissent and Communion," 14) has recognized that "our First Amendment culture is also [less happily], and not coincidentally, an individualistic culture," with negative consequences that make "a sense of community and concern for the common good fragile and vulnerable." If M. Steinfels must recognize the way Western individualism seems "to trump all social bonds" (14) in her own culture, it is hardly any wonder that Christians in cultures that value social bonds and communal identity even more instinctively are resisting the moral patterns and proposals of Western Christians.

100. See Philip Jenkins, *The Next Christendom: The Coming of Global Christianity* (Oxford and New York: Oxford University Press, 2002); Jenkins, "Defenders of the Faith," *Atlantic Monthly* 292, no. 4 (November 2003): 46, 49. For a helpful survey of how southward shifts in the demographics of global Christianity are affecting Catholicism in particular, see Sophie Arie, "Global South as Growing Force in Catholic Church," *Christian Science Monitor*, April 5, 2005, www.csmonitor.com/2005/0405/p01s03-wogi.html.

101. Quotation comes from P. Steinfels, *A People Adrift*, 37. While P. Steinfels agreed that there was a danger in this regard, his own assessment was more measured and nuanced than those whose reaction he was reporting.

102. P. Steinfels, *A People Adrift*, 6.
103. Alberigo, *History of Vatican II*, 5:421, 423; quoting from 421.
104. Toolan, "The Catholic Taboo against Schism," 36–50.
105. Alberigo, *History of Vatican II*, 5:4–9, 23, 360–61, 541, 543.
106. Toolan, "The Catholic Taboo against Schism," 37.
107. Toolan, "The Catholic Taboo against Schism," 36.
108. Toolan, "The Catholic Taboo against Schism," 37.
109. Toolan, "The Catholic Taboo against Schism," 40.
110. Toolan, "The Catholic Taboo against Schism," 45.
111. Toolan, "The Catholic Taboo against Schism," 48.
112. Toolan, "The Catholic Taboo against Schism," 48.
113. Toolan, "The Catholic Taboo against Schism," 49.
114. Toolan, "The Catholic Taboo against Schism," 39.

Chapter 5 Stability in Hard Times: Loyal Dissent

1. Dorothy Day, "The Case of Father Duffy," *The Catholic Worker*, December 1949.
2. Toolan, "The Catholic Taboo against Schism."
3. Leonardo Boff, quoted in Toolan, "The Catholic Taboo against Schism," 48.
4. The account of this meeting comes from another Sant'Egidio leader, Andrea Bartoli, who shared it at the 2003 conference of Bridgefolk, a grassroots movement for dialogue and unity between Mennonites and Catholics, meeting at St. John's Abbey in Minnesota, July 17–20. Bartoli also provided specific details to me in personal correspondence of October 11, 2006. For general information on Sant'Egidio, see the community's Web site, www.santegidio.org, and the following articles: Robert P. Imbelli, "The Community of Sant'Egidio: Vatican II Made Real," *Commonweal*, November 18, 1994, 20–22; John L. Allen Jr., "Host Sant'Egidio Community in Familiar Mediator Role," *National Catholic Reporter*, October 6, 2000, 15; David S. Toolan, SJ, "Of Many Things," *America*, February 19, 2001, 2; John L. Allen Jr., "Interview with Sant'Egidio Founder Andrea Riccardi," online article, *National Catholic Reporter*, July 23, 2004, www.natcath.org/mainpage/specialdocuments/riccardi.htm.
5. Because this letter has often been reprinted and is available on numerous Web sites, I will not be providing page-by-page citations. Its original published location, however, is Martin Luther King Jr., "Letter from the Birmingham Jail," in *Why We Can't Wait* (New York: Harper & Row, 1964), 77–100.
6. Martin Luther King Jr., *Stride toward Freedom: The Montgomery Story* (New York: Harper, 1958), 31–35.
7. Actually, the full charge was that of "bringing or attempting to bring into hatred or contempt or exciting or attempting to excite disaffection towards His Majesty's Government established by law in British India." Because "hatred or contempt" seems so out of character with Gandhi's moral and religious philosophy, it seems safe to assume that when he pled guilty, he saw himself as doing so simply for exciting disaffection. It was part of the injustice of the law under which he was tried that the repeated "or" in the law erased all distinction between these acts.
8. Richard Attenborough, producer and director, *Gandhi* (Burbank, CA: RCA/Columbia Pictures Home Video, 1982), 1:55:45–1:58:31; John Briley, *Gandhi: The Screenplay*, foreword by Sir Richard Attenborough (New York: Grove Press, 1983), 121–24. A full account of "The Great Trial," utilizing court transcripts, is available in Gandhi, *The Collected Works of Mahatma Gandhi*, vol. 23 (1922–1924) ([Delhi]: Publications Division, Ministry of Information

and Broadcasting, Government of India, 1967), 110–20. Also see Judith M. Brown, *Gandhi: Prisoner of Hope* (New Haven: Yale University Press, 1989), 173.

9. Robert Payne, *The Life and Death of Mahatma Gandhi* (New York: Dutton, 1969), 174; Gandhi, *An Autobiography or the Story of My Experiment with Truth*, trans. Mahadev H. Desai, 2nd ed. (Ahmedabad: Navajivan, 1940), 305.

10. Gandhi, *Collected Works*, 23:115.

11. Gandhi, *An Autobiography or the Story of My Experiment with Truth*, 305. A moment before, Gandhi had paired his respect for the rule of law with his resolute disobedience: "I am fully conscious of the fact that a person, holding, in the public life of India, a position such as I do, has to be most careful in setting an example. It is my firm belief that in the complex constitution under which we are living, the only safe and honourable course for a self-respecting man is, in the circumstances such as face me, to do what I have decided to do, that is, to submit without protest to the penalty of disobedience."

12. For an account of the friendship between Jean and Hildegaard Goss-Mayr and Cardinal Ottaviani, see Tom Cornell, "How Catholics Began to Speak Their Peace," *Salt of the Earth* 16, no. 5 (September/October 1996): 17–18. On the role of Ottaviani's speech in favor of what became part II, chap. 5, section 1, of *Gaudium et spes* on the avoidance of war (§§79–82), see Alberigo, *History of Vatican II*, 5:173–75.

13. As my own project was in progress, Catholic moral theologian Charles E. Curran published a memoir titled with this same term, *Loyal Dissent: Memoir of a Catholic Theologian*, Moral Traditions Series (Washington, DC: Georgetown University Press, 2006).

14. Robert McClory, *Faithful Dissenters: Stories of Men and Women Who Loved and Changed the Church* (Maryknoll, NY: Orbis Books, 2000).

15. James Patrick Shannon, *Reluctant Dissenter* (New York: Crossroads, 1998).

16. R. Scott Appleby, Patricia Byrne, and William L. Portier, eds., *Creative Fidelity: American Catholic Intellectual Traditions* (Maryknoll, NY: Orbis Press, 2002).

17. Paul Wilkes, *The Good Enough Catholic: A Guide for the Perplexed* (New York: Ballantine Books, 1996), 277, 292.

18. Janet Somerville, "The Grace of Mutual Respect," 2004–5 Somerville Lecture on Christianity and Communication (St. Jerome Centre, Saint Jerome's University, Waterloo, Ontario, 2004).

19. Murray, "Freedom, Authority, Community," 741.

20. Toolan, "The Catholic Taboo against Schism," 39.

21. Richard R. Gaillardetz, "Marital and Ecclesial Commitment," *America*, August 4, 2003, 8–11. Gaillardetz's essay is among the most succinct descriptions I know of the practices and virtues I am associating with stability and fidelity.

22. David Gibson, *The Coming Catholic Church: How the Faithful Are Shaping a New American Catholicism* (San Francisco: HarperSanFrancisco, 2003), 82–108.

23. Gibson, *The Coming Catholic Church*, 84.

24. John Chrysostom, *De incomprehensibili* 3.6.

25. Gibson, *The Coming Catholic Church*, 91.

26. Gibson, *The Coming Catholic Church*, 94–96.

27. Cowdin, "Religious Liberty, Religious Dissent and the Catholic Tradition," 35; see 27 for a summary of Cowdin's larger argument.

28. M. Steinfels, "Dissent and Communion," 10–11.

29. Robert McClory, "Yves Congar: A Passion for Unity," in *Faithful Dissenters*, 130; Alberigo, *History of Vatican II*, 5:166.

30. Writing on All Saints' Day 2006, James Martin noted that it was "a good time to remember that while most saints led lives of quiet service, some led the life of the noisy

prophet, speaking the truth to power—even when that power was within the church." On this feast day, he continued, "the Catholic Church rightly honors all of its saints, even those it once mistreated, silenced or excommunicated." J. Martin's example was the most recently canonized American saint, Mother Théodore Guérin (October 16, 2006), who had stubbornly led her community and its ministries in rural Indiana in the 1800s in defiance of the local bishop. James Martin, SJ, "Saints That Weren't," *New York Times*, November 1, 2006, www.nytimes.com/2006/11/01/opinion/01martin.html.

31. McClory, "Yves Congar: A Passion for Unity," 129. Cf. Jossua, *Yves Congar*, 54.

32. Thomas O'Meara, "'Raid on the Dominicans': The Repression of 1954," *America*, February 5, 1994, 8–16.

33. Quoted in Jossua, *Yves Congar*, 55.

34. Quoted in Jossua, *Yves Congar*, 55–56.

35. Jossua, *Yves Congar*, 53–54.

36. McClory, "Yves Congar: A Passion for Unity," 129.

37. Jossua, *Yves Congar*, 109.

38. I find it significant that Congar, from early in his career, refused one tactic that others have commonly used to avoid ecclesiastical censure, that of writing under a pseudonym (Jossua, *Yves Congar*, 32). Though I can certainly imagine circumstances in which a practitioner of Gandhian nonviolence would appropriately use a pseudonym, Congar's reluctance suggests eminently Gandhian principles not only of accepting the consequences of one's actions, but also of transparency, truth telling, and the correspondence of means with ends.

39. McClory, "Yves Congar: A Passion for Unity," 32.

40. Yves Congar, "Silenced for Saying Things Rome Didn't Like to Have Said," excerpt of letter written by the author to his mother, *National Catholic Reporter*, June 2, 2000, 20.

41. Quoted in McClory, "Yves Congar: A Passion for Unity," 132.

42. Cf. Appleby, Byrne, and Portier, *Creative Fidelity*, 165.

43. David Tracy, *The Analogical Imagination: Christian Theology and the Culture of Pluralism* (New York: Crossroad, 1981), 247n27.

44. Dorothy Day, "In Peace Is My Bitterness Most Bitter," *Catholic Worker*, January 1967, 1–2.

45. Robert Coles, *Dorothy Day: A Radical Devotion*, Radcliffe Biography Series (Reading, MA: Addison-Wesley, 1987), 65–67.

46. William D. Miller, *All Is Grace: The Spirituality of Dorothy Day* (Garden City, NY: Doubleday, 1987), 112, 114.

47. Coles, *Dorothy Day: A Radical Devotion*, 75.

48. Dorothy Day, "The Case of Father Duffy," *Catholic Worker*, December 1949, 1, 4.

49. Dorothy Day, "Holy Obedience," in *Dorothy Day, Selected Writings: By Little and by Little*, ed. Robert Ellsberg (Maryknoll, NY: Orbis Books, 1992), 170.

50. W. Miller, *All Is Grace: The Spirituality of Dorothy Day*, 82.

51. Coles, *Dorothy Day: A Radical Devotion*, 82, 85–86, 88.

52. Dorothy Day, "On Pilgrimage," *Catholic Worker*, January 1962, 1, 7–8.

53. Coles, *Dorothy Day: A Radical Devotion*, 68; Dorothy Day, "Bread for the Hungry," *Catholic Worker*, September 1976, 1, 5.

54. Dorothy Day, "Day after Day: Thoughts on Breadlines and on the War," *Catholic Worker*, June 1940, 1, 4.

55. Dorothy Day, "The Council and the Mass," *Catholic Worker*, September 1962, 2.

56. Coles, *Dorothy Day: A Radical Devotion*, 76.

57. Day, "Holy Obedience," 168–70.

58. Hélder Câmara, *The Conversions of a Bishop: An Interview with José de Broucker*, trans. Hilary Davies (London and Cleveland: Collins, 1979), 181.

59. Long inspired by Dom Hélder Câmara's notion of Abrahamic minorities, I have written at greater length on these themes elsewhere: see Gerald W. Schlabach, *To Bless All Peoples: Serving with Abraham and Jesus*, Peace and Justice Series 12 (Scottdale, PA: Herald, 1991); "The Blessing of Abraham's Children: A Theology of Service," *Mission Focus* 19, no. 4 (December 1991): 52–55; "Beyond Two- versus One-Kingdom Theology: Abrahamic Community as a Mennonite Paradigm for Engagement in Society," *Conrad Grebel Review* 11, no. 3 (Fall 1993): 187–210; "Deuteronomic or Constantinian: What Is the Most Basic Problem for Christian Social Ethics?" in *The Wisdom of the Cross: Essays in Honor of John Howard Yoder*, ed. Stanley Hauerwas et al. (Grand Rapids: Eerdmans, 1999), 456–61, 463–64.

60. Câmara, *Conversions of a Bishop*, 13.

61. José de Broucker, introduction to Câmara, *Conversions of a Bishop*, 13. For Câmara's biographical trajectory, also see Benedicto Tapia de Renedo, ed., *Hélder Câmara: Proclamas a la Juventud*, Serie PEDAL 64 (Salamanca: Ediciones Sígueme, 1976), 10–18.

62. Câmara, *Conversions of a Bishop*, 211.

63. Tapia de Renedo, *Hélder Câmara: Proclamas a la Juventud*, 35–36.

64. The three speeches were: "Un pacto digno de coronor vuestra marcha" [A covenant worthy to crown your march], message to the *Mani Tese* youth movement climaxing a march on November 5, 1972; "¿Comunidad europea o imperio europeo?" [European community or European Empire?], speech at Turin, Italy, November 6, 1972; "La degradación de los mundos y la urgente renovación de la tierra" [The degradation of the worlds and the urgent renovation of the earth], speech at Turin, Italy, November 7, 1972. They appear in Tapia de Renedo, *Hélder Câmara: Proclamas a la Juventud*, 185–204. The original Portuguese version of the speeches appears in Dom Hélder Câmara, *Justiça e paz: Viagens 1972–1973*, Servicio de Apostillas 36 (1973). English translations of the full texts at http://courseweb .stthomas.edu/gwschlabach/docs/manitese.htm.

65. Tapia de Renedo, *Hélder Câmara: Proclamas a la Juventud*, 189. Also see Câmara, *Conversions of a Bishop*, 180–81, 187, 212–13.

66. Tapia de Renedo, *Hélder Câmara: Proclamas a la Juventud*, 189. Also see Câmara, *Conversions of a Bishop*, 212–13.

67. Câmara, *Conversions of a Bishop*, 98–99. Among the "advocates of prudence and patience" whom Câmara had in mind were "the commissioners in Rome [who were] busy making up rules and regulations for our lives [while] the young seminarists [*sic*], the new priests, the laity, the people and Christian communities, go on ahead, far ahead." Representing the second group was the then-influential priest Ivan Illich, author of *Deschooling Society* and other books. Câmara spoke of his deep respect and admiration for his friend Illich, but saw him attacking "schools, or hospitals, or medicine" as currently constituted to such an extent that "his idea of making life more human again seems to involve rejecting society completely and returning more or less to a natural state."

68. Unless otherwise noted, references in the next three paragraphs are from Tapia de Renedo, *Hélder Câmara: Proclamas a la Juventud*, 197–98.

69. See also Câmara, *Conversions of a Bishop*, 120, 184.

70. Tapia de Renedo, *Hélder Câmara: Proclamas a la Juventud*, 203.

71. Tapia de Renedo, *Hélder Câmara: Proclamas a la Juventud*, 98–99, 117–18.

72. Câmara, *Conversions of a Bishop*, 142–45.

73. Câmara, *Conversions of a Bishop*, 159–60.

74. To understand rural poverty in the underdeveloped regions of the third world, Câmara insisted, study the neglected rural areas of one's own country. Make the connections between unemployment, migrant labor, displacement of jobs, and the hoarding of technology both at home and abroad. "Since we must obtain justice as a condition of peace, may each one begin by examining whether one is at peace with justice, or whether one is committing injustices." Tapia de Renedo, *Hélder Câmara: Proclamas a la Juventud*, 190, 203.

75. Tapia de Renedo, *Hélder Câmara: Proclamas a la Juventud*, 191.

76. Tapia de Renedo, *Hélder Câmara: Proclamas a la Juventud*, 190–91. Again we see here Câmara's willingness to critique the critics as well as those in power. Reject false solutions that only perpetuate the problems of humanity, he continued here. War and consumerism were two of his examples, but so was an elitist form of environmentalism that fails to include impoverished human beings in its concern. Capitalist extremism and socialist distortions were other false and ideological solutions he named. Finally, for all his sympathy for the desperation that was irrupting in revolution at many places in the world, he clearly considered violent insurrection to be a false solution too. Mere words on behalf of peaceful solutions, "as beautiful and ringing as they may be," would not do either. If active nonviolence could not "demonstrate its validity or resolve the structures of oppression, the winner will be armed violence. And then the empire of injustice will long continue, oppressing most of humanity."

77. Tapia de Renedo, *Hélder Câmara: Proclamas a la Juventud*, 203.

78. Tapia de Renedo, *Hélder Câmara: Proclamas a la Juventud*, 203.

79. Tapia de Renedo, *Hélder Câmara: Proclamas a la Juventud*, 204.

80. Terrence W. Tilley, "The Institutional Element in Religious Experience," *Modern Theology* 10 (April 1994): 185–212.

81. Tilley, "Institutional Element," 185. The overarching arguments in Tilley's article provide further backing for my own analysis in the first two chapters of this book. After all, Tilley has exposed the fallacy of sharply distinguishing between charisma and office that runs not only through Weberian typologies but also through Tillich's Protestant Principle and the "heroic pneumatology" of Mennonites in the Concern Group.

82. "It may be obvious, but it is often ignored: institutions are not necessarily 'deteriorations' of charismatic authority or real religion, but [may well be] transformations of authority without which there is *no practically possible retrieval* of that authority and *no practically possible access* to that charismatic figure, and *no practically possible continuity of* his or her distinctive gifts and insights, once the charismatic figure and immediate memory of her or him is gone." Tilley, "Institutional Element," 188, with original emphasis. An important footnote to this paragraph includes the additional case of founding charismatic figures themselves, who never spring forth purely through charisma alone (or "manna," to use the metaphor we encountered in chaps. 1–2):

Charismatic figures' charisma are constituted, in part, by institutional authorities, communal relationships, and believe/practice traditions. Their contributions are never, and never could be, *purely* original, as a "monodirectional" reading of the relationship between charismatic and institutional authority would suggest. Charismatic authority emerges in social contexts which are *given*. Such inherited traditions are the lodes from which meanings are *taken*. The power of charismatic persons comes, in part, from their ability to reshape the given by taking meaning from it in new, unconventional ways, to communicate that meaning to others, and thus to inspire a new community with a nascent tradition. (208n8)

83. Tilley, "Institutional Element," 205.

84. Marie Dennis, Scott Wright, and Renny Golden, *Oscar Romero: Reflections on His Life and Writings*, Modern Spiritual Masters Series (Maryknoll, NY: Orbis Books, 2000), 34.

85. Dennis, Wright, and Golden, *Oscar Romero*, 8–9.

86. Dennis, Wright, and Golden, *Oscar Romero*, 24.

87. James R. Brockman, *Romero: A Life* (Maryknoll, NY: Orbis Books, 1989), 145.

88. Dennis, Wright, and Golden, *Oscar Romero*, 27–28.

89. Dennis, Wright, and Golden, *Oscar Romero*, 11.

90. Tilley, "Institutional Element," 202–5. Quotations of Jean Donovan are cited from Ana Carrigan, *Salvador Witness: The Life and Calling of Jean Donovan* (New York: Simon & Schuster, 1984), 109, 121.

91. Tilley, "Institutional Element," 203. Jean Donovan's transformation committed her to nonviolence, renewed her life of prayer, and restored her respect for the institutional church; Tilley wrote of all this: "It is hard to imagine any of that happening without an institution which would evoke her desire to do missionary work, sponsor her work in El Salvador, expose her to a Church structure rather different from that in the first world, introduce her to a leader whose institutional authority made him a hero and saint, and enable her to learn authentic humility by realizing that she was being ministered to by the people of El Salvador as much as ministering to them" (204).

92. For a fuller account of this exchange, see Margot Patterson, "Saying 'No' to the Vatican: Obedience Is a Complex Matter," *National Catholic Reporter*, July 27, 2001, 5.

93. To be clear, what Chittister was refusing to wait for was not the ordination of women, but a churchwide discussion of the topic. As she told a radio interviewer, "At the end of that discussion, we may all decide we want it just the way it is, for whatever reason, but not for a false reason. The very fact that you don't discuss it is the problem. It's not the answer that's the problem." Krista Tippett, "Obedience and Action," interview with Joan Chittister, OSB, *Speaking of Faith* (Minnesota Public Radio, 2006), http://speakingoffaith.publicradio.org/programs/obedienceandaction/index.shtml.

94. Joan Chittister, *Called to Question: A Spiritual Memoir* (Lanham, MD: Sheed & Ward, 2004), 170–74.

95. Chittister, *Called to Question*, 135–36.

96. Chittister, *Called to Question*, 128, 136, 169–70.

97. Chittister, *Called to Question*, 170.

98. Joan Chittister, "What's Right with the Catholic Church?" in *Womanstrength: Modern Church, Modern Women* (Kansas City, MO: Sheed & Ward, 1990), 41.

99. Chittister, "What's Right with the Catholic Church?" 42–43.

100. Chittister, "What's Right with the Catholic Church?" 45.

101. Tippett, "Obedience and Action." In her interview with Chittister, Tippett noted her Benedictine "long view of time, that progress sometimes takes hundreds of years," and remarked: "This is not an instinct that Americans have culturally." When Chittister agreed, Tippett continued: "But, you know, you're extremely passionate, you're out there working on this, but I don't hear you being impatient in the way our culture might be impatient."

102. Joan Chittister, *Light in the Darkness: New Reflections on the Psalms for Every Day of the Year* (New York: Crossroad, 1998), 20, 22–24.

103. Sample: "Does anybody think that it may be time for Sr. Joan to simply admit that she and the Catholic Church have irreconcilable differences and move to another denomination?" In response: "Absolutely, if not past time. . . . It is past time to force the protesting 'Catholics' out of the Church." See http://blog.ancient-future.net/2006/09/sr-joan-chittister-the-game-is-up.html (accessed August 3, 2009).

104. A reader familiar with philosopher Alasdair MacIntyre's notion of the "rationality of traditions" would be right to note his influence here. I will say more about MacIntyre in my final chapter.

105. I refer mainly to Joan Chittister, *Wisdom Distilled from the Daily: Living the Rule of St. Benedict Today* (San Francisco: Harper & Row, 1990), but others recommend her commentary, *The Rule of Benedict: Insights for the Ages*, The Crossroad Spiritual Legacy Series (New York: Crossroad, 1992).

106. Chittister, *Called to Question*, 134–35.

107. Joan Chittister, "In Search of Belief," *National Catholic Reporter*, December 31, 1999, 11. Here is the quotation in context:

What has for long years been considered "dissent" in the churches by those who want more answers than questions, more clerical authority than spiritual investment, may not be real dissent at all. People are not challenging Christianity and leaving the church. They are not arguing against the need for a spiritual life. They are not denying God, Jesus, the Holy Spirit. They are not ridiculing religion and going away. On the contrary. People currently considered "excommunicated" or "suspect" or "heretical" or "smorgasbord" believers are, in many ways, among the most intense Christians of our time. They do more than sing in the choir or raise money for the parish center or fix flowers for the church. They care about it and call it to be its truest self. They question it, not to undermine it, but to strengthen it. They call for new ways of being church together. They do not dismiss the need for the spiritual life. They crave it. What's more, they look for it in their churches. But they crave more than ritual. They crave meaning. They look for more than salvation. They look for authenticity and the integrity of the faith.

108. Recall Margaret O'Brien Steinfels's suggestion ("Dissent and Communion," 10) that dissent "is very seldom an exercise in pure speculation, or the self-aggrandizing acts of disobedience, rebellion, or disloyalty commonly portrayed. More frequently, dissent's origins are found in painful disjunctures between pastoral experience and existing teaching." This carries the implication that challenges to the church are most likely to come from those most deeply engaged in the life and ministry of the church.

109. Even if one remains convinced that Chittister and the case she makes for Christian feminism is wrong, a Catholic worldview ought to recognize mistakes—even sinful ones—as misdirected goods to be redirected with pastoral generosity, not as substantive evils to be squashed. It is precisely this worldview, rooted in Augustine's rejection of Manichaeism, that distinguishes orthodox Catholicism from any kind of fundamentalism.

110. Gibson, *The Coming Catholic Church*, 82–83.

Chapter 6 Giving the Gift of Stability to a Globalizing World

1. Day, "In Peace Is My Bitterness Most Bitter."

2. Benjamin R. Barber, *Jihad vs. McWorld: How Globalism and Tribalism Are Reshaping the World* (New York: Random House, 1995). Also see Barber, "Jihad vs. McWorld," *The Atlantic* 269 (March 1992): 53–65.

3. Benjamin R. Barber, "Beyond *Jihad Vs. McWorld*," *Nation*, January 21, 2002, 17.

4. The *Oxford English Dictionary*'s earliest instances of "globalise" or "globalisation" are from 1959 through 1965. Vatican II instances of "*interdependentia*" appear in *Gaudium et spes* 25–26.

5. Even the early "befriending" sections of *Gaudium et spes* recognize the ambivalence of "modern man" about its achievements: "In wonder at their own discoveries and their own

might [human beings] are today troubled and perplexed by questions about current trends in the world, about their place and role in the universe, about the meaning of individual and collective endeavor, and finally about the destiny of nature and of [humanity]" (§3). To scrutinize "the signs of the time" unblinkingly was to see that too often the "critical and swift upheavals" that humanity's technological achievements were achieving "recoil" back upon us (§4). It was precisely this ambivalence that called forth the church's offer of friendship and solidarity with humanity on its journey, not a starry-eyed celebration of all things modern.

6. Vatican Council, *Gaudium et spes* 53–62. All quotations of the Second Vatican Council are from Second Vatican Council, *Vatican Council II*.

7. Vatican Council, *Gaudium et spes* 54.

8. Vatican Council, *Gaudium et spes* 55.

9. See Barber, *Jihad vs. McWorld*, 8–20, for Barber's own summary of his book-length argument.

10. Rahner, "Towards a Fundamental Theological Interpretation of Vatican II." In chap. 4 see "Religious Liberty" in the larger section "Authority and Dissent."

11. Vatican Council, *Sacrosanctum concilium* 39–40, 63; *Ad gentes* 9, 15–22, 26, 64; *Gaudium et spes* 44, 58.

12. Trish O'Kane, *Guatemala in Focus: A Guide to the People, Politics, and Culture* (London: Latin America Bureau; New York: Interlink Books, 1999), 79.

13. The very title of a recent book by *New York Times* columnist Thomas Friedman reflects this thesis: *The World Is Flat: A Brief History of the Twenty-First Century* (New York: Farrar, Straus & Giroux, 2005).

14. As the reader will soon see, I am most indebted here to the work of philosopher Alasdair MacIntyre. On the point at hand, see MacIntyre on the problem of incommensurability and the inevitability of making judgments from within some tradition: *Whose Justice? Which Rationality?* 1–4, 122–23, 133–34, 166.

15. Cf. MacIntyre, *Whose Justice? Which Rationality?* chap. 17, "Liberalism Transformed into a Tradition."

16. MacIntyre has paid most attention to the Nietzschean critique. See MacIntyre, *After Virtue: A Study in Moral Theory*, chaps. 9 and 18; MacIntyre, *Three Rival Versions of Moral Enquiry: Encyclopedia, Genealogy, and Tradition*, The Gifford Lectures 1988 (Notre Dame, IN: University of Notre Dame Press, 1990), chap. 2.

17. MacIntyre, *Whose Justice? Which Rationality?* 395–96.

18. Cf. Bellah et al., *Habits of the Heart*, 20–26.

19. MacIntyre's argument extends through a trilogy of his books: *After Virtue: A Study in Moral Theory*; *Whose Justice? Which Rationality?*; and *Three Rival Versions of Moral Enquiry*. A reader new to MacIntyre's thought can gain a good introduction to his overall project in "The Privatization of Good: An Inaugural Lecture," *The Review of Politics* 32 (1990): 344–61; and a good introduction to "the rationality of traditions" in the final three chapters of *Whose Justice? Which Rationality?*

20. MacIntyre, *After Virtue: A Study in Moral Theory*, 96–97; cf. 31–33, 236, 250; MacIntyre, *Whose Justice? Which Rationality?* 141.

21. MacIntyre, *After Virtue: A Study in Moral Theory*, 204–19.

22. MacIntyre, *After Virtue: A Study in Moral Theory*, 220–24, 349; *Whose Justice? Which Rationality?* 12; "The Privatization of Good," 355, 358.

23. MacIntyre, *After Virtue: A Study in Moral Theory*, 221; MacIntyre, *Whose Justice? Which Rationality?* 54.

24. Kelvin Knight, *Aristotelian Philosophy: Ethics and Politics from Aristotle to MacIntyre* (Cambridge, UK; Malden, MA: Polity, 2007).

25. MacIntyre, *Whose Justice? Which Rationality?* 172, 327–28.

26. MacIntyre, *Whose Justice? Which Rationality?* 172–73, 326–27, 388.

27. MacIntyre, *After Virtue: A Study in Moral Theory*, 164.

28. MacIntyre, *After Virtue: A Study in Moral Theory*, 171.

29. MacIntyre, *After Virtue: A Study in Moral Theory*, 276–77. Cf. *Whose Justice? Which Rationality?* 12, 326.

30. MacIntyre, *Whose Justice? Which Rationality?* 36.

31. MacIntyre, *After Virtue: A Study in Moral Theory*, 222, 226.

32. For a more detailed account of the stages through which a tradition navigates its challenges and debates, see MacIntyre, *Whose Justice? Which Rationality?* 354–62.

33. MacIntyre, *After Virtue: A Study in Moral Theory*, 98–99.

34. MacIntyre, *Whose Justice? Which Rationality?* 361–62.

35. MacIntyre dedicated an entire chapter to the possibilities and limitations of translation—both literally between languages and figuratively between traditions—because the issue illuminates the dynamics and rationality of traditions so well. See *Whose Justice? Which Rationality?* 370–88. Also cf. MacIntyre's running commentary on the problem of "incommensurability," as in *After Virtue: A Study in Moral Theory*, 245; *Whose Justice? Which Rationality?* 1–3, 166–67, 327, 350–51.

36. MacIntyre, *Whose Justice? Which Rationality?* 350.

37. MacIntyre, *Whose Justice? Which Rationality?* 394, 398.

38. MacIntyre, *Whose Justice? Which Rationality?* 394, 397.

39. MacIntyre, *After Virtue: A Study in Moral Theory*, 194–95.

40. MacIntyre, *After Virtue: A Study in Moral Theory*, 203.

41. MacIntyre, *Whose Justice? Which Rationality?* 394–95.

Bibliography

Alberigo, Giuseppe, ed. *History of Vatican II.* English version edited by Joseph Komonchak. 5 vols. Maryknoll, NY: Orbis Books; Leuven, Belgium: Peeters, 1996.

Allen, John L., Jr. "Host Sant'Egidio Community in Familiar Mediator Role." *National Catholic Reporter,* October 6, 2000, 15.

———. "Interview with Sant'Egidio Founder Andrea Riccardi." *National Catholic Reporter,* July 23, 2004, www.natcath.org/mainpage/specialdocuments/riccardi.htm.

Appleby, R. Scott, Patricia Byrne, and William L. Portier, eds. *Creative Fidelity: American Catholic Intellectual Traditions.* Maryknoll, NY: Orbis Books, 2002.

Arie, Sophie. "Global South as Growing Force in Catholic Church." *Christian Science Monitor,* April 5, 2005, www.csmonitor.com/2005/0405/p01s03-wogi.html.

Attenborough, Richard, producer and director. *Gandhi.* Burbank, CA: RCA/Columbia Pictures Home Video, 1982.

Barber, Benjamin R. "Beyond *Jihad vs. McWorld.*" *Nation,* January 21, 2002, 11–18.

———. "Jihad vs. McWorld." *Atlantic* 269 (March 1992): 53–65.

———. *Jihad vs. Mcworld: How Globalism and Tribalism Are Reshaping the World.* New York: Random House, 1995.

Bellah, Robert N. *The Broken Covenant: American Civil Religion in a Time of Trial.* The Weil Lectures 1971. New York: Seabury, 1975.

———. "Religion and the Shape of National Culture: Flaws in the Protestant Cultural Code." *America,* July 31–August 7, 1999, 9–14.

Bellah, Robert N., Richard Madsen, William M. Sullivan, Ann Swidler, and Steven M. Tipton. *Habits of the Heart: Individualism and Commitment in American Life.* New York: Harper & Row, 1985.

Bender, Harold S. "The Anabaptist Vision." *Church History* 13 (March 1944): 3–24.

———. "The Anabaptist Vision." *Mennonite Quarterly Review* 18 (April 1944): 67–88.

———. "The Anabaptist Vision." In Hershberger, *Recovery of the Anabaptist Vision,* 29–54.

Benedict, Saint. *RB 1980: The Rule of St. Benedict in English.* Edited by Timothy Fry, OSB. Collegeville, MN: Liturgical Press, 1982.

Bennett, John C. *Christian Ethics and Social Policy.* The Richard Lectures in the University of Virginia. New York: Charles Scribner's Sons, 1946.

Berkman, John, and Michael G. Cartwright, eds. *The Hauerwas Reader.* Durham, NC: Duke University Press, 2001.

Bernardin, Joseph. "Address on the Common Ground Project," October 24, 1996, *Origins: CNS documentary service* (November 14, 1996), 353; www.us.catholic.net/rcc/Periodicals/Homiletic/07-97/america.html.

———. "The Impact of Vatican II: Church in the Modern World." *Origins*, October 17, 1985, 306–8.

Berry, Wendell. "The Body and the Earth." In *The Unsettling of America: Culture and Agriculture*, 97–140. New York: Avon, 1977.

———. "The Work of Local Culture." In *What Are People For?* 153–69. San Francisco: North Point, 1990.

Biesecker-Mast, Gerald. *Separation and the Sword in Anabaptist Persuasion: Radical Confessional Rhetoric from Schleitheim to Dordrecht*. The C. Henry Smith Series 6. Telford, PA: Cascadia; Scottdale, PA: Herald, 2006.

Briley, John. *Gandhi: The Screenplay*. Foreword by Sir Richard Attenborough. New York: Grove Press, 1983.

Brockman, James R. *Romero: A Life*. Maryknoll, NY: Orbis Books, 1989.

Brown, Judith M. *Gandhi: Prisoner of Hope*. New Haven: Yale University Press, 1989.

Brunk, George R., III. "The Credibility of Leadership." In Esau, *Understanding Ministerial Leadership*, 114–23.

Calvin, John. *The Necessity of Reforming the Church*. In *Tracts and Treatises*. Translated by Henry Beveridge, 123–234. Grand Rapids: Eerdmans, 1958.

Câmara, Hélder. *The Conversions of a Bishop: An Interview with José de Broucker*. Translated by Hilary Davies. London and Cleveland: Collins, 1979.

Carrigan, Ana. *Salvador Witness: The Life and Calling of Jean Donovan*. New York: Simon & Schuster, 1984.

Carson, Rachel. *Silent Spring*. Boston: Houghton Mifflin, 1962.

Carter, Craig A. *The Politics of the Cross: The Theology and Social Ethics of John Howard Yoder*. Grand Rapids: Brazos, 2001.

Cartwright, Michael G. *The Royal Priesthood: Essays Ecclesiological and Ecumenical*. Grand Rapids: Eerdmans, 1994.

Casey, Michael, OCSO. "The Value of Stability." *Cistercian Studies Quarterly* 31, no. 3 (1996): 287–301.

Cavanaugh, William. "Stan the Man: A Thoroughly Biased Account of a Completely Unobjective Person." In Berkman and Cartwright, *Hauerwas Reader*, 17–32.

Chittister, Joan. *Called to Question: A Spiritual Memoir*. Lanham, MD: Sheed & Ward, 2004.

———. "In Search of Belief." *National Catholic Reporter*, December 31, 1999, 10–12.

———. *Light in the Darkness: New Reflections on the Psalms for Every Day of the Year*. New York: Crossroad, 1998.

———. *The Rule of Benedict: Insights for the Ages*. The Crossroad Spiritual Legacy Series. New York: Crossroad, 1992.

———. "What's Right with the Catholic Church?" In *Womanstrength: Modern Church, Modern Women*, 41–50. Kansas City: Sheed & Ward, 1990.

———. *Wisdom Distilled from the Daily: Living the Rule of St. Benedict Today*. San Francisco: Harper & Row, 1990.

Ciulla, Joanne B. "Leadership and the Problem of Bogus Empowerment." In *Ethics, the Heart of Leadership*, edited by Joanne B. Ciulla, 63–86. Westport, CT: Quorum Books, 1998.

Coles, Robert. *Dorothy Day: A Radical Devotion*. Radcliffe Biography Series. Reading, MA: Addison-Wesley, 1987.

Congar, Yves. "Silenced for Saying Things Rome Didn't Like to Have Said." Excerpt of letter written by the author to his mother. *National Catholic Reporter*, June 2, 2000, 20.

Cornell, Tom. "How Catholics Began to Speak Their Peace." *Salt of the Earth* 16, no. 5 (September/October 1996): 17–18.

Cowdin, Daniel M. "Religious Liberty, Religious Dissent and the Catholic Tradition."

Heythrop Journal 32, no. 1 (January 1991): 26–61.

Curran, Charles E. *Loyal Dissent: Memoir of a Catholic Theologian.* Moral Traditions Series. Washington, DC: Georgetown University Press, 2006.

Day, Dorothy. "Bread for the Hungry." *Catholic Worker*, September 1976, 1, 5.

———. "The Case of Father Duffy." *Catholic Worker*, December 1949, 1, 4.

———. "The Council and the Mass." *Catholic Worker*, September 1962, 2.

———. "Day after Day: Thoughts on Breadlines and on the War." *Catholic Worker*, June 1940, 1, 4.

———. "Holy Obedience." In *Dorothy Day, Selected Writings: By Little and by Little*, edited by Robert Ellsberg, 168–73. Maryknoll, NY: Orbis Books, 1992.

———. "In Peace Is My Bitterness Most Bitter." *Catholic Worker*, January 1967, 1–2.

———. "On Pilgrimage." *Catholic Worker*, January 1962, 1, 7–8.

Dennis, Marie, Scott Wright, and Renny Golden. *Oscar Romero: Reflections on His Life and Writings.* Modern Spiritual Masters Series. Maryknoll, NY: Orbis Books, 2000.

Doerksen, Paul. "Share the House: Yoder and Hauerwas among the Nations." In Ollenburger and Koontz, *Mind Patient and Untamed*, 187–204.

Dolan, Jay P. *In Search of an American Catholicism: A History of Religion and Culture in Tension.* Oxford and New York: Oxford University Press, 2002.

Driedger, Leo. *Mennonites in the Global Village.* Toronto and Buffalo: University of Toronto Press, 2000.

Driedger, Leo, and Leland Harder. *Anabaptist-Mennonite Identities in Ferment.* Elkhart, IN: Institute of Mennonite Studies, 1990.

Dulles, Avery Robert. "The Vatican II Revolution: Authority and Obedience." *Tablet*, December 18, 1982, 1264–65.

Esau, John A. "Recovering, Rethinking, and Re-Imagining: Issues in a Mennonite Theology for Christian Ministry." In Esau, *Understanding Ministerial Leadership*, 1–27.

———, ed. *Understanding Ministerial Leadership.* Foreword by Ross T. Bender. Text Reader Series 6. Elkhart, IN: Institute of Mennonite Studies, 1995.

Flannery, Austin, ed. *Vatican Council II: The Conciliar and Post-Conciliar Documents.* New revised edition. Vatican Collection 1. Newport, NY: Costello; Dublin, Ireland: Dominican Publications, 1996.

Friedmann, Robert. *The Theology of Anabaptism: An Interpretation.* Studies in Anabaptist and Mennonite History 15. Scottdale, PA: Herald, 1973.

Friedman, Thomas L. *The World Is Flat: A Brief History of the Twenty-First Century.* New York: Farrar, Straus & Giroux, 2005.

Gaillardetz, Richard R. *By What Authority? A Primer on Scripture, the Magisterium, and the Sense of the Faithful.* Collegeville, MN: Liturgical Press, 2003.

———. "Marital and Ecclesial Commitment." *America*, August 4, 2003, 8–11.

Gandhi, Mahatma. *An Autobiography or the Story of My Experiment with Truth.* Translated by Mahadev H. Desai. 2nd ed. Ahmedabad: Navajivan, 1940.

———. *The Collected Works of Mahatma Gandhi.* Vol. 23 (1922–1924). Delhi: Publications Division, Ministry of Information and Broadcasting, Government of India, 1967.

Gibson, David. *The Coming Catholic Church: How the Faithful Are Shaping a New American Catholicism.* San Francisco: HarperSanFrancisco, 2003.

Goldberg, Michael. "Corporate Culture and Corporate Cult." In *Against the Grain: New Approaches to Professional Ethics*, edited by Michael Goldberg, 13–36. Valley Forge, PA: Trinity Press International, 1993.

Graber, J. D. *The Church Apostolic: A Discussion of Modern Missions.* Scottdale, PA: Herald, 1960.

Graff, Ann Elizabeth O'Hara. "Transforming Today's Church." *Chicago Studies* 32, no. 2 (August 1993): 127–42.

Grisar, Hartmann. *Martin Luther, His Life and Work.* Adapted from the second German edition, 1930. Westminster, MD: Newman, 1950.

Gunderson, Gary. *Deeply Woven Roots: Improving the Quality of Life in Your Community.* Minneapolis: Fortress, 1997.

Guroian, Vigen. "Tradition and Ethics: Prospects in a Liberal Society." *Modern Theology* 7, no. 3 (April 1991): 205–24.

Harink, Douglas K. "For or against the Nations: Yoder and Hauerwas, What's the Difference?" *Toronto Journal of Theology* 17, no. 1 (Spring 2001): 167–85.

Hauerwas, Stanley. "Abortion, Theologically Understood." 1991. Reprinted in Berkman and Cartwright, *Hauerwas Reader*, 603–22.

———. "Abortion: Why the Arguments Fail." In Hauerwas, *Community of Character*, 212–29.

———. *After Christendom?* 2nd ed. Nashville: Abingdon, 1999.

———. *Against the Nations: War and Survival in a Liberal Society.* Minneapolis: Winston, 1985.

———. *Character and the Christian Life: A Study in Theological Ethics.* Trinity University Monograph Series in Religion 3. San Antonio: Trinity University Press, 1975.

———. "Character, Narrative, and Growth in the Christian Life." In Hauerwas, *Community of Character*, 129–52.

———. "A Christian Critique of Christian America." 1986. Reprinted in Berkman and Cartwright, *Hauerwas Reader*, 459–80.

———. "The Christian Difference: Or, Surviving Postmodernism." In *A Better Hope: Resources for a Church Confronting Capitalism, Democracy, and Postmodernity*, 35–51. Grand Rapids: Brazos, 2000.

———. *Christian Existence Today: Essays on Church, World, and Living in Between.* Durham, NC: Labyrinth, 1988.

———. "Christianity: It's Not a Religion, It's an Adventure." 1991. Reprinted in Berkman and Cartwright, *Hauerwas Reader*, 522–35.

———. "Clerical Character." In Hauerwas, *Christian Existence Today*, 133–48.

———. *A Community of Character: Toward a Constructive Christian Social Ethic.* Readings in Moral Theology 4. Notre Dame, IN: University of Notre Dame Press, 1981.

———. "The Family: Theology and Ethical Reflections." In Hauerwas, *Community of Character*, 167–74.

———. "The Importance of Being Catholic: Unsolicited Advice from a Protestant Bystander." In Hauerwas, *In Good Company*, 91–108.

———. *In Good Company: The Church as Polis.* Notre Dame, IN: University of Notre Dame Press, 1995.

———. "The Liturgical Shape of the Christian Life: Teaching Christian Ethics as Worship." In Hauerwas, *In Good Company*, 153–68.

———. "The Moral Authority of Scripture: The Politics and Ethics of Remembering." In Hauerwas, *Community of Character*, 53–71.

———. "The Moral Value of the Family." In Hauerwas, *Community of Character*, 155–66.

———. "Must a Patient Be a Person to Be a Patient? Or, My Uncle Charlie Is Not Much of a Person but He Is Still My Uncle Charlie." In *Truthfulness and Tragedy: Further Investigations in Christian Ethics*, 127–31. Notre Dame, IN: University of Notre Dame Press, 1977.

———. "On Keeping Theological Ethics Theological." 1983. Reprinted in Berkman and Cartwright, *Hauerwas Reader*, 51–74.

———. "The Pastor as Prophet: Ethical Reflections on an Improbable Mission." In Hauerwas, *Christian Existence Today*, 149–67.

———. *The Peaceable Kingdom: A Primer in Christian Ethics.* Notre Dame, IN: University of Notre Dame Press, 1983.

———. "Reconciling the Practice of Reason: Casuistry in a Christian Context." In Hauerwas, *Christian Existence Today*, 67–87.

———. "Reforming Christian Social Ethics: Ten Theses." 1981. Reprinted in Berkman and Cartwright, *Hauerwas Reader*, 111–15.

———. "Response." In *On Baptism: Mennonite-Catholic Theological Colloquium, 2001–2002*, edited by Gerald W. Schlabach. The Bridgefolk Series 101–3. Kitchener, ON: Pandora, 2004.

———. "A Retrospective Assessment of an 'Ethics of Character': The Development of Hauerwas's Theological Project." 1985. Reprinted in Berkman and Cartwright, *Hauerwas Reader*, 75–89.

———. "Situation Ethics, Moral Notions, and Moral Theology." In *Vision and Virtue: Essays in Christian Ethical Reflection*, 11–29. Notre Dame, IN: Fides, 1974. Reprint, Notre Dame, IN: University of Notre Dame Press, 1981.

———. "What Could It Mean for the Church to Be Christ's Body? A Question without a Clear Answer." In Hauerwas, *In Good Company*, 19–31.

———. "Whose Church? Which Future? Whither the Anabaptist Vision?" In Hauerwas, *In Good Company*, 65–78.

———. "Why Truthfulness Requires Forgiveness: A Commencement Address for Graduates of a College of the Church of the Second Chance." 1992. Reprinted in Berkman and Cartwright, *Hauerwas Reader*, 307–17.

———. *With the Grain of the Universe: The Church's Witness and Natural Theology.* Grand Rapids: Brazos, 2001.

Hauerwas, Stanley, and Samuel Wells, eds. *The Blackwell Companion to Christian Ethics.* Blackwell Companions to Religion. Malden, MA: Blackwell, 2004.

———. "Christian Ethics as Informed Prayer." In Hauerwas and Wells, *Blackwell Companion to Christian Ethics*, 3–12.

———. "The Gift of the Church and the Gifts God Gives It." In Hauerwas and Wells, *Blackwell Companion to Christian Ethics*, 13–27.

———. "How the Church Managed before There Was Ethics." In Hauerwas and Wells, *Blackwell Companion to Christian Ethics*, 39–50.

Hauerwas, Stanley, and William H. Willimon. "Why *Resident Aliens* Struck a Chord." In Hauerwas, *In Good Company*, 51–63.

Hershberger, Guy F., ed. *The Recovery of the Anabaptist Vision: A Sixtieth Anniversary Tribute to Harold S. Bender.* Scottdale, PA: Herald, 1957.

———. *War, Peace, and Nonresistance.* 3rd ed. Scottdale, PA: Herald, 1969.

Hovey, Craig R. "The Public Ethics of John Howard Yoder and Stanley Hauerwas: Difference or Disagreement." In Ollenburger and Koontz, *Mind Patient and Untamed*, 205–20.

Imbelli, Robert P. "The Community of Sant'Egidio: Vatican II Made Real." *Commonweal*, November 18, 1994, 20–22.

Jenkins, Philip. "Defenders of the Faith." *Atlantic Monthly* 292, no. 4 (November 2003): 46, 49.

———. *The Next Christendom: The Coming of Global Christianity.* Oxford and New York: Oxford University Press, 2002.

John XXIII, Pope. *Gaudet mater ecclesia* [Mother Church Rejoices]. Opening speech to the Second Vatican Council, October 11, 1962. In *The Documents of Vatican II*, edited by Walter M. Abbott, SJ, 710–19. New York: Guild, 1966.

———. *Humanae salutis* [Of Human Salvation]. Apostolic Constitution convoking the Second Vatican Council, 1961. In *The Documents of Vatican II*, edited by Walter M. Abbott, SJ, 705–9. New York: Guild, 1966.

Johnson, Maxwell E., and the monks of Saint John's Abbey, eds. *Benedictine Daily Prayer: A Short Breviary.* Collegeville, MN: Liturgical Press, 2005.

Jossua, Jean Pierre. *Yves Congar: Theology in the Service of God's People.* Chicago: Priory Press, 1968.

259

Kanagy, Conrad L. *Road Signs for the Journey: A Profile of Mennonite Church USA.* Scottdale, PA: Herald, 2007.

Kardong, Terrence G. *Benedict's Rule: A Translation and Commentary.* Collegeville, MN: Liturgical Press, 1996.

———. "RB 71.6–9 in the Light of Gandhi's Non-Violence." *Tjurunga* 27 (1984): 3–16.

Kasper, Walter Cardinal. "Current Problems in Ecumenical Theology." *Reflections* 6 (Spring 2003): 56–88.

Kauffman, Ivan. "On Being a Mennonite Catholic." *Mennonite Quarterly Review* 77, no. 2 (April 2003): 235–55, www.goshen .edu/mqr/pastissues/apr03kauffman.html.

Kauffman, J. Howard, and Leo Driedger. *The Mennonite Mosaic: Identity and Modernization.* Foreword by Donald B. Kraybill. Scottdale, PA: Herald, 1991.

Kauffman, J. Howard, and Leland Harder. *Anabaptists Four Centuries Later: A Profile of Five Mennonite and Brethren in Christ Denominations.* Scottdale, PA: Herald, 1975.

Kaveny, M. Cathleen. "The Perfect Storm: 'The Vagina Monologues' and Catholic Higher Education." *America*, May 8, 2006, 14–19.

Keim, Albert N. *Harold S. Bender, 1897–1962.* Scottdale, PA: Herald, 1998.

King, Martin Luther, Jr. "Letter from the Birmingham Jail." In *Why We Can't Wait*, 77–100. New York: Harper & Row, 1964.

———. *Stride toward Freedom: The Montgomery Story.* New York: Harper, 1958.

Kittelson, James M. *Wolfgang Capito: From Humanist to Reformer.* Studies in Medieval and Reformation Thought 17. Leiden: Brill, 1975.

Knight, Kelvin. *Aristotelian Philosophy: Ethics and Politics from Aristotle to MacIntyre.* Cambridge, UK; Malden, MA: Polity, 2007.

Komonchak, Joseph A. "Ordinary Papal Magisterium and Religious Assent." In *The Magisterium and Morality*, edited by Charles E. Curran and Richard A. McCormick, 67–90.

Readings in Moral Theology 3. New York: Paulist Press, 1982.

———. "What Road to Joy? How Vatican II Changed the Church, Pt. 8." *Tablet*, November 30, 2002, 11–12.

Kotva, Joseph J., Jr. "For or against the Nations? John Howard Yoder vs. Stanley Hauerwas on the Nature of Christian Politics." Conference presentation at the Society of Christian Ethics, Chicago, 2001.

Kraus, C. Norman, and John W. Miller. "Intimations of Another Way—a Progress Report." *Concern: A Pamphlet Series* 3 (1956): 5–19.

Kraybill, Ronald S. "The 'Concern' Group: An Attempt at Anabaptist Renewal." History Seminar paper. Mennonite Historical Library, Goshen College, Goshen, IN, 1976.

Lauerien, Hanna-Renata. "The Benedictine Monastery—a Challenge for Society?" In *As We Seek God: International Reflections on Contemporary Benedictine Monasticism*, edited by Stephanie Campbell, 62–76. Cistercian Studies Series 70. Kalamazoo, MI: Cistercian Publications, 1983.

Lortz, Joseph. "The Basic Elements of Luther's Intellectual Style." In *Catholic Scholars Dialogue with Luther*, edited by Jared Wicks, SJ, 1–33. Chicago: Loyola University Press, 1970.

———. *Die Reformation als religiöses Anliegen heute: Vier Vorträge im Dienste der Una Sancta.* Trier, [W. Germany]: Paulinus Verlag, 1948.

———. *The Reformation: A Problem for Today.* Translated by John C. Dwyer. Westminster, MD: Newman, 1964.

Lovin, Robin W. "Niebuhr at 100: Realism for New Realities." *Christian Century*, June 17, 1992, 604–5.

Luther, Martin. "The Babylonian Captivity of the Church." Translated by Charles M. Jacobs. Revised by James Atkinson. In *Three Treatises*. 2nd ed., 113–260. Philadelphia: Fortress, 1970.

———. "The Freedom of a Christian." Translated by W. A. Lambert. Revised by Harold J. Grimm. In *Luther's Works*. Vol. 31, edited by Harold J. Grimm, 327–77. Philadelphia: Fortress, 1957.

———. "Treatise on Good Works." Translated by W. A. Lambert. Revised by James Atkinson. In *Luther's Works*. Vol. 44, *The Christian in Society I*, edited by James Atkinson, 15–114. Philadelphia: Fortress, 1966.

MacIntyre, Alasdair. *After Virtue: A Study in Moral Theory*. 2nd ed. Notre Dame, IN: University of Notre Dame Press, 1984.

———. "The Privatization of Good: An Inaugural Lecture." *The Review of Politics* 32 (1990): 344–61.

———. *Three Rival Versions of Moral Enquiry: Encyclopedia, Genealogy, and Tradition*. The Gifford Lectures 1988. Notre Dame, IN: University of Notre Dame Press, 1990.

———. *Whose Justice? Which Rationality?* Notre Dame, IN: University of Notre Dame Press, 1988.

Madigan, Patrick. Review of John Howard Yoder, *The Jewish-Christian Schism Revisited*. *Heythrop Journal* 47, no. 2 (April 2006): 301–2.

Marsh, Charles. *God's Long Summer: Stories of Faith and Civil Rights*. Princeton, NJ: Princeton University Press, 1997.

Martin, Dennis D. "Journey to a Far Country: Premodern History as Crosscultural Education." *Conrad Grebel Review* 11, no. 3 (Fall 1993): 249–63.

———. "Nothing New under the Sun? Mennonites and History." *Conrad Grebel Review* 5, no. 1 (Winter 1987): 1–28.

Martin, James, SJ. "Saints That Weren't." *New York Times*, November 1, 2006, www.nytimes.com/2006/11/01/opinion/01martin.html.

McCarraher, Eugene. *Christian Critics: Religion and the Impasse in Modern American Social Thought*. Ithaca, NY: Cornell University Press, 2000.

McClory, Robert. *Faithful Dissenters: Stories of Men and Women Who Loved and Changed the Church*. Maryknoll, NY: Orbis Books, 2000.

———. "Yves Congar: A Passion for Unity." In *Faithful Dissenters: Stories of Men and Women Who Loved and Changed the Church*, 119–32. Maryknoll, NY: Orbis Books, 2000.

McSorley, Harry J., CSP. "Erasmus versus Luther: Compounding the Reformation Tragedy." In *Catholic Scholars Dialogue with Luther*, edited by Jared Wicks, SJ, 106–17. Chicago: Loyola University Press, 1970.

Merton, Thomas. *The Sign of Jonas*. New York: Harcourt, Brace & Company, 1953.

Miller, John W. "Concern Reflections." *Conrad Grebel Review* 8, no. 2 (Spring 1990): 139–54.

———. "Organization and Church." *Concern: A Pamphlet Series* 4 (1957): 33–41.

Miller, Marlin E. "Priesthood of All Believers." In *Mennonite Encyclopedia*. Vol. 5, 721. Scottdale, PA: Herald, 1990.

———. "The Recasting of Authority: A Biblical Model for Community Leadership." In *Theology for the Church*, edited by Richard A. Kauffman and Gayle Gerber Koontz, 109–16. Elkhart, IN: Institute of Mennonite Studies, 1997.

———. "Some Reflections on Pastoral Ministry and Pastoral Education." In Esau, *Understanding Ministerial Leadership*, 57–69.

Miller, Susan Fisher. *Culture for Service: A History of Goshen College, 1894–1994*. Goshen, IN: Goshen College, 1994.

Miller, William D. *All Is Grace: The Spirituality of Dorothy Day*. Garden City, NY: Doubleday, 1987.

Murray, John Courtney. "Freedom, Authority, Community." *America*, December 3, 1966, 734–41.

———. *We Hold These Truths: Catholic Reflections on the American Proposition*. New York: Sheed & Ward, 1960.

Nation, Mark Thiessen. *John Howard Yoder: Mennonite Patience, Evangelical Witness, Catholic Convictions*. Grand Rapids: Eerdmans, 2006.

Nichols, Terence L. "Participatory Hierarchy." In *Common Calling: The Laity and Gov-*

261

ernance of the Catholic Church, edited by Stephen J. Pope, 111–27. Washington, DC: Georgetown University Press, 2004.

———. That All May Be One: Hierarchy and Participation in the Church. Collegeville, MN: Liturgical Press, 1997.

Niebuhr, H. Richard. Christ and Culture. New York: Harper & Row, 1956.

———. The Purpose of the Church and Its Ministry: Reflections on the Aims of Theological Education. In collaboration with Daniel Day Williams and James M. Gustafson. New York: Harper & Row, 1956.

Niebuhr, Reinhold. "Why the Christian Church Is Not Pacifist." In Christianity and Power Politics, 1–32. New York: Charles Scribner's Sons, 1940.

Nolt, Steven M. "Anabaptist Visions of Church and Society." Mennonite Quarterly Review 69 (July 1995): 283–94.

Norris, Kathleen. Amazing Grace: A Vocabulary of Faith. New York: Riverhead Books, 1998.

———. The Cloister Walk. New York: Riverhead Books, 1987.

O'Donovan, Oliver. The Problem of Self-Love in St. Augustine. New Haven: Yale University Press, 1980.

O'Kane, Trish. Guatemala in Focus: A Guide to the People, Politics, and Culture. London: Latin America Bureau; New York: Interlink Books, 1999.

Ollenburger, Ben C., and Gayle Gerber Koontz. A Mind Patient and Untamed: Assessing John Howard Yoder's Contributions to Theology, Ethics, and Peacemaking. Telford, PA: Cascadia, 2004.

O'Malley, John W. "Developments, Reforms, and Two Great Reformations: Towards a Historical Assessment of Vatican II." Theological Studies 44, no. 3 (1983): 373–406.

O'Meara, Thomas. "'Raid on the Dominicans': The Repression of 1954." America, February 5, 1994, 8–16.

Patterson, Margot. "Saying 'No' to the Vatican: Obedience Is a Complex Matter." National Catholic Reporter, July 27, 2001, 5.

Payne, Robert. The Life and Death of Mahatma Gandhi. New York: Dutton, 1969.

Peachey, Paul. "The Modern Recovery of the Anabaptist Vision." In Hershberger, Recovery of the Anabaptist Vision, 327–40.

———. "Preface." Concern: A Pamphlet Series 2 (1955): 3.

———. "Spirit and Form in the Church." Concern: A Pamphlet Series 2 (1955): 15–25.

———. "Toward an Understanding of the Decline of the West." Concern: A Pamphlet Series 1 (1954): 8–44.

———. "What Is Concern?" Concern: A Pamphlet Series 4 (1957): 14–19.

Rahner, Karl. "Towards a Fundamental Theological Interpretation of Vatican II." Theological Studies 40, no. 4 (December 1979): 716–27.

Ratzinger, Cardinal Joseph. Church, Ecumenism, and Politics: New Essays in Ecclesiology. New York: Crossroad, 1988.

Reno, Russell R. In the Ruins of the Church: Sustaining Faith in an Age of Diminished Christianity. Grand Rapids: Brazos, 2002.

Sanders, Scott Russell. Hunting for Hope: A Father's Journey. Boston: Beacon, 1998.

———. "Settling Down." In Staying Put: Making a Home in a Restless World, 95–122. Boston: Beacon, 1994.

Sawatsky, Erick. "Helping Dreams Come True: Toward Wholeness—Articulating the Vision." In Esau, Understanding Ministerial Leadership, 28–39.

Schlabach, Gerald W. "Beyond Two- versus One-Kingdom Theology: Abrahamic Community as a Mennonite Paradigm for Engagement in Society." Conrad Grebel Review 11, no. 3 (Fall 1993): 187–210.

———. "The Blessing of Abraham's Children: A Theology of Service." Mission Focus 19, no. 4 (December 1991): 52–55.

———. "Breaking Bread: Peace and War." In Hauerwas and Wells, Blackwell Companion to Christian Ethics, 360–74.

———. "The Bridgefolk Movement in Ecumenical Context." *Ecumenical Trends* 32, no. 3 (March 2003): 14–15.

———. "Catholic and Mennonite: A Journey of Healing." *One in Christ* 42, no. 2 (Winter 2008): 318–40.

———. "Deuteronomic or Constantinian: What Is the Most Basic Problem for Christian Social Ethics?" In *The Wisdom of the Cross: Essays in Honor of John Howard Yoder*, edited by Stanley Hauerwas et al., 449–71. Grand Rapids: Eerdmans, 1999.

———. *For the Joy Set before Us: Augustine and Self-Denying Love*. Notre Dame, IN: University of Notre Dame Press, 2001.

———. "Stability amid Mobility: The Oblate's Challenge and Witness." *American Benedictine Review* 52, no. 1 (March 2001): 3–23.

———. *To Bless All Peoples: Serving with Abraham and Jesus*. Peace and Justice Series 12. Scottdale, PA: Herald, 1991.

———. "The Vow of Stability: A Premodern Way through a Hypermodern World." In *Anabaptists and Postmodernity*, edited by Susan Biesecker-Mast and Gerald Biesecker-Mast. Foreword by J. Denny Weaver, 301–24. The C. Henry Smith Series 1. Telford, PA: Pandora Books, 2000.

———. "You Converted to What? One Mennonite's Journey." *Commonweal*, June 1, 2007, 14–17.

Schlabach, Theron F. *Peace, Faith, Nation: Mennonites and Amish in Nineteenth-Century America*. Vol. 2 of *The Mennonite Experience in America*. Scottdale, PA: Herald, 1988.

———. "To Focus a Mennonite Vision." In *Kingdom, Cross, and Community: Essays on Mennonite Themes in Honor of Guy F. Hershberger*, edited by John Richard Burkholder and Calvin Redekop, 15–50. Scottdale, PA: Herald, 1976.

———. *War, Peace, and Social Conscience: Guy F. Hershberger and Mennonite Ethics*. Scottdale, PA: Herald, 2009.

Senarclens, Jacques de. *Heirs of the Reformation*. Philadelphia: Westminster, 1964.

Shannon, James Patrick. *Reluctant Dissenter*. New York: Crossroads, 1998.

Smith, Derek G. "Oblates in Western Monasticism." *Monastic Studies* 13 (Autumn 1982): 47–72.

Snyder, C. Arnold. *The Life and Thought of Michael Sattler*. Studies in Anabaptist and Mennonite History 26. Scottdale, PA: Herald, 1984.

Somerville, Janet. "The Grace of Mutual Respect." 2004–5 Somerville Lecture on Christianity and Communication. St. Jerome Centre, Saint Jerome's University, Waterloo, Ontario, 2004.

Steinfels, Margaret O'Brien. "Dissent and Communion: You Can't Have One without the Other." *Commonweal*, November 18, 1994, 9–15.

———. "The Unholy Alliance between the Right and the Left in the Catholic Church." *America*, May 2, 1992, 376–82.

Steinfels, Peter. *A People Adrift: The Crisis of the Roman Catholic Church in America*. New York: Simon & Schuster, 2003.

Stout, Jeffrey. *Democracy and Tradition*. New Forum Books. Princeton, NJ: Princeton University Press, 2004.

———. *Ethics after Babel: The Languages of Morals and Their Discontents*. Boston: Beacon, 1988.

———. "Liberal Society and the Languages of Morals." In *Community in America: The Challenge of Habits of the Heart*, edited by Charles H. Reynolds and Ralph V. Norman, 127–46. Berkeley: University of California Press, 1988.

Tapia de Renedo, Benedicto, ed. *Hélder Câmara: Proclamas a la Juventud*. Serie PEDAL 64. Salamanca: Ediciones Sígueme, 1976.

Tilley, Terrence W. "The Institutional Element in Religious Experience." *Modern Theology* 10 (April 1994): 185–212.

Tillich, Paul. *The Protestant Era*. Translated by James Luther Adams. Chicago: University of Chicago Press, 1948.

Tippett, Krista. "Obedience and Action." Interview with Joan Chittister, OSB.

Speaking of Faith. Minnesota Public Radio, 2006, http://speakingoffaith.pub licradio.org/programs/obedienceandac tion/index.shtml.

Toews, Paul. "The Concern Movement: Its Origins and Early History." *Conrad Grebel Review* 8, no. 2 (Spring 1990): 109–26.

———. *Mennonites in American Society, 1930–1970: Modernity and the Persistence of Religious Community.* Vol. 4 of *The Mennonite Experience in America.* Scottdale, PA: Herald, 1996.

Toolan, David S. "The Catholic Taboo against Schism: Strained but Holding." *Religion and Intellectual Life* 7, no. 1 (Fall 1989): 36–50.

———. "Of Many Things." *America,* February 19, 2001, 2.

Tracy, David. *The Analogical Imagination: Christian Theology and the Culture of Pluralism.* New York: Crossroad, 1981.

Troeltsch, Ernst. *The Social Teaching of the Christian Churches.* Translated by Olive Wyon, with an introduction by H. Richard Niebuhr. New York: Macmillan, 1931. Reprint, Chicago: University of Chicago Press, 1981.

Vatican Council, Second. *Ad gentes* [Decree on the Church's Missionary Activity]. 1965. In Flannery, *Vatican Council II.*

———. *Apostolicam actuositatem* [Decree on the Apostolate of the Laity]. 1965. In Flannery, *Vatican Council II.*

———. *Dei Verbum* [Dogmatic Constitution on Divine Revelation]. 1965. In Flannery, *Vatican Council II.*

———. *Dignitatis humanae* [Declaration on Religious Liberty; or, On the Right of the Person and Communities to Social and Civil Liberty in Religious Matters]. 1965. In Flannery, *Vatican Council II.*

———. *Gaudium et spes* [Pastoral Constitution on the Church in the Modern World]. 1965. In Flannery, *Vatican Council II.*

———. *Lumen gentium* [Dogmatic Constitution on the Church]. 1964. In Flannery, *Vatican Council II.*

———. *Optatam totius* [Decree on Priestly Training]. 1965. In Flannery, *Vatican Council II.*

———. *Presbyterorum ordinis* [Decree on the Ministry of Priests]. 1965. In Flannery, *Vatican Council II.*

———. *Sacrosanctum concilium* [Constitution on the Sacred Liturgy]. 1963. In Flannery, *Vatican Council II.*

———. *Unitatis redintegratio* [Decree on Ecumenism]. 1965. In Flannery, *Vatican Council II.*

Visser 't Hooft, Willem A. "Teachers and the Teaching Authority: The Magistri and the Magisterium." *Ecumenical Review* 38, no. 2 (April 1986): 152–202.

Whitley, Oliver Read. *Trumpet Call of Reformation.* St. Louis: Bethany, 1959.

Wilken, Robert L. *Remembering the Christian Past.* Grand Rapids: Eerdmans, 1995.

Wilkes, Paul. *The Good Enough Catholic: A Guide for the Perplexed.* New York: Ballantine Books, 1996.

Wilson, Jonathan R. *Living Faithfully in a Fragmented World: Lessons for the Church from MacIntyre's "After Virtue."* Harrisburg, PA: Trinity Press International, 1997.

Wuthnow, Robert. *The Restructuring of American Religion: Society and Faith since World War II.* Princeton, NJ: Princeton University Press, 1988.

Yoder, John Howard. "The Ambivalence of the Appeal to the Fathers." In *Practiced in the Presence: Essays in Honor of T. Canby Jones,* edited by Neil Snarr and Daniel Smith-Christopher, 245–55. Richmond, IN: Friends United Press, 1994.

———. "Anabaptism and History." In Yoder, *Priestly Kingdom,* 123–34.

———. "The Anabaptist Dissent: The Logic of the Place of the Disciple in Society." *Concern: A Pamphlet Series* 1 (1954): 45–68.

———. "Anabaptist Vision and Mennonite Reality." In *Consultation on Anabaptist-Mennonite Theology: Papers Read at the 1969 Aspen Conference,* edited by A. J. Klassen.

Fresno, CA: Council of Mennonite Seminaries, 1970.

———. "The Authority of Tradition." In Yoder, *Priestly Kingdom*, 63–79.

———. "Binding and Loosing." In Cartwright, *Royal Priesthood*, 323–58.

———. *Body Politics: Five Practices of the Christian Community before the Watching World*. Nashville: Discipleship Resources, 1992.

———. "The Burden and the Discipline of Evangelical Revisionism." In *Nonviolent America: History through the Eyes of Peace*, edited by Louise Hawkley and James C. Juhnke, 21–37. Cornelius H. Wedel Historical Series 5. North Newton, KS: Bethel College, 1993.

———. "The Christian Case for Democracy." In Yoder, *Priestly Kingdom*, 151–71.

———. "Christian Education: Doctrinal Orientation." Prepared as beginning of conversation about Mennonite Church-administered high schools. Historical mss. 1–48, section 1, box 02, unpublished writings 1947–1997. John H. Yoder Collection. Mennonite Church USA Archives, Goshen, IN, 1958.

———. "Discerning the Kingdom of God in the Struggles of the World." In *For the Nations: Essays Public and Evangelical*, 237–45. Grand Rapids: Eerdmans, 1997.

———. "The Free Church Syndrome." In *Within the Perfection of Christ: Essays on Peace and the Nature of the Church; In Honor of Martin H. Schrag*, edited by Terry L. Brensinger and E. Morris Sider, 169–76. Nappanee, IN: Evangel Press; Grantham, PA: Brethren in Christ Historical Society, 1990.

———. *The Fullness of Christ: Paul's Revolutionary Vision of Universal Ministry*. Elgin, IL: Brethren Press, 1987.

———. "The Hermeneutics of Peoplehood: A Protestant Perspective on Practical Moral Reasoning." *Journal of Religious Ethics* 10–11 (1982–83): 40–67.

———. "Historiography as a Ministry to Renewal." *Brethren Life and Thought* 42 (Summer–Fall 1997): 216–28.

———. "Is There Historical Development of Theological Thought?" In *The Witness of the Holy Spirit: Proceedings of the Eighth Mennonite World Conference, Amsterdam, The Netherlands, July 23–30, 1967*, edited by Cornelius J. Dyck, 379–88. Elkhart, IN: Mennonite World Conference, 1967.

———. "The Kingdom as Social Ethic." In Yoder, *Priestly Kingdom*, 80–101.

———, ed. *The Legacy of Michael Sattler*. Classics of the Radical Reformation 1. Scottdale, PA: Herald, 1973.

———. "Methodological Miscellany #2: Have You Ever Seen a True Church?" Historical mss. 1–48, box 187, section: ethics, 1938–1997. John H. Yoder Collection. Mennonite Church USA Archives, Goshen, IN, 1988.

———. "A People in the World." In Cartwright, *Royal Priesthood*, 65–101.

———. *The Priestly Kingdom: Social Ethics as Gospel*. Notre Dame, IN: University of Notre Dame Press, 1984.

———. "The Prophetic Dissent of the Anabaptists." In Hershberger, *Recovery of the Anabaptist Vision*, 93–104.

———. "The Recovery of the Anabaptist Vision." In *Radical Reformation Reader*, issued as *Concern: A Pamphlet Series* 18 (Scottdale, PA: [n.p.], 1971): 5–23.

———. "Reflections on the Irrelevance of Certain Slogans to the Historical Movements They Represent. Or, the Cooking of the Anabaptist Goose[.] Or, Ye Garnish the Sepulchres of the Righteous." Historical mss. 1–48, box 6, file 1. John H. Yoder Collection. Mennonite Church USA Archives, Goshen, IN, 1952.

———. "That Household We Are." Keynote address at the conference on "Is There a Believers' Church Christology?" Bluffton College, Bluffton, OH, 1980.

———. "To Serve Our God and to Rule the World." In Cartwright, *Royal Priesthood*, 127–40.

———. "What Are Our Concerns?" *Concern: A Pamphlet Series* 4 (1957): 20–32.

Index

BV 652.9 .S278 2010
Schlabach, Gerald.
Unlearning Protestantism

Index